OXFORD
FREEMASONS

Published for and on behalf of Apollo University Lodge

First published in 2018 by the Bodleian Library
Broad Street, Oxford OX1 3BG
www.bodleianshop.co.uk

ISBN: 978 1 85124 467 6

Cover design by Dot Little at the Bodleian Library
Designed and typeset by Ocky Murray in 11 on 16 Minion
Printed and bound by Great Wall Printing Co. Ltd., Hong Kong on 157gsm Neo Matt paper

British Library Catalogue in Publishing Data
A CIP record of this publication is available from the British Library

OXFORD FREEMASONS

A Social History of
Apollo University Lodge

JOE MORDAUNT CROOK
AND JAMES W. DANIEL

Bodleian Library
UNIVERSITY OF OXFORD

CONTENTS

A MESSAGE FROM
HRH THE DUKE OF KENT, KG
GRAND MASTER,
UNITED GRAND LODGE OF ENGLAND

The Oxford University Freemasons' lodge is remarkable. Described by Sir James Stubbs, my first Grand Secretary, as 'the Sandhurst of Masonry', over the two centuries that it has been in existence it has seemed to be just that: Apollo University Lodge No.357 has initiated some 4,500 candidates into the Craft. That is a phenomenal achievement. Even more remarkable are the tales that surround so many of its members during that time. Membership of 'the Apollo' has frequently been found amongst the antecedents of Oxford alumni who reached the top of their professions, service life, the church and politics. And that is still the case: men who have embraced Freemasonry during their undergraduate days (many quietly continuing their membership) have been unearthed in great numbers as research proceeded in this first scholarly examination of the social history and significance of the Apollo.

Properly absorbed, the principles and tenets of Freemasonry have a tendency to improve its members' performance in society; we members will recognise these words from our ritual: '… [a Freemason] is one to whom the burdened heart may pour forth its sorrow, to whom the distressed may prefer their suit, whose hand is guided by justice and whose heart is expanded by benevolence'. It is a comfort to note that these sentiments can be identified in the roles of many of those mentioned in this history. It is particularly poignant that the names are recorded of the 81 Apollo men who paid the greatest sacrifice during the First World War.

Professor Crook has made an admirable job of this little book – he has an engaging style and has clearly enjoyed what has been revealed in this work. Another of my Grand Secretaries, Dr Jim Daniel, could not have been a better choice to add an intimacy to the contents that will please the widest readership.

HRH The Duke of Kent, KG
Grand Master
The United Grand Lodge of England

FOREWORD

APOLLO UNIVERSITY LODGE HAS lain quietly amongst the clubs and societies of Oxford for two centuries now; indeed, its germination was even earlier. But, in 1818, with the blessing of the then vice chancellor, a group of Freemasons within the University petitioned their Masonic rulers in London in order to begin the lodge that has initiated many thousands of members of the University, who have taken their masonry to the furthest quarters of the globe, often occupying the highest offices in clerical, military and political life. Apollo University Lodge holds its place with dignity amongst the oldest of the Oxford societies. This is the first social history of the lodge.

In choosing our authors, a historian was sought amongst whose publications could be found ample evidence of an interest in the societies of the University coupled with a sound knowledge of the small change of Oxford student life during the period in question. The research profile of Professor Joe Mordaunt Crook, CBE, FBA, suited our needs excellently: he is not a Freemason, but he is an eminent social and architectural historian, who has written authoritatively on a number of Oxford societies and produced the definitive history of his alma mater, Brasenose College, where, incidentally, the first meetings of Apollo took place.

Dr James Wallace Daniel FRHistS was initiated in Apollo as an undergraduate over fifty years ago; after a career with the British Council, 'Jim' was appointed Grand Secretary (chief executive) at Grand Lodge, serving on its General Board, under my chairmanship, for a number of years. His doctoral thesis was 'The 4th Earl of Carnarvon (1831–1890): Statesman and Freemason' and he has a respected profile in Masonic publication. He, too, is an alumnus of Brasenose; despite that, he is also a close colleague and friend.

The result of this collaboration is a triumph. *Oxford Freemasons: A Social History of Apollo University Lodge* can only be the beginning of much further research. The complete lodge archive, which is preserved amongst the Bodleian Library's Special Collections, has yielded a treasure trove of detail which our authors have woven into the fascinating book you have in your hands. Professor Mordaunt Crook's inimitable style exploits not only the richness of Oxford gossip, but also hints at networks that were hitherto only speculative. Dr Daniel, on the other hand, speaks to us not only as a proud member of Apollo, but also as an academic Freemason who has had the advantage of an overview of the Craft through familiarity with its central headquarters organization. It is therefore fitting that the Bodleian Library should be our publisher.

I was much touched to be elected to honorary membership of the lodge in 2004 and I regularly attend meetings with an enthusiasm that springs from the hallmark privacy and disinterested friendship of the fraternity, combined with the unique sharing of the Oxford experience.

The Rt Hon. the Earl Cadogan, KBE, DL
Past Deputy Grand Master, United Grand Lodge of England
Magdalen College, Oxford

PREFACE

AS APOLLO UNIVERSITY LODGE approaches its bicentenary, it is timely to record its history. Freemasonry is described by the United Grand Lodge of England (UGLE) as 'one of the world's oldest secular fraternal societies, whose members are concerned with moral and spiritual values'. For two centuries, year after year, Apollo University Lodge (or more familiarly 'Apollo') has recruited undergraduates and graduates: some 4,500 young men, hand-picked, sworn never improperly to reveal the 'secrets' of Freemasonry, bound each to each by ties of loyalty and good fellowship.[1] The impact of such a network – in politics, law, religion and philanthropy – cannot have been negligible. The whole subject, however, has generally been ignored by historians. In the monumental *History of the University of Oxford* [2] – four volumes cover the eighteenth, nineteenth and twentieth centuries alone – the very word 'Freemasonry' is missing from each successive index. It is only recently that academic historians and cultural sociologists have paid any attention to the subject, despite the historian J.M. Roberts, a fellow of Merton College, signalling Freemasonry as a 'neglected topic' as long ago as 1969.[3] Roberts argued that 'the preliminary to any historical construction must be the establishment of firm sociological knowledge about English Freemasonry' and that the 'first and most important facts to establish are who became Freemasons, and why'.[4] Here an attempt is made to answer the first of these questions. But Roberts's second question as to why these men became Freemasons in the first place is now often unanswerable.

Every candidate for initiation in one of the 7,400 or so lodges under the UGLE must declare that he believes in God – in Masonic language, 'the Great Architect of the Universe' – and that his application has not been prompted by 'the improper solicitation of friends against ... [his] own inclination'; nor influenced by 'mercenary or any other unworthy motives' but by 'a favourable

(opposite) Charter of The Apollo Lodge No. 711, signed 28 December 1818.

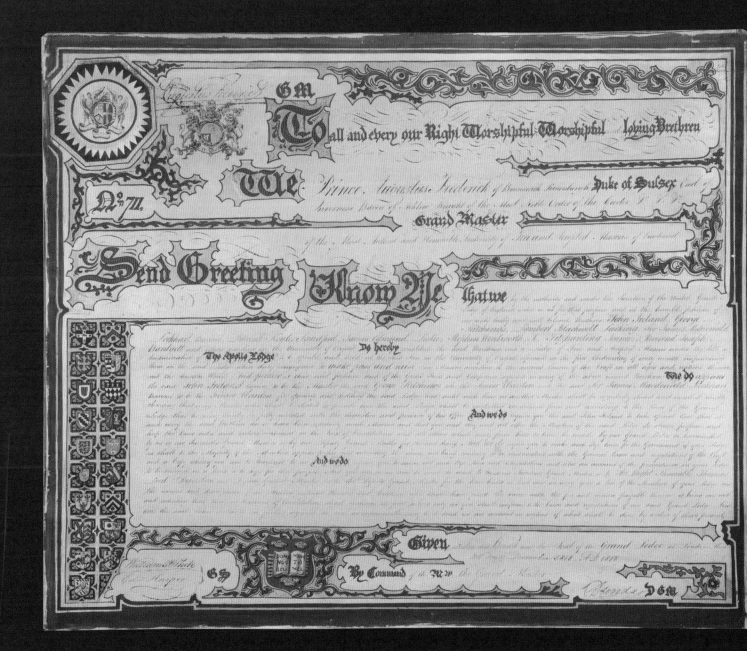

Undergraduates posing on the steps of Brasenose College chapel in 1861. Six are members of Apollo: J. Dunn (standing, first left), P.H. Lee (standing, fourth left), W.H. Erskine (standing, sixth left), P. Arden (standing, seventh left), J.H. Gumbleton (sitting, first left), J.B. Orme (sitting, fourth left).

opinion preconceived of the institution, a general desire of knowledge' and 'a sincere wish to render … [himself] more extensively serviceable' to his 'fellow-creatures'. But why do so many retain membership of the Craft long after their initiation? A recent survey conducted by the UGLE showed that the main reasons why Freemasons enjoy their membership of the Craft include love of tradition, respect for its principles and purposes, its ceremonies, fellowship, fraternity and charitable work.

In some ways there is almost too much material. Detailed records of Freemasonry in the University since 1769 survive and are now in the Bodleian Library. Lists of members; minutes of countless meetings; the ephemera of entertainment and celebration – all these have been preserved. Membership of Apollo, however, is in constant flux as most of its initiates are young men between 18 and 22 years of age who cease to attend its meetings when they go down. Few continue to live close enough to Oxford to be able to fill the senior offices of Worshipful Master, Treasurer, Secretary and Director of Ceremonies (DC). Even if they then join other lodges elsewhere, their subsequent Masonic careers are difficult to discover unless one is lucky enough to find their names in the UGLE's Masonic Year Book – which lists those who have reached national ('Grand') rank within the institution – or else in its Historical Supplement, last published in 1969.[5] There are few other sources to tap for the modern period. The regular coverage of Freemasonry in the printed press is today far less than it was in the period up to the 1920s; indeed, that source of information has almost dried up. And in the later chapters we have also had to proceed more selectively as many of those who became members of the lodge after 1946 are still alive and we must respect both their personal wishes and the laws regarding data protection. That the professional careers and personal lives of some of the thousands of members or former members of Apollo are highlighted in this history is thus to some extent a matter of chance: their names in the lodge's Minute Books rang a sufficiently loud bell for the authors to notice them.

This book is therefore just a first attempt to grapple with the evidence. Inevitably, it falls short. Too much – particularly the private side of innumerable careers – is now irrecoverable. But this survey does try to capture a little of the flavour of what – in terms of longevity if nothing else – must surely be counted a unique fraternity. This is history in a minor key; but a minor narrative with major implications. It might even unscramble that impenetrable concept: 'the Oxford mind'. At the very least this book will answer one long-unanswered question: just who were these Oxford Freemasons?

Joe Mordaunt Crook and James W. Daniel

ACKNOWLEDGEMENTS

Acknowledgements are due to the following for their help with this book:

Committee of Apollo University Lodge; Geoffrey Bourne-Taylor, former lodge Secretary and coordinator of Apollo bicentenary, at whose initiative this history was written; Lord Cadogan, who generously paid for this production and assisted in further fund-raising; Diane Clement (director), Martin Cherry (librarian), Peter Aitkenhead (assistant librarian), Susan Snell (archivist), Library and Museum, Freemasons' Hall; Colin Dunn, Scriptura, photographer; Chris Fletcher and the team at Bodleian Library Publishing; Peter Laurence, archivist, Oxford Masonic Centre; Susan Mayor, for assistance to Joe Mordaunt Crook; Colin Perrin, who compiled the list of Apollo World War I fatalities found in Appendix 3; Robin Fellerman, who compiled the list of Apollo Olympians found in Appendix 4.

TIMELINE

1717   The Grand Lodge is formed in London.

1769   'The Lodge of Alfred in the University of Oxford' is formed in Brasenose College.

1782   'The Lodge of Alfred in the University of Oxford' ceases to function as an inter-college institution.

1818   'Apollo Lodge' is formed in Brasenose College on 24 May 1818.

1819   The first meeting of 'Apollo Lodge' is held on 19 February 1819 in the Star Hotel (later the Clarendon Hotel) in Cornmarket, where it remains until 1832.

1820   'Apollo Lodge' is renamed 'Apollo University Lodge' (AUL).

1829   AUL meets at the Angel Inn, High Street.

1832   AUL moves to the Maidenhead Inn, Turl Street.

1833   AUL moves to the Masonic Hall, Alfred Street.

1865   AUL moves to the University Masonic Hall, Frewin Court.

1919   AUL's centenary celebration is held in the Assembly Room of the Town Hall.

1926   When the lease on the University Masonic Hall in Frewin Court is terminated, AUL moves into the Masonic Hall at 50A High Street.

1939   (Autumn) The Masonic Hall on the High Street is requisitioned by the War Office.

1940   (March) AUL meetings are resumed, but at the Congregational Church, Cowley Road.

1942–46   AUL meets in Magdalen College except for the last three meetings in 1946, which it holds at the Randolph Hotel.

1947   AUL returns to the Masonic Hall at 50A High Street.

1961   AUL moves to Freemasons' Hall at 333 Banbury Road.

2012   Since the sale of Freemasons' Hall on the Banbury Road in 2012 AUL has met in the Ballroom of the Randolph Hotel – except once, in 2015, when it held a meeting (followed by a garden party) at the Oxford Union.

εὑρήκα

1 ORIGINS AND THE EARLY MASONS, 1717–99

THE GRAND LODGE OF England dates from 1717; of Ireland from 1725; of Scotland from 1736. But records relating to previous lodges go back to the sixteenth century; traditions to the Dark Ages; and legends even to prehistory. There is much dispute over this early history, and much ink has been spilt in disputation. What is clear, however, is that before the Grand Lodge era the content and context of Freemasonry were fundamentally Christian. And so, to an extent, it remains to this day. Anglo-Saxon Freemasonry – unlike the political and anti-clerical 'Latin' Freemasonry of Continental Europe – continued and continues to be at least para-Christian. The mysteries of Masonic ritual have been interpreted allegorically as the quest of the soul for mystic union with the Supreme Being. But that is only one among many explanations, and no such overarching metaphysic is attempted here. More simply, Freemasonry defines itself as 'a peculiar system of morality veiled in allegory and illustrated by symbols'.[6]

THE BOOK OF CONSTITUTIONS

The defining manifesto of Freemasonry in its Grand Lodge incarnation appeared in 1723. It is usually known as the first *Book of Constitutions*,[7] edited and largely compiled by Bro. The Revd Dr James Anderson. Anderson – a Calvinist Presbyterian by upbringing – did not work alone. His book of injunctions – based on a number of venerable manuscript *Old Charges* [8] – seems to have been fortified by advice from at least fourteen learned Brothers. Indeed the *Constitutions* is perhaps best regarded as a summation of Masonic thinking at one particular point of time. In 1738 a second edition appeared, dedicated to Frederick Prince of Wales, 'a *Master* Mason and *Master* of a Lodge'.[9] By means of these two volumes English Freemasonry first clarified its ground rules, then nailed its colours to a royalist, indeed Unionist, mast. Between 1737 and 1907 the Brotherhood would be led by no fewer than sixteen princes of the blood royal. And for three centuries every meeting would be solemnly marked by a loyal toast.

The *Constitutions* of 1723 and 1738 are bolstered with esoteric lore, but they do set out the essential Masonic code in agreeably homely terms:

> A *Mason* is oblig'd … to observe the Moral Law …; and if he rightly understands the Craft, he will never be a Stupid Atheist, nor an Irreligious Libertine, nor act against Conscience. In ancient Times, the *Christian Masons* were charged to comply with the *Christian* usages of each Country where they travell'd or work'd … But Masonry being found in all Nations, even of divers Religions, they are now only charged to adhere to that Religion in which all Men agree (leaving each Brother to his own particular opinions) that is to be Good men and true, Men of Honour and Honesty, by whatever Names, Religions or Persuasions they may be distinguish'd … Thus *Masonry* [becomes] the Centre of their Union and the happy Means of conciliating persons that otherwise must have remained at a perpetual Distance.[10]

Much of this so-called 'First Charge' – 'Concerning God and Religion' – is vague, and for very good reason. After generations of discord, Augustan Grand Masters prized harmony above all else; harmony, tolerance and discretion. At lodge meetings, therefore, private and public disputes were to be set aside:

> No private Piques, no Quarrels about Nations, Families, Religions or Politicks must be brought within the Door of the Lodge: For as *Masons*, we are of the oldest *Catholick Religion* … and [thus] we are resolv'd against political Disputes …[11]

Again, the language is vague. 'Catholick' here implies an ancient or primitive Christianity; hence the prohibition of '*all politicks* … especially ever since the *Reformation* in Britain, or the Dissent and Secession of these Nations from the *Communion* of Rome'.[12] Roman Catholics and Jews could indeed gain admission to the Masonic circle. Two early-eighteenth-century Grand Masters – the 8th Duke of Norfolk and the 2nd Duke of Montagu – were practising Catholics. But, for the sake of harmony, competing ideologies – to say nothing of Jacobite proclivities – were in practice best ignored.

Within the lodge discussions of politics and religion were thus avoided from the start. 'Ours is the best Policy … the Policy of the holy Jesus, … [Because] the religion we profess … is the law of Nature, which is the law of God, for God is Nature … [Therefore] love God above all things, and our neighbour as ourself; this is the true, primitive, catholick and universal religion.'[13]

There is some circular thinking here. But the message of the *Constitutions* – as developed in successive editions – is clear enough. Charity, in a general sense, is taken as a given; loyalty to authorized government is assumed as a prerequisite. 'Let a man's religion or mode of worship be what it may', the only specified commitment was to be a belief in 'the Great Architect of the Universe';[14] that and the practice of 'the sacred duties of morality'.[15]

Of course such injunctions involved several degrees of ambivalence. And this ambivalence – Anglicanism with a dash of deism – seems to have been both conscious and calculated. It suited the pragmatism of the age of Walpole. It also suited the rationalism of the age of Locke. From Locke's irenic embrace, however, Roman Catholics and atheists were theoretically excluded: the former because of their allegiance to foreign powers; the latter because of their equivocal attitude to the sanctity of oaths. Otherwise, the barriers were elastic.

As early as 1667, such ambivalent attitudes had indeed been admitted by Thomas Sprat, Bishop of Rochester: 'All wise men should have two religions, the one a publick, for their conformity with the people; the other, a private, to be kept to their own breasts.'[16] The wisest historians of English Freemasonry – Douglas Knoop (a Mason) and G.P. Jones (a non-Mason) – came therefore to an appropriately common-sense conclusion: 'Apparently [these early Masons] saw no clash between the deistic principle of the First Charge, which was valid on Lodge Nights, and a sincere profession of revealed [theistic] religion, which was valid on Sundays.'[17] To this day the Bible – the Volume of Sacred Law – remains open in every lodge.

In the late seventeenth and early eighteenth centuries, by increasingly opening up Freemasonry to non-artisan gentry, English Masonry became – in

CONSTI
TU
TIONS

THE
NEW BOOK
OF
CONSTITUTIONS
OF THE
Antient and *Honourable* FRATERNITY
OF
FREE and ACCEPTED MASONS.

CONTAINING

Their *History, Charges, Regulations,* &c.

COLLECTED and DIGESTED

By Order of the GRAND LODGE from their old *Records*,
faithful *Traditions* and *Lodge-Books,*

For the Use of the LODGES.

By JAMES ANDERSON, D. D.

L O N D O N:
Printed for Brothers CÆSAR WARD and RICHARD CHANDLER,
Bookfellers, at the *Ship* without *Temple-Bar* ; and fold at their
Shops in *Coney-Street*, YORK, and at SCARBOROUGH-SPAW.
M DCC XXXVIII.
In the *Vulgar* Year of Masonry 5738.

the language of the lodge – not just Free but Accepted; not just Operative but Speculative. It was indeed 'a Speculative Science founded on an Operative Art'. Its ceremonies – the three degrees of Entered Apprentice, Fellow Craft, Master Mason – became increasingly formulaic; guarantees of secrecy, mechanisms of mutualized self-interest.[18] Formulaic too were their songs and entertainments: 'The Enter'd 'Prentice's Song', for example, probably dates back to the initiation of one future Grand Master – John, 2nd Duke of Montagu – in 1720.

Montagu's influence at court – he was a noted patron of the arts and a celebrated bon viveur – did much to establish Grand Lodge as a fashionable coterie. During the mid-eighteenth century the fraternity as a whole became

Meissen figurines of the Senior Warden (pink coat) and Worshipful Master (white coat). Attributed to Johann Kändler, 1740? Presented by Past Master Sir George Cooper in 1961.

increasingly prestigious and politically influential; wide enough indeed to include both John Wilkes and George Washington. Its prosperity inevitably provoked hostility. But by the later eighteenth century Grand Lodge and its network of subsidiary lodges had clearly gained acceptance at the highest levels of society. And in the face of threats from Revolutionary France, it proceeded to set its face against most forms of political change. Hence its exemption from the Unlawful Societies Act of 1799.[19] It became a kind of shadowy praetorian guard, an invisible buttress to the Establishment. In years to come English Freemasons would sing the 'The Enter'd 'Prentice's Song' (1720), not the anthems of Continental Freemasonry: 'La Marseillaise' (1791) or 'L'Internationale' (1872). Fealty to Crown and Creator, charity from Brother to Brother: these became the watchwords of Grand Lodge affiliates; the yardsticks of Masonic morality. Such, by cultural transference, was the inheritance of the earliest Oxford Freemasons.

No. 71.

2 FOUNDING AN OXFORD LODGE, 1769–1818

WITH A WARRANT FROM the 5th Duke of Beaufort, MA, DCL, Oxon, Grand Master and Jacobite, 'The Lodge of Alfred in the University of Oxford' was established at Brasenose College (BNC) in 1769. There had of course been Oxford Freemasons before. One associate of the college, Elias Ashmole – royalist founder of the Ashmolean Museum – had been initiated, though not in Oxford, as early as 1646. Other varsity masons can be traced elsewhere: in Dublin as early as 1688, in London as early as 1722 and in Cambridge as early as 1763.[20] But 'The Lodge of Alfred in the University of Oxford' was the first English lodge with a stated university connection, King Alfred being the University's legendary founder. Its originators were a group of six Brasenose Masons, four of them fellows: Hercules Durham, a gentleman commoner from Scotland; the Revd Dr Robert Markham, junior bursar; the Revd James Wood, fellow; the Revd John Napleton, vice principal and future University reformer; the Revd Giles Haddon, senior bursar; and John Willis, a commoner who happened to be the son of George III's doctor. This was the group that James Woodforde of New College – the future Parson Woodforde – joined in 1774. 'It is a very honourable and charitable Institution', he wrote; 'much more than I could conceive it was. Am very glad being a Member of it.' His quarterly subscription was 13s., his entrance fee £3 5s., perhaps equivalent to £350 today.

Monthly meetings, which had initially been held at the King's Head in Cornmarket, were by this time held at the New Inn, sometimes with postprandial singing at the Mitre. Woodforde's dining companions – apart from Wood and Napleton – included several other Brasenose literati: Bennett Dorset, Charles Francis and Ralph Cawley.[21] Membership was mixed, town and gown together, with an occasional oddity like Paniattotti Ballanchi, the University fencing master. It seems to have been a prosperous and convivial society. Its roster of initiates ran to more than 100 members. But its life turned out to be short, and full records do not survive. In about 1782 it ceased to exist as an inter-college institution. It vanished completely in 1790, only to re-emerge in 1814 in the form of a non-University lodge.[22] Today it is the oldest surviving lodge in the city of Oxford, quite separate from – though fraternally related to – Apollo University Lodge.

At this juncture one point needs to be made clear. The Lodge of Alfred in the University of Oxford contained Jacobites – Brasenose, after all, was a traditionally Jacobite place. But that does not make it a vehicle for Jacobite conspiracy. By 1769 it was really too late for such things. With the collapse of the 1745 Rebellion, and with the accession in 1760 of King George III – an identifiably English monarch – Jacobite sentiment had retreated into dining clubs and drinking parties. Among these, it seems, were several of the Masonic lodges that multiplied in increasing numbers around 1760. In 1769 – the very year of the foundation of Alfred Lodge – there appeared in Brasenose hall a massive portrait of King Alfred himself, eponymous patron of the lodge and mythical founder of the 'King's Hall and College of Brasenose'. It was paid for by the Smith-Barry family of Cheshire and County Cork, Jacobites and Freemasons through several generations. It takes only a small leap of imagination to see Oxford's Alfred Lodge as part of a wider mythopoeic process: the University's legendary patron, and the equally mythical founder of Brasenose, becoming together a focus for the loyalty of Old England. Here, it seems, was an escape from the humiliation of Hanoverian rule.[23]

Lambert Blackwell Larking, 1857. In his rooms at Brasenose College, on 24 May 1818, Apollo Lodge was founded.

Be that as it may, such atavistic sentiments had by the 1790s – even in Oxford, even in Brasenose – long been subsumed into something rather more substantial: hostility to Revolutionary and Napoleonic France. The protean nature of late-eighteenth-century Freemasonry – Whiggish, Radical, Jacobite, even Jacobin – enabled it to survive as a kind of social fixative: a cohesive ingredient in evolving nationhood.[24] By 1818, when Freemasonry was formally re-established in Oxford University, 'Church and King' – a toast popularly directed to the maintenance of the Anglican Settlement and the continuance of the Hanoverian dynasty – can have aroused few objections in Apollo. After all, the Grand Master of the order was now a royal duke.

FOUNDING OF APOLLO

Alfred Lodge turned out to be a false start (to be revived subsequently as a 'City' or non-University lodge). Four years after that episode, five Oxford undergraduates met on 24 May 1818 in the rooms of Lambert Blackwell Larking and founded Apollo Lodge. Technically it was No. 711; from 1833 No. 460; from 1863 No. 357.[25] From 1820 it was known as Apollo University Lodge. Once again Brasenose was the college of choice. The rooms chosen were not particularly impressive; they were situated in the attic storey of Old Quad, just above the Library staircase. But the setting was sublime. Through narrow casements young Larking could look out over Radcliffe Square, past the dome of the Radcliffe Camera, towards the magical twin towers of All Souls.

Larking, an Etonian, with a lengthy clerical and antiquarian career ahead of him, had the time – and means – to devote himself for the next few years to establishing Apollo as an integral part of Oxford's social fabric. Bearing a warrant from the Duke of Sussex – a royal duke, no less; a Unitarian; and Grand Master of the Masonic Order – this new lodge held its first formal meeting in the Star Hotel (later the Clarendon), in Cornmarket, on 19 February 1819. So the lodge was now established, and it had the blessing of the vice chancellor.

According to Greek mythology, Apollo was the son of Zeus. Born on the Island of Delos, he was – among many other things – the god of song and music, art and poetry; by extension he was responsible for the education of the young. Legendarily, he was even the father of Plato. Iconographically, Apollo's image was therefore an image of youth, in particular an ideal image of male beauty. By choosing Apollo as their prophet – he also happened to be the god of prophesy – these early Oxford Freemasons no doubt aimed to characterize their lodge as a nursery for the leaders of the future.[26] Here was an opportunity to enlist the *jeunesse dorée* – term after term – and turn them into sturdy pillars of the constitution. In effect, Apollo's agenda was the shaping of an elite; a veritable Sandhurst among Masonic lodges. As a University agency, it was unique: not until 1861 would Cambridge boast a comparable institution.

The five founders who met together that night in Brasenose in 1818 were already Freemasons. They consisted of two Brasenose College gentry, Larking himself and Charles Macdonald Lockhart, heir to a Scottish baronetcy, plus three armigerous Christ Church undergraduates: Daniel Sandford from Edinburgh, James Leslie from Belfast and William St Aubyn from Cornwall (already a member of the Union des Coeurs Lodge, Geneva).[27] To this nucleus were added two more gentlemanly undergraduates, one from Exeter College (Robert Jenner of Gloucestershire) and one from Wadham (John Jones of Herefordshire), plus one 'plebeian' Oxford cleric (Joseph Bardgett of All Souls and Merton). These might all be described as constituent founder members. But in addition there were four members imported from the town: John Ireland 'Esquire', apothecary, first Master of the Alfred Lodge, by then aged 71; George Hitchings, 'surveyor' (also of Alfred Lodge); Stephen Wentworth, 'pharmacopola' or 'medical practitioner'; and Hiram Holden, 'printer' and 'serving brother'. Ireland became Apollo's first Master, Bardgett its first Chaplain, Larking its first Secretary, Wentworth its first Treasurer and Holden its first Tyler. At the first formal meeting, on 19 February 1819, two more members were initiated: James Case, a future cleric from Manchester Grammar School and Brasenose; and Thomas Purrick of Oxford, 'clothes cleaner' and 'serving brother'.

What conclusions can we draw from these first fourteen members? From the beginning the characteristic membership of Apollo was already apparent: a mixture of gentry, academic clergy and artisan associates, with hints of Freemasonry's Celtic fringe. The fraternity is not yet exclusive. Within this founding group, however, we should note two figures who foreshadow the lodge's elitist future: Larking and Sandford. Larking had social connections and presumably some talent for organization. He was already a member of the St Frederick Lodge, Boulogne. His role was that of initiator. But his health was never robust. His career would lead him far away from public prominence, to

Brasenose College,
Oxford, from *Picturesque
Views of Oxford* by Thomas
Malton, 1822.

a rural vicarage in Kent and a private chaplaincy to Viscountess Falmouth at
Mereworth Castle in the same county. Sandford's destiny was rather different.
We first encounter him – unusually – as an untitled member of Loder's, a
privileged Christ Church dining club (of which more later). By upbringing he
was a Scottish liberal, second son of an Episcopalian Bishop of Edinburgh.

Members of the Apollo Lodge
open'd Feb: 10th 1819
A. L. 5819

		Age	Profession	Abode	Admitted
Honorary	John Ireland	71	Esquire	Oxford	May 24 - 1818
	George Hitchings	29	Surgeon	Oxford	—
Resigned	Lambert Blackwell Larking	21	Esquire	Oxford B.N.C	—
Resigned	Daniel Keyte Sandford		Esquire	— R.C.C	—
Resigned	James Cammond Leslie		Esquire	— Ch. Ch.	—
Resigned	Charles Macdonald Lockhart		Baronet	— B.C.C	—
	Joseph Badgett	43	Clerk	— Merton	—
Resigned	William John St Aubyn	24	Esquire	— Univ. Coll	—
Resigned	Robert Fitzharding Inner	21	Esquire	— — Ex. Coll	—
	Stephen Wentworth	36	Surgeon	Oxford	—
Resigned	Hiram Holden		Printer	Oxford	—
Deceased	John Green Jones	21	Esquire	— Wad. Coll	Feb: 10th 1819
Resigned	James Case	22	Ugr. B.A.	B.N.C	Feby. 19th 1819
	Thomas Carrick	50	Clothes Cleaner	Oxford	Feby. 19/19
Resigned	Henry Barrett Lennard	21	Ugr.	Merton C.	Feby 24th 19
Resigned	Richard Humphrey	22	Ugr.	Merton C.	Feby 24/19
Resigned	Thos Somerville		Ugr.	Univ. C.	March 3d/19

(opposite) Page from a
Minute Book showing a
list of members in 1819.

After a First in Greats in 1820, he went in for a fellowship at Oriel – at that time
one of the few open fellowships in Oxford – and was rejected. Thereafter his
reformist instincts took on a personal edge. As a Scot and an Episcopalian, he
felt himself outside the Anglican Establishment. Writing anonymously for the
Edinburgh Review in 1821, he attacked the unreformed University mercilessly.
Here, he announced, we see 'the true spirit of the Monkish system in full and
flagrant operation'. Power, apparently, could still rest unaccountably in 'the
hands of [some] conceited, ignorant, illiberal recluse'. In pursuit of preferment,
any would-be academic must learn to 'comb his hair smooth, avoid cleanliness
and essences, be regular at Latin prayers, and sedulous in capping'; for success
is 'determined in proportion to the scrapings, grins, and genuflections of the
… competitors'. In terms of syllabus reform, he concluded, 'Oxford [may have]
improved upon its former self; but in all points of right sentiment or liberal
feeling, it [is] still the same University that stripped Locke of a studentship, and
refused Johnson a degree.'[28]

That put paid to Sandford's prospects in Oxford. But it did not hinder his
securing a professorship of Greek at Glasgow. And in 1829, when Sir Robert
Peel faced down the wrath of Anglican Oxford by emancipating Roman
Catholics, Sandford rushed south to his defence – and was rewarded with a
knighthood. Next came the battle for the Great Reform Bill. As a vigorous
supporter of constitutional change, he soon found himself, in 1834, newly
elected MP for Paisley in Renfrewshire. Four years later he was dead. But
his influence in the Apollo network lived on: in 1821 his younger brother – a
Liberal church reformer – had also joined Apollo; and in 1823 his sister had
married a fellow-founder of the lodge, James Leslie of Leslie Hill near Belfast,
High Sheriff of County Antrim – a locality not unknown to Freemasonry.

APOLLO'S EARLY YEARS

After a few apologies to Grand Lodge – confessing 'inexperience' and
'ignorance' of procedure – Apollo embarked upon a pattern of meetings that
would continue almost unchanged: weekly or fortnightly nominations, ballots
and initiations during term time; modest suppers (with a bowl of negus – that
is, mulled wine – at each end of the table); occasionally rather more lavish
dinners, garden fêtes and summer balls; and regular acts of charity, mostly but
not always directed within Masonic circles.[29]

Fees were not substantially more than that of Alfred Lodge: initiation cost £3 12s.; the annual subscription £4 4s.; life membership thereafter £5 5s.; plus a variety of lesser charges. This was a gentlemen's lodge. But the lodge establishment was by no means extravagant. They met first in the Star Hotel, Cornmarket; then, from 1829 in the Angel Inn, High Street; then, from 1832, at the Maidenhead Inn, Turl Street; then, from 1833, in modest rooms of their own, the Masonic Hall in Alfred Street. When a new dinner service was required in 1849, the Brethren contributed individually: 38 members each donated a single silver fork.[30] Not until 1865 would Apollo move into its own premises in Frewin Court – the University Masonic Hall – built on land leased from the Clarendon Hotel. There they would stay – apart from fraternal visits to the Alfred Lodge's Masonic Hall in High Street – until shortly after World War I.

Of course, like any other lodge, Apollo's secrecy aroused occasional suspicion. To outsiders its ceremonies may sometimes have seemed sinister; to insiders they were in practice a series of bonding mechanisms, emblems

Interior of the Temple of the Masonic Hall in Alfred Street, Oxford. These modest premises were the headquarters of Apollo University Lodge from 1833 to 1865, adjoining the City Book Club Library.

Illustration from 'Mr. Verdant Green is made a Mason', in Cuthbert Bede, *The Adventures of Mr. Verdant Green*, 1853.

of fellowship, ritual expressions of a deeper commitment. One widely read parody occurs in *The Adventures of Mr. Verdant Green* (1853). This popular squib was written not by an Oxford man, still less by an Oxford Freemason. Its author was the Revd Edward Bradley (1827–89), a graduate of Durham, publishing under the pseudonym 'Cuthbert Bede'. At the start the reader is introduced to a naive Brasenose man, fresh from the provinces, who is badgered by hearty friends into joining Apollo. In one chapter – 'Mr. Verdant Green is made a Mason' – he enters the 'Lodge of Cemented Bricks': a house [in Alfred Street] 'not a hundred miles from the High Street'. There he endures a series of 'rituals' orchestrated by his boisterous friend Bouncer. First he is introduced to the 'Swordbearer and Deputy Past Pantile', then to the 'Provincial Grand Mortar Board', then to the 'Past Grand Hodman', then finally to all the other Brethren: 'Each held a drawn and gleaming sword; each wore aprons, scarves or mantels; each was decorated with mystic masonic jewellery.'[31] Bradley's humorous sketches, with their lively pen-and-ink illustrations, delighted generations of undergraduates – by 1870 it had sold 100,000 copies. One hundred and fifty years later, they still have a certain talent to amuse. But they are really no more than student humour.

The early members of Apollo took their oaths solemnly. In his farewell address as Worshipful Master, Brother Ireland – 'the elder statesman of Oxford Masonry' – 'gave a short lecture to the Brethren with regard to their behaviour out of the Lodge'. He warned them 'to be particularly cautious in all their conduct'.[32] That advice echoed an injunction in the Order's earliest *Constitutions*. In years to come, the Brethren of Apollo would be sociable rather than sybaritic, and took care to 'proceed to their meetings in their Academics'.[33] They might seem sometimes absurd, sometimes even a little menacing. But they would remain fundamentally patriotic, fundamentally loyal. And, whatever happened, their caution could generally be relied on.

(above) Jewels, including the Deacon's jewel (dove bearing an olive branch) bearing the cipher of the Prince of Wales; centenary jewel (light blue with '357' on ribbon); steward's jewel presented to Apollo University Lodge No. 711, 1832.

(opposite) The Past Master's jewel, presented to William Beach, 1853.

3 GRANDEES AND GENTLEMEN, 1819–90

APOLLO WAS NOW INDEED established. But its ambitions had yet to be realized. This was to change dramatically during the next two decades. A first straw in the wind came with the second formal meeting on 24 February 1819. Only two members, Mertonians both, were initiated. However, one, Richard Humfrey, was an Eton King's Scholar, and the other was a baronet's son from a romantic Gothic manor at Belhus in Essex: Henry Barrett-Lennard. Thereafter the lodge's social trajectory moved significantly upwards.

The figures are striking. Between March 1819 and June 1821 no fewer than seventeen initiates were heirs to hereditary titles: ten baronets (Hayes, Ogle, Graham, Fludyer, Malet, Borough, Cotton, Ridley, Sterling and Musgrave); one viscount (Templetown); four earls (Ellesmere, Shaftesbury, Galloway and Clanricarde); one Marquess (Cholmondeley); and one duke (Leeds). During the same two years Apollo was also able to claim the brother of a viscount (Strathallan), the son of an earl (Harley) and the son of a baron (Despencer). And then there were the future clerics and academics: a solicitor-general (Dundass), an Eton housemaster (Coleridge), a principal of Brasenose (Harington), a Regius Professor of Medicine (Ogle), a professor of Anglo-Saxon (Ridley), a Bishop of Madras (Spencer), a Regius Professor of Hebrew (Nicol), a vice principal of Trinity (Short), a Canon of Windsor (Markham), and a chaplain at Heidelberg and Cannes (Ford). All these elections to Apollo took place within a period of only thirteen months in 1819–21.

These men were all grandees, but three of them were very grand indeed: Henry, 3rd Marquess of Cholmondeley; Francis, 1st Earl of Ellesmere; and Anthony Ashley Cooper, Baron Ashley, 7th Earl of Shaftesbury. Each of them – but especially Shaftesbury – combined formidable wealth with a powerful sense of social responsibility. As hereditary Great Chamberlain of England, Cholmondeley presided over the coronations first of William IV and then of Queen Victoria. A strong Evangelical Tory MP, landlord of 34,000 acres in Cheshire (Cholmondeley Castle) and Norfolk (Houghton Hall), he took his philanthropic responsibilities seriously. His name was regularly to be found in subscription lists alongside that of his exact Apollo contemporary, the great Lord Shaftesbury.

Shaftesbury's contribution to social improvement was legendary even in his own lifetime. An evangelical Conservative, paternalist and progressive, he devoted his life to helping the disadvantaged. Factories, mines, slavery; public health, education, penal reform; 'lunatics', chimney sweeps, costermongers – the range of Shaftesbury's concern was more than impressive: it was almost saintly. He had his blindspots. His evangelical instincts did rather inhibit his appreciation of both ritualism and rationalism. He was no friend of Rome, and no friend of Broad Church biblical criticism. He bitterly opposed the restoration of Catholic hierarchy in 1850; and he notoriously condemned J.R. Seeley's *Ecce Homo* (1865) as 'the most pestilential book ever vomited from the jaws of Hell'. Still, the achievements of this 'poor man's Earl' are rightly commemorated today by the statue of Eros in Piccadilly Circus.[34]

Lord Francis Leveson-Gower – Francis 1st Earl of Ellesmere, a younger son of the 1st Duke of Sutherland – was devoted more to art and literature than to material charity. Even so, his social commitment was impressive. He inherited a large slice of the gigantic Bridgewater fortune, plus quite

Portrait of Anthony Ashley Cooper, Lord Shaftesbury (Apollo, 1819). Evangelical Conservative, reformer and philanthropist, commemorated in Piccadilly Circus, London.

ELLIOTT & FRY   Copyright   55, BAKER S?
PORTMAN SQ?

a few of the family titles – he signed himself 'Egerton Ellesmere' – and lived in very great state at Bridgewater House, London. In politics he was a Liberal Conservative, a Canningite; in the world of art and scholarship, he was both patron and collector on a princely scale. Shy and withdrawn, something of an artist, and more than something of a poet, Ellesmere certainly did enough to justify his inheritance. The paintings in Bridgewater House were famously available to all.

It is perhaps not too fanciful to credit a little of the sense of purpose possessed by this remarkable trio – Cholmondeley, Shaftesbury and Ellesmere – to the influence of pre-Oxford Movement Anglicanism. Their careers tell us something about the moral earnestness – and highly privileged paternalism – of Apollo Lodge in its earliest years.

As we shall see in Chapter 4, recruitment was then – and would long remain – predominantly clerical. But the tone of the lodge at this time cannot have been wholly ascetic. Three initiates, all of 1820 – Richard Harington, St Vincent Cotton and Ulick de Burgh – clearly led indulgent lives. De Burgh, later 14th Earl and later still 1st Marquess of Clanricarde, was apparently 'tall, thin … bald and bland … [known for his] tight pantaloons, striped silk socks and pumps … [and for the fact that he was] immensely rich … clever, and … fond of low company'.[35] Harington – cousin of a baronet, three times Master of the lodge – eventually became principal of Brasenose and vice chancellor of Oxford, as well as a vehement opponent of University reform. But he was marked down by Mark Pattison of Lincoln College as an idler: a 'fine gentleman, who sailed his own pinnace on the river and dined out too much'. Nor were his manners particularly refined: he used to pick his teeth while talking to ladies.[36] As for Cotton, a future baronet, he comes down to us as an archetypal Regency rake: 'well-known in the hunting, racing and shooting, cricket and pugilistic world'; an officer in the 10th Hussars; a celebrated 'whip' on the Brighton run; and 'a great gambler' who 'dissipated all his property' before marrying at death's door his erstwhile creditor, one Hephzibah Dimmick.[37]

The pace of titled recruitment showed little sign of slackening during the 1820s. In 1823 Apollo secured five future baronets (Cotterell, Jervoise, Des Voeux, Howard and Peyton), one future baron (Meredyth), two sons of barons (Vernon and Scarsdale), one son of an earl (Bathurst) and one future earl (Meath); in 1825–6 one son of a baronet (Wilmot), one son of a baron (Southampton), one son of an earl (Roden) and one son of a royal duke

(Clarence); in 1827–8 two future barons (Southampton and Monson), one future earl (Craven) and one future duke (Bedford); in 1829 two future baronets (Geary and Filmer), one son of a baronet (Piggott) and one son of an earl (Roden); and in 1830 two future baronets (Johnstone and Acland) and one son of a baronet (another Acland), three future barons (Zouche, Dunsandle and De Tabley), two future viscounts (Falmouth and Lifford) and one future duke (Abercorn). In only one year during this entire decade – namely 1824 – was there no aristocratic initiate. There was still the occasional artisan (William Thompson, 'carver and gilder'; John Townsend, John Hart and John Doughty, 'waiters' or 'serving brothers' at the Star and the Angel). There was even a dash of new money: Algernon Perkins (brewing) and John Temple Leader (distilling),[38] both initiated in 1830. But mostly it was landed wealth. Apollo was now not only well established; it was formidably well connected.

1830S–1870S INITIATES: ARISTOCRACY, NEW MONEY AND NEW TALENT

During the 1830s and 1840s Apollo's canter through the peerage becomes a veritable gallop. The list of titled initiates – out of a general intake of some 200 – is worth a moment's pause. Indeed, without a detailed roll-call of titled members it is impossible to appreciate just how exclusive – and just how influential – Victorian Apollo could claim to be. During the 1830s and 1840s the list was as follows: four younger sons of baronets (Sutton, Honywood, Boughey and Russell), as well as seventeen baronets or future baronets (Beaumont, Beach, Boyd, Brownrigg, Buxton, Domville, Harrington, Hazlerigg, Hopkins, Hunter, Knighton, Lechmere, Marjoribanks, Meux, Puleston, Simeon and Taylor); one younger son of a baron (Ravensworth) and six future barons (Carew, Emly, Wolverton, Northbourne, Northwick and Suffield); one younger son of a viscount (Gage) and two future viscounts (Fitzgibbon and Sherbrooke); six younger sons of earls (Cadogan, Cork and Orrery, Delawarr, Granville, Huntingdon and Malmesbury) and four future earls (Canning, Granville, Radnor and Shrewsbury), two younger sons of marquesses (Bath and Ely), as well as three marquesses or future marquesses (Ely, Londonderry and Waterford); and finally, to complete the roster with a flourish, no fewer than four future dukes (Hamilton, Leinster, Marlborough and Newcastle). Of these, only

Sherbrooke – a future Liberal Chancellor of the Exchequer – could be counted as newly noble.[39]

During the 1850s the pace scarcely slackens. Overall recruitment is higher – some 360 over a single decade – but the proportion of titled initiates remains much the same: sixteen baronets or future baronets (Bailey, Bernard, Clarke-Jervoise, Clay, Cope, Cust, Fergusson, Grant, Hicks Beach, Johnstone, Leighton, Maxwell, Pottinger, Vane, Vernon and Vincent), as well as twelve younger sons of baronets (Barrow, Beaumont, Cave-Browne Cave, Chetwode, Crewe, Knatchbull-Hugessen, Malet, Pasley, Scott, Walsh, Welby-Gregory and Williamson); seven future barons (Brabourne, Clonbrook, Grantley, Lilford, North, Poltimore, Saye and Sele), plus six younger sons of barons (Byron, Hambro, Howard de Walden, Monson, Suffield and Vernon); eight future earls (Brassey, Cowper, Dunraven, Effingham, Erne, Galloway, Lathom and Lisburne), plus five younger sons of earls (two Carnarvon brothers, Delawarr, Sheffield and Strafford); one younger son of a marquess (Ailesbury); and at last – another final flourish – two future dukes (Abercorn and Newcastle). There is occasional new money here, notably Brassey (railways); but these are nearly all traditional landed families.

The 1860s, however, mark a significant transition. Apollo's overall number of recruits expands considerably: more than 300 in the first half of the decade alone. The proportion of titled initiates, therefore, drops sharply. The nobility are still there: in the earlier 1860s, one future baronet (Sebright), five future barons (Headley, Northcote, Hothfield, Norton and Tredegar), one future viscount (Galway), six future earls (Bective, Donoughmore, Egmont, Jersey, Kilmorey, and Mar and Kellie) and one future Duke (Northumberland). But the balance has shifted. Apollo was still a lodge populated by gentry; very much so. But the bulk of its emerging membership had for some years been predominantly clerical and legal; now it was increasingly infiltrated by new money.

There had been a few advance indicators of change. For instance Joseph Bailey, heir to a dynasty of ironmasters, a future MP and baronet; or John Currey, a tobacco manufacturer; or Sir Henry Meux, 2nd Bt, 'the eminent brewer'; or the Portal brothers, George and Wyndham, whose family mills supplied the paper for the banknotes of the Bank of England (a third brother, Melville Portal, was elected to Apollo but never initiated). But from now on the trickle became a tide. Second-generation money, mostly: money from banking (Mills and Drummond, Glyn, Baring, Chapman, Grenfell, Marjoribanks,

Praed and Hambro); money from spinning (Arkwright, Ackroyd, Brocklehurst and Gott); money from shipping (Bective), wool (Salting), paper (Wrigley), hat-making (Wagner), laxatives (Henry), wine (Woodhouse), beer (Allsopp, Tollemache and Guinness), guano (Gibbs), engineering (Field), building (Cubbitt), printing (Clowes), insurance (Chance), publishing (Hansard and Kegan Paul), newspapers (Walter), copper (Illingworth), iron (Whitmore), more iron (Bailey), and still more iron (Hardy). All these were initiates of the 1860s and 1870s. The tone of the lodge was definitely changing.

And not just new money; there was new talent too. Lurking among the gentry of the mid-Victorian intake occurs the name of Walter Parratt, organist at Magdalen College. A musical prodigy from Huddersfield, he succeeded John Stainer at Magdalen in 1872, became a Bachelor of Music in 1873 and a member of Apollo in 1875. Thereafter his career blossomed gloriously. As Sir Walter Parratt, he became Master of the Queen's Music. His anthem 'Confortare' was played at the coronations of both Edward VII and George V. He ended as Professor of Music at Oxford, acknowledged as the greatest organist of his generation. Appropriately, he appears next to Stainer in Holman Hunt's painting *May Morning on Magdalen Tower* (1888–91).

So change in Apollo was possible, but not too fast. At least two factors made for continuity. First, Apollo continued to recruit from families that were already Masonic. Between 1819 and 1843 no fewer than thirty-three initiates were recorded as 'son of a Mason'. And many of them were both Masonic and noble: Augustus Fitzclarence, for example, an illegitimate son of the future King William IV. Then there was the Christ Church Society. Comparisons between the Apollo lists and those of the Christ Church Society show a persistent degree of correlation. The Christ Church Society – or Loder's as it was known, in memory of its earliest clubhouse proprietor – was an exclusive college club. It continued to supply well-born members of Apollo right through the nineteenth century. Each year from its foundation in 1814 it elected perhaps a dozen members of the college, all landed or nobly born. Here, in the words of Sir Keith Feiling, the 'sons of the country houses sacrificed at their ancestral altars of fox-hunting, Church and King'.[40] On average, two or three joined Apollo each year. In 1830, for example, out of six elected to Loder's, three were quickly initiated in Apollo: the future Lord Canning, the future Lord De Tabley and the future Duke of Newcastle. Each will stand as an Apollo stereotype of the 1830s. George Leicester, 2nd Baron

Charles 'Clemency' Canning (Apollo, 1831). Canning was Governor General of India during the Mutiny. Portrait by George Richmond.

De Tabley, inherited a large swathe of Cheshire. He became a Lord in Waiting to the Queen, then Treasurer of the Royal Household, and died in debt. Henry Pelham-Clinton, Earl of Lincoln, 5th Duke of Newcastle, was Secretary to the Viceroy of Ireland during the Famine, Secretary to the War Department during the Crimea, and Provincial Grand Master to the Freemasons of Nottinghamshire. He lies today in a formidable Doric mausoleum at Markham Clinton, overlooking what remains of his estate in the Dukeries at Clumber Park, Nottinghamshire. Charles Canning – 'Clemency' Canning, 'Canning the just', Governor General of India during the Mutiny – bore a famous name, and was well aware of its distinction. When he moved up from viscount to earl in 1859 he was by no means pleased: 'I am rather low at

No. 17. STATESMEN, No. 4. Price 6d.

"An enemy to democracy, yet a professor of liberal principles, which tend to democracy ; the combination will one day make him Prime Minister of England."

Robert Lowe, 1st Baron Sherbrooke (Apollo, 1833). Lowe was Chancellor of the Exchequer in Gladstone's Liberal Ministry of 1868–74. He dreamed of turning the civil service into a 'freemasonry' of highly educated governors (*Vanity Fair*, 1869).

leaving the Viscounts, whom I have always looked upon as a more select caste than the Earls.'[41] He rests today in Westminster Abbey, close to the grave of his more famous father. Politically, all three – Canning, De Tabley and Newcastle – were Peelites; that is, Liberal Tories. Their early careers, in different ways, link Apollo in the 1830s to the Christ Church of Peel and Gladstone; to Oxford in the days before reform.

Of course, apart from future grandees and numbers of worthy clergy – of whom more later – mid-Victorian Apollo attracted quite a few young men who wasted their substance in pleasurable living. Step forward George Trafford Heald, of Eton and Corpus. Son of a wealthy London barrister, he matriculated as a gentleman-commoner in 1846, joined Apollo in 1848, went down without a degree, then cut a dash in metropolitan society as an eligible young cornet in the 2nd Life Guards. At the age of 21, at St George's Hanover Square, he flickered briefly in the glare of international fame: he married Lola Montez. But Lizzie Gilbert – for that was Lola's real name – was unfortunately already married. A self-styled Spanish dancer – in fact a notorious demi-mondaine – she quickly fled abroad and soon found a third husband in California. While she travelled the world in pursuit of higher and higher game – her liaisons were rumoured to include Liszt, Wagner and Ludwig I of Bavaria – Cornet Heald returned to obscurity; poorer no doubt, if not a little wiser.[42]

But for every Apollo recruit turned wastrel, a countervailing example of industry and ambition could be produced. Robert Lowe, for instance, was a dogmatic meritocrat. A half-blind albino with a fierce intellect and a biting tongue, he represented a brand of Liberalism immune to vested interests. He dreamed of an elite system of administration based on rigorous examinations and an ethos of secular altruism. In this respect his Masonic background was by no means irrelevant. In Parliament he argued for a purged civil service, a 'freemasonry' of highly educated governors. His blind spot, however, was parliamentary reform: he had no faith in the wisdom of a mass electorate. But as Chancellor of the Exchequer and Home Secretary – eventually Baron Sherbrooke – he more than held his own in Gladstone's great ministry of 1868–74.[43]

ANGLO-SCOTTISH AND ANGLO-IRISH RECRUITS

If we look at the first 1,100 Apollo men, recruited between 1818 and 1865 – round numbers, of course, excluding 'serving Brethren' – two statistics are immediately striking. First, there are some 200 Etonians, not far short of one in five of the total intake: mid-Victorian Apollo was very much a gentlemen's club. Even those without native titles had claims to nobility: Henry Walrond (Apollo, 1860), for example, was 'a Spanish Marquis and Count, and a Grandee of the first class'. Second, there are a considerable number of initiates from the Anglo-Irish and, to a lesser extent, Anglo-Scottish establishment.

From the start Scottish landed families were notably represented: Hamilton, Galloway, Maxwell, Erskine, Mackenzie. But it was the Anglo-Irish who stood out. Of the first 200 recruits, in 1818–30, no fewer than twenty were Irish landowners. One in ten: a significant proportion. Of the next 200, in 1831–45, almost exactly the same proportion can be counted. Thereafter there is a noticeable diminution. Of the following 200, in 1846–53, only three belonged to the Irish ascendancy; and of the next 200, in 1853–57, only nine. The causes are clear. By mid-century, Apollo had much increased its intake. Its membership could still be categorized as gentry; but the majority were less landed, more professionally moneyed. And the Anglo-Irish element, demarcated from its Roman Catholic context – in England if not wholly in Ireland – had very significantly diminished. The final tranche in this analysis of the first 1,100 – a larger sample of 300 or so in 1858–65 – contains no more than fourteen initiates who could claim to be members of the old Irish Ascendancy.

But when these statistics are weighed rather than counted, they become more interesting still, particularly as regards Apollo's continuing influence in the upper echelons of Freemasonry. Not only did the lodge recruit regularly – especially in its early days – from the titled and landed aristocracy of Scotland and Ireland; in the mid-Victorian period it managed to enrol several undergraduates who would soon become key figures in the Masonic hierarchy of Britain.

North of the border, the highest Masonic office was that of Grand Master Mason of the Grand Lodge of Scotland. Between the 1830s and the 1880s this was twice held by Apollo men, both leading Conservatives. William Hamilton, Marquess of Douglas, later 11th Duke of Hamilton – elected Grand Master in 1833 – was certainly very grand. In fact he was noted for his 'grandeeship' of manner'. Lord Brougham thought him 'Very Duke of Very Duke'. When he married, he

James Hamilton, 2nd Marquess and 1st Duke of Abercorn (Apollo, 1830). Grand Master of Irish Freemasons and leader of the Conservative Party in Ireland.

chose the daughter of the Grand Duke of Baden, whose wife was Napoleon's adopted daughter.[44] The second Scottish Grand Master from the Apollo stable was Walter Erskine, a Brasenose initiate of 1860. He rose – via a complicated series of decisions in the House of Lords – to be, in 1872, 11th Earl of Mar and 13th Earl of Kellie; in 1873 a Conservative Representative Peer; and then in 1882 Grand Master of the Freemasons of Scotland.[45]

The Scottish Grand Mastership was more symbolic than political. But its Irish equivalent in those days carried serious political clout. Here Apollo could claim first Charles Fitzgerald, Marquess of Kildare, heir to the 3rd Duke of Leinster (1791–1874), Grand Master of Irish Freemasons; and secondly Leinster's two immediate successors in the Irish Masonic hierarchy: the 1st and 2nd Dukes of Abercorn.

It was Leinster's fate to try, and fail, to bridge the sectarian divide between Catholics and Protestants within the structure of Irish Freemasonry. In politics he was a Liberal, supporting Catholic emancipation and Parliamentary reform. He was also a nephew of Edward Fitzgerald, the United Irishman. But the Irish Rebellion of 1798 marked a watershed. Despite papal disapproval – in 1760 for instance – late-eighteenth-century Irish Freemasonry included a sizeable minority of Catholics: 20 per cent in Munster, 40 per cent in Dublin; and not only gentry, but artisans and shopkeepers too.[46] After the 1820s, Catholic participation in Irish Freemasonry decreased dramatically: Daniel O'Connell's Catholic Association dates from 1823; the Liberator himself, under pressure from Rome, withdrew from the Order in 1837. Irish lodges became increasingly Protestant, increasingly Tory, increasingly bourgeois, increasingly Orange. And changes among the lodges of Ireland were paralleled by changes in English Freemasonry too. Georgian lodges had been surprisingly diverse; socially, religiously, politically. Victorian lodges became increasingly uniform: Protestant, patriotic, professional. In Oxford, the shifting membership of Apollo clearly reflected this trend, a change that has been characterized as the 'great reshaping of Masonry'.[47]

Leinster's successor, James Hamilton, 2nd Marquess and 1st Duke of Abercorn (1811–1885), inherited therefore – at least in Masonic terms – a narrower, more dogmatic kingdom. He was for many years the leader of the Conservative Party in Ireland. Lord Lieutenant of Donegal and Hon. Colonel of the Donegal Militia; heir to the great estate of Barons Court, Co. Tyrone; Groom of the Stole to Prince Albert; Privy Councillor and Knight of the

Garter; twice Lord Lieutenant of Ireland; as well as Grand Master of Irish Freemasons – Abercorn was the very embodiment of Unionism. In fact, along with that of his son, the 2nd Duke (1838–1913) – who succeeded him in every one of those offices and honours except the Lord Lieutenancy – his career can now be seen as the high watermark of Apollo; that is, Apollo as an agency of the British Establishment.[48]

APOLLO MEMBERS IN LONDON

Generations of Apollo grandees – especially those with ambitions in Whitehall and St James's – beat a path from Oxford to London. In particular, they joined the Westminster and Keystone Lodge (No. 10). In 1855 this was a lodge that was largely moribund. In February that year there were only three members. By the end of 1856 there were 65: Apollo accounted for 37 of them, with the rest from the Alfred, Churchill and Cherwell Lodges in and around Oxford. By the late 1860s membership totalled upwards of 140, with Apollo recruitment gradually slimming down thereafter, from one-half to one-third. Lt Col. H.A. Bowyer (d.1871) of Christ Church, Provincial Grand Master of Oxfordshire, seems to have acted as chief recruiting sergeant. Meetings were held at Freemasons' Tavern in Great Queen Street, normally on the first Wednesday of each month. Summer banquets took place downriver at Greenwich, or at the Star and Garter in Richmond. But not in 1858: that year the venue was moved to the Mitre Hotel at Hampton Court, because of 'the offensive condition of the Thames' at Greenwich. Initiation and joining fees were £10 (£15 from 1867; 15 guineas from 1880).

Some idea of the ceremonial arrangements of this revitalized lodge can be gathered from its inventory of furniture and regalia (see List 1 opposite).[49] All these seem to have been Westminster and Keystone property. Extra items had then to be purchased as the lodge began to grow (see List 2 opposite). Membership of the augmented Westminster and Keystone Lodge – at times almost an Apollo in London – included numbers of Oxford grandees: Sir Michael Hicks Beach ('Black Michael', a future Tory Chancellor of the Exchequer); Viscount Adare, soon to be 4th Earl of Dunraven; Viscount Newry (as 3rd Earl of Kilmorey a future leader of Ulster's anti-Home Rulers); Prince Leopold, Duke of Albany, youngest son of Queen Victoria;[50] Lord Kenlis, Earl of Bective, heir to the City fortune – and Parliamentary seat – of

LIST 1:
INVENTORY OF FURNITURE AND REGALIA

- Three Pedestals … £15 0s. 0.
- Three Candlesticks … £8 8s. 0.
- Two columns for Wardens £3 3s. 0.
- Wands for Deacons and D.C. [Director of Ceremonies] £2 5s. 0.
- Two kneeling stools … £2 10s. 0.
- Sheet for 3rd Degree … £1 10s. 0.
- Sword for Tyler … £1 10s. 0.
- Four Slippers and Three Cable Tows 12s. 0.
- Lodge Banner … £5 0s. 0.
- Banners for W.M. and Wardens £12 0s. 0.
- Mosaic Flooring £4 4s. 0.
- Three framed Tracing Boards £2 3s. 0.
- Shears for Perfect Ashlar £2 10s. 0.
- Square, Level and Plumb for W.M. and Wardens £1 0s. 0.
- Cushion for Volume of Sacred Law [Bible] £1 0s 0.
- Secretary's Table with cover and emblems £3 10s. 0.
- Repairs to Furniture £5 0s. 0.
- Three Gavels for use at Banquets 12s. 0.
- Total estimate outlay £72 17s. 0.

LIST 2:
EXTRA ITEMS PURCHASED FOR THE LODGE

- Three Chairs for the W.M. [Worshipful Master] and Wardens.
- Three platforms for ditto.
- One Chair for the I.P.M. [Immediate Past Master]
- One large mahogany and two small pedestals
- Working tools in mahogany case
- A set of sixteen Officers' silver jewels with silver square and compasses in case
- Another set of sixteen Officers' collars in tin box
- Volume of Sacred Law [Bible], with velvet cushion and cover
- Three ivory Gavels
- Rough Ashlar. Perfect Ashlar
- Alms Box and Alms Dish
- Emblems of Mortality in Box
- Poignard in sheath
- Twenty-four Inch Gauge, level, brass square and compasses
- Two black velvet bandages and box
- Two E.A. [Entered Apprentice] and F.C. [Fellow Craft] aprons
- Pair of small globes and gilt ornament for W.M.'s Chair in case
- Mahogany Ballot Box in deal case
- Antique tracing in Marble
- Book of the Constitutions
- Minute, Declaration and Signature Books
- Secretary's Portable Case

(left) Silver tankard (London, 1705, by John Read) presented in 1850 to Apollo University Lodge No. 460. It is still used to collect alms.

(right) Silver salver (London 1854, Hands and son). A legacy from Revd C.J. Ridley, 1854, Provincial Grand Master of Oxfordshire.

(left) Rock brought from Mount Parnassus (location of the ancient Temple of Apollo) and presented to the lodge by William Lane Fox and Ralph Fawcett.

A LEGACY
from the late
Provincial Grand Master of Oxfordshire
The Revᵈ. C.I. Ridley M.A.
TO THE
Apollo University Lodge
Nᵒ 460 OXFORD
1854.

William Thompson of Underley Hall, Westmoreland; J.H. Arkwright, scion of a spinning dynasty translated via Eton and Christ Church to the battlements of Hampton Court, Herefordshire;[51] Sutton Chichester of the War Office, a name to conjure with in Tory circles, Secretary of the Carlton Club – a place not unknown to Apollo men;[52] and City magnate Alban Gibbs – the future 2nd Baron Aldenham – who had married a daughter of Beresford Hope and lived for a while in Arcadian isolation at St Dunstan's in Regent's Park. In addition, there was a scattering of backbench Conservative MPs (William Evelyn from Surrey, George Cornewall Legh from Cheshire and John Malcolm from Argyll) and a long cohort of lawyers (Leopold Robbins, Philip Scratchley,

Reverse of a nineteenth-century Apollo University Lodge plate, marked 'Apollo 460'.

LIST 3:
DINNER MENU PRICE LIST

– Dinner and Dessert 8s. 6d.

– Waiters 1s. 0d.

– Tea and Coffee 1s. 0d.

– Refreshments after the Tyler's toast, by individual arrangement.

Prices of Wines

– Sherry: Gonzalez at Dinner 7s. per bottle.

– Gold at Dessert 6s. …

– Steinwein 7s. …

– Claret: at Dinner 6s.

– at Dessert 8s. …

– Port to be decanted

– Champagne any brand 10s.

– Hockheim 6s.

– Rudesheim 6s.

– Bills of Fare to be charged 5s.

– For Dinner with Turtle Soup 3s. per head extra.

George Cary, Albert Pearson, William Salting, Charles Tahourdin, Charles Webster, George Dodd, Alfred Cripps and George Murray).

Some idea of a Westminster and Keystone dinner menu can be gleaned from the price list agreed in 1870 with Mr Francatelli, manager of the Freemasons' Tavern Co. (see List 3 left). Dinners were clearly substantial rather than lavish. In 1871 there was some discussion as to whether or not the menu should include 'Black Puddings' or 'Marrow Bones'.[53]

Apollo grandees naturally attracted luminaries from other lodges. In this way the Westminster and Keystone became increasingly fashionable. Ferrers, Holmesdale, Milltown, Pevensey, Powerscourt, Sudeley, Valletort, Tyrone and Clonmell: such young noblemen – with links, often enough, to fashionable regiments – could mix readily enough with their compeers from Apollo. Valletort (later 4th Earl of Mount Edgcumbe, 1832–1917), for instance, became Lord Chamberlain and Lord Steward as well as a Deputy Grand Master of Grand Lodge. But there were other non-Apollo men too, famous in rather different fields. For example, in the 1860s, a clutch of clubbable gentlemen-architects: William Burges, F.P. Cockerell, R.W. Edis, W.E. Nesfield and Matthew Digby Wyatt. Dinners in Great Queen Street, river trips to Greenwich: such occasions must have been enlivened by these talented members from outside the Oxford circle. But it was the Apollo men who tended to dominate, at least between 1855 and 1878.[54]

COURT, CABINET AND THE EMPIRE

Among the Apollo group in London, two in particular played major parts in court, Cabinet and lodge: the 2nd Baron Skelmersdale and the 4th Earl of Carnarvon. Carnarvon was initiated in Westminster and Keystone Lodge in 1856 and joined Apollo (sponsored by his friend George Portal) in 1857; Skelmersdale was initiated in Apollo in 1856 and joined the Westminster and Keystone in 1857.

Edward Bootle-Wilbraham, later Skelmersdale, later still 1st Earl of Lathom (1837–1898), was never a professional politician. But as a Lord in Waiting, Capt. of the Yeomen of the Guard and Lord Chamberlain of the Household, he lived his life in the ambience of the court. At Lathom House, Lancashire, he exercised the traditional responsibilities of landowning; as a leading Freemason he acted as Deputy Grand Master to his close friend, Edward, Prince of Wales. 'As handsome as he was good and generous', noted Lord Redesdale; 'very courtly

(below left) Edward Bootle-Wilbraham, later 2nd Baron Skelmersdale, later still 1st Earl of Lathom (Apollo, 1856).

(below right) Henry Herbert, 4th Earl of Carnarvon (Apollo, 1857).

Earl of Carnarvon

and resourceful' agreed Queen Victoria; Skelmersdale joined with Lords Limerick and Mount Edgcumbe in forming a Masonic coterie of some power among the Conservative peers in the House of Lords.[55] Limerick was actually twice Capt. of the Yeomen of the Guard as well as Lord in Waiting to Lord Chamberlain Lathom and Conservative Whip in the House of Lords, 1889–96.[56]

Henry Herbert, known at Oxford as Lord Porchester; known to a wider world as Lord Carnarvon – Skelmersdale's close contemporary and immediate predecessor at the top of the Masonic hierarchy – occupied a somewhat larger stage. Three times he held government office: at the Colonial Office – under Derby and Disraeli – and then again as Lord Lieutenant of Ireland under Lord Salisbury. His political career spanned several decades. But he was only spasmodically successful. If he succeeded in Canada, he failed in Southern Africa and – predictably no doubt – in Ireland. 'Possessed as he was by a great charm of manner, of eloquence and industry', noted Lord George Hamilton, 'yet he had a microbe of incurable fidgetiness in his composition. Three times in twenty years did he resign from office.'[57] He was really a Whig embedded in a sequence of Tory governments. In terms of political affiliation, he had more in common with Gladstone than with Disraeli. By temperament and instinct he preferred his library at Highclere to the cut and thrust of Westminster. But he was happiest of all in Great Queen Street. There, as Deputy and later Pro Grand Master – 'the working chieftain of the Masonic Order in England' – he laboured persistently for the good of what he liked to call 'the kingdom' of Freemasonry.[58] India, Canada, South Africa, Australia and New Zealand – what tied these new worlds 'to the old mother country', he believed, was 'the link of English Freemasonry'.[59]

Freemasonry's proudest boast as fraternity and charity – that it encompassed all religions, all classes, all races – was to come nearest to fulfilment in this high tide of Empire before the Great War; but it was part of a tradition of internationalism stretching back into the eighteenth century. When in 1802 the Chevalier Bartholomew Ruspini had led into the great hall of Grand Lodge a procession of 'charity girls' – children funded by the Royal Cumberland School (now part of the Royal Masonic Trust for Girls and Boys) – the audience was significantly global. Next to British royalty and nobility, the Lord Mayor of London and the capital's chief magistrate, stood the Ottoman ambassador (Yusuf Agah Efendi) and the Chief of the Embassy for Creek and Cherokee Nations (General Bowles).

By the late Victorian period the reach of Freemasonry had extended even further, led first as Grand Master by the future Edward VII, and then by his successor (brother and Brother) Prince Arthur, Duke of Connaught and Strathearn. As Lord Carnarvon put it, in an appropriately Masonic metaphor, the Prince of Wales's ceremonial duties as Grand Master – notably his travels in the Indian subcontinent – had truly 'cemented those blocks – those colossal blocks – of empire'. Here indeed was 'the convergence of Masonry, empire and monarchy'.[60]

Others would play more famous parts in the great imperial drama: Kipling, Kitchener, Roberts, Wolseley, Rhodes himself (Apollo, 1877); empire builders and Freemasons to a man. But it was Carnarvon and his circle, operating from their command base in Grand Lodge, who orchestrated this global Masonic network. By the 1890s there were more than 400 English lodges overseas.[61]

In camp and trading post, in colony and dominion, the lodge followed the flag. In all this, Apollo University Lodge had a not inconsiderable part to play. When in 1892 a slim volume appeared entitled *Tennyson and Our Imperial Heritage*, it was quite appropriately written by an Apollo man, the Revd William Greswell of Brasenose.[62]

The Apollo diaspora was worldwide. Lodge members, for example, found themselves planted out in chaplaincies across the globe. Peter Hansell (Apollo, 1826) at Caen; Henry Tristram (Apollo, 1844) in Bermuda; Robert Leach (Apollo, 1859) at Oporto; Archibald Knollys (Apollo, 1874) at Florence; Augustus Blundell (Apollo, 1862) at Odessa; William Beach (Apollo, 1863) in Hong Kong; John Brunesson (Apollo, 1863) in the Punjab and Henry Midwinter (Apollo, 1869) in Baroda; John Robbins (Apollo, 1852) and William Emmett (Apollo, 1867) at Wiesbaden and Freiburg respectively; William Hobart (Apollo, 1876) in Madras; Edmund Jermyn (Apollo, 1868), John Scobell (Apollo, 1864) and Ernest Brown (Apollo, 1875), all in Calcutta; John Clough (Apollo, 1857) at Rangoon and Tounghoo; and finally Francis Stewart (Apollo, 1864) – clearly a most discerning traveller – first at Versailles and then in Monaco. Some of Apollo's wandering clergy roamed particularly far afield: Richard Norman (Apollo, 1851) spent years as an incumbent in Montreal; Arthur Rivers (Apollo, 1877) and Robert Stanford (Apollo, 1862) stayed half a lifetime in Sydney, Australia and Dunedin, New Zealand. And even those who remained nearer home sometimes ended their days in places which must have seemed peculiarly remote: Herbert Richardson (Apollo, 1856) spent the bulk of

(opposite) Edward, Prince of Wales, later King Edward VII (Apollo, 1873). Grand Master of the United Grand Lodge of England. 'Secret societies as a rule are to be deprecated', he told Queen Victoria in 1868; 'but I can assure you that this has unpolitical significance … [and] I feel convinced that I should have many opportunities of doing great good.'

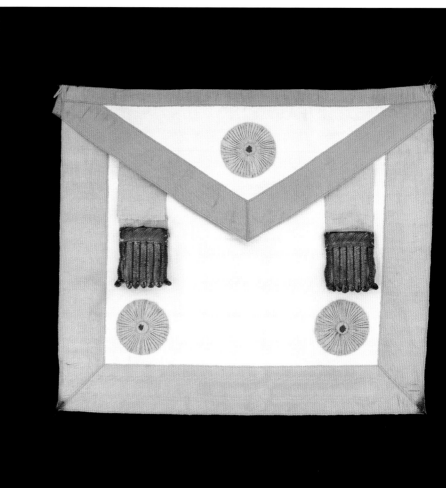

his life as chaplain and canon at the College of the Holy Spirit on the Scottish island of Cumbrae.

The Masonic career of Cecil Rhodes deserves particular mention. On the very day – 2 June 1877 – when he became a member of the exclusively Christian branch of Freemasonry familiarly known as the Rose Croix, he set out his personal 'Confession of Faith'. In effect this proved to be the germ of a whole sequence of subsequent wills and testaments. The future Rhodes Trust was to embody an implicitly Masonic spirit. Rhodes' memorandum envisioned the formation of a global brotherhood, 'with but one object, the furtherance of the British Empire and the bringing of the whole uncivilised world under British rule; [it would work] for the recovery of the United States [and] for the making of the Anglo-Saxon race [into] one Empire … [After all] the more of the world we inhabit, the better it is for the human race'.

Here Rhodes – still an undergraduate, but already a formidable figure in the politics of Africa – was conjuring up an imperial elite, a network of leaders embodying the discipline of the Jesuits, the mystery of Freemasonry, the racial

(above left) Cecil Rhodes (Apollo, 1877). On 2 June he was 'perfected' into the 18th Degree (Rose Croix); that night he prepared a personal 'Confession of Faith', in effect the germ of several subsequent wills and ultimately of the Rhodes Trust.

(above right) Cecil Rhodes's apron. This formed part of a wreath deposited on the bier of Cecil John Rhodes, inscribed: 'The Apollo University Lodge mourns her son of noble soul', presented to the lodge by Bros C. Fred Silberbauer and C. Christian Silberbauer.

fantasies of Winwood Reade, and the romance of Ruskin's first Slade Lecture. It was a vision that – at least for a while – seemed almost a possibility. In 1873 the future Edward VII – King and Emperor – had become Worshipful Master of Apollo Lodge; in 1875, before 8,000 Freemasons in the Royal Albert Hall, London, he was installed as Grand Master of the United Grand Lodge of England.[63]

ROYAL PATRONAGE AND NEW PREMISES

The future king first entered the Masonic fraternity in 1868. He was initiated not in England but in Stockholm, by the Swedish monarch – Charles XV – in his capacity as Grand Master of the Grand Lodge of Sweden. Queen Victoria was at first not pleased. 'I quite agree', replied the prince soothingly, 'that secret societies as a rule are to be deprecated, but I can assure you that this has unpolitical significance. More than that I cannot say, [but] I feel convinced that I shall have many opportunities of doing great good.'[64] Oxford Freemasons had sensed their opportunity some years before. In 1859–60 – while technically registered at Christ Church – the prince had lived outside college at Frewin Hall, close to the Clarendon Hotel, while undergoing a little gentle tuition. In March 1863 the Brethren of Apollo held a torchlight procession to celebrate his wedding.[65] And in June that year the prince and princess were guests of honour at a Masonic Commemoration Ball in Oxford's new Corn Exchange.

The new Exchange was a sub-Ruskinian structure of brick and iron. It required some additional decoration to turn it into a ballroom. Flags and banners, mirrors and wreaths, carpets, chandeliers and curtains: the principal room was made festive without being frivolous. Ladies wore crinoline ball dresses. Gentlemen were garbed in Masonic regalia. Tickets were priced at 1 guinea each. But the cost of staging the whole operation turned out to be rather more than the lodge had bargained for. Three years previously, a musical fête and a summer ball had both been financially successful.[66] But in 1863, to match the prospect of royal patronage, no expense was spared. The final cost – a staggering £2,046 for the ball alone: nearly as much as the cost of the Corn Exchange itself – had to be shared between Apollo and Christ Church, with Apollo making up its own contribution by drawing on the surplus profits of their fête of the same year.

Some idea of the arrangements for the ball can be gathered from the list of materials which had to be sold off afterwards. Apparently, a processional entrance through a corridor marquee led via a carpeted staircase into the ballroom itself. For the purpose of sitting out between dances, and taking light refreshment, a separate room was specially fitted up for the principal guests.[67] The fittings were impressive (see List 4 below).

Not everything was disposed of. The lodge retained a good many items for use on future occasions. Their cost was carefully noted (see List 5 below).[68]

Afterwards the lodge had to hold an enquiry into the cost. The Secretary felt obliged to resign. And it would be eight years and more before the prince actually joined Apollo. But whatever the immediate expense, a precedent had now been set. Henceforward the annual Masonic Ball and the Garden Party or Musical Fête became the highlights of Commemoration Week. In 1866, no fewer than 750 attended the ball in the Clarendon Hotel: the takings amounted to £751. 19s. 11d., with a profit of £65. 13s. 5d. In the same year as many as 3,212

LIST 4:
ITEMS SOLD AFTER THE
COMMEMMORATION BALL

– 4 large chimney glasses £ 25. 4. 0.

– 2 oval mirrors 7. 17. 6.

– 20 banners, poles and ends 31. 10. 0.

– Carpet for gallery 5. 14. 10.

– Glass Chandelier in the Prince's room 21. 0. 0.

– Carpet for Prince's room 10. 14. 2.

– 3 White Mats 1. 11. 6.

– 3 Gilt Lamps, used in the corridor 9. 9. 0.

– Table Cloths 2. 10. 0.

– Glass for the Royal Table 14. 7. 0.

   Total: 135. 8. 4.

LIST 5:
ITEMS RETAINED AFTER THE
COMMEMMORATION BALL

– 17 Silvered Mirrors (without frames) £65. 10. 0.

– 2 Armorial Devices 7. 17. 6

– Masonic Mottoes 5. 5. 0.

– Large diaper cloth 20. 2. 0.

– Brussels carpet to go round it 14. 7. 10

– Pink Calico 10. 0. 0.

– 25 Panels with fluted calico 6. 10. 0.

– 17 Pairs of Curtains 14. 10 6.

– 6 Sofas (as fitted) 9. 0. 0.

– Corridor and papering 61. 4. 10.

– Roses for decorating 14. 5. 0.

– Carpet for Corridor 28. 9. 3.

– Flower Baskets 2. 2. 0.

– Brussels Carpet for Staircase 3. 7. 0.

   Total: 262. 10. 11

(above) The 'Arch of Steel': reception of the Prince and Princess of Wales at the Commemoration Ball given by Apollo University Lodge in June 1863. The Prince and Princess were guests of honour and tickets were priced at one guinea each. Engraving from the *Illustrated London News*.

(overleaf) The Corn Exchange, Oxford, as decorated for the Commemoration Ball, June 1863. Engraving from the *Illustrated London News*.

were present at the Fête in New College garden: that meant 1,912 subscribing members' tickets; 1,300 tickets by invitation; with takings of £402. 15s. 6d., producing a profit of £140. 5s. 8d.[69] In 1883 the Ball was actually held – much to Ruskin's displeasure – in the University's New Examination Schools,[70] designed by an appropriately Masonic architect, Brother T.G. Jackson (Apollo, 1856). In 1884 no fewer than 1,597 people attended the Fête in Worcester College gardens.[71] Such figures give us some idea of Apollo's prominence and status at this time: Freemasonry was integral at the grandest level to the social life of late-Victorian Oxford. Not until after the close of the Great War would the vice chancellor's Encaenia Garden Party replace the Masonic Fête as Oxford's premier social event of the year. The last Oxford University Masonic Ball took place, symbolically enough, in the summer of 1914.[72]

As early as 1864 Apollo clearly sensed it had outgrown its homely headquarters in Alfred Street. A new site was leased from the Clarendon Hotel, facing the Oxford Union; and by 1866 a new University Masonic Hall had been

finished to the designs of Brother E.G. Bruton.[73] Four-square late Gothic in appearance, with a 'large Lodge Room and other buildings', Apollo's new home cost as much as £1,400. Here Cecil Rhodes was initiated in 1876. Here the lodge would meet until 1926. Here as many as 2,000 undergraduates would join the Masonic Order.

As Apollo grew, its traditions of philanthropy were not forgotten. Contributions to Masonic charities – small but regular – continued to appear in the minutes of nearly every meeting. And occasionally there are donations to outside charities as well. In November 1862, for instance, £20 was voted 'towards the fund for the Lancashire Distress'.[74] The American Civil War – or rather its consequent Cotton Famine blockades – impinged even on undergraduate conclaves in an obscure Oxford backstreet.

The University Examination Schools (1876–82), designed by Brother T.G. Jackson (Apollo, 1856), and the venue for the Masonic Ball of 1883.

Signed photograph of
Prince Leopold, presented
to the lodge by W.A.F.
Hendrick, 1874.

NOTMAN & SANDHAM—MONTREAL

H.R.H. Prince Leopold was Initiated into
Apollo University Lodge as an undergraduate
of Christ Church on 1 May 1874. He was
Worshipful Master in 1876 and Provincial
Grand Master for Oxfordshire from 1876 until
his death in 1884.

This signed photograph was presented to the
Lodge by W.Bro. W.A.F.Hendrick on 29 xii 74.

In February 1872 Apollo diplomatically congratulated the Prince of Wales on recovery from serious illness; in April the same year – eight years and eight months after the Commemoration Ball – they elected him an Hon. Life Member; by March 1873 he had been made Worshipful Master.[75] That clinched the social standing of the Brethren in Oxford. Unlike Prince Leopold, later Duke of Albany (Apollo, 1874; installed as Provincial Grand Master in the Sheldonian Theatre in 1876), the future King Edward VII was a symbolic rather than an active member of the lodge. But his role in wider Masonic circles was conducted with panache. In 1875, Earl Percy, later 7th Duke of Northumberland (Apollo, 1866), began a decade in office as Treasurer of the Queen's Household. Meanwhile, Grand Lodge itself was now led by a trio of Apollo men: Carnarvon, Skelmersdale and, of course, the prince himself.[76] And among lesser courtiers Freemasons were by no means rare. In 1874 Sir Robert Collins (Apollo, 1877), previously tutor to Prince Leopold, became the prince's (by then the Duke of Albany's) Comptroller of Household. In the same year the Hon. Alexander Grantham Yorke (Apollo, 1867), 5th son of the Earl of Hardwicke, became the duke's equerry and thus, in 1884, Groom in Waiting to the queen. Forgotten now, he has his own niche in history. It was Alec Yorke's off-colour repartee which provoked on one occasion that most famous of royal dismissals: 'We are not amused'.[77]

THE LODGE AND PARLIAMENTARY GRANDEES

In the Conservative administrations of the 1880s and 1890s, Apollo played a very strong hand. In the 1860s the lodge had been able to point to G.W. Hunt (Apollo, 1848), Disraeli's Chancellor of the Exchequer. 'Sensible and laborious', as Lord Stanley described him, he was a ponderous 25-stone giant – an expert on foot-and-mouth disease – who died of gout while taking the waters at Homburg in 1877. The next generation proved equally impressive and rather more resilient. Sir Michael Hicks Beach, 1st Earl St. Aldwyn (Apollo, 1856; Senior Grand Warden, 1865; Provincial Grand Master for Gloucestershire, 1880–1916), was twice Lord Salisbury's Chancellor of the Exchequer as well as twice Chief Secretary for Ireland.[78] Then there was William Beach (Apollo, 1848; Provincial Grand Master for Hampshire and the Isle of Wight, 1869–1901), who lived to become both a Privy Councillor and 'Father' of the House of Commons.

Walter Long, 1st Viscount Long (Apollo, 1874). A Tory Cabinet minister for a quarter of a century in five departments of state; forty years an MP in seven different constituencies; and a leading Irish Unionist.

That was just the beginning, however. It has been estimated that by the 1880s as many as 330 out of 360 Tory MPs had Masonic connections;[79] and quite a number of these were Apollo men holding key parliamentary offices. In the persons of two Tory chief whips, Freemasons controlled the organization of the Conservative Party in both Houses of Parliament. The 3rd Earl of Limerick was chief whip in the Lords; Aretas Akers-Douglas (Apollo, 1871) in the Commons.[80] In Walter Long (Apollo, 1874), Oxford Freemasonry could claim its typal Tory grandee: twenty-six years on the Conservative front bench; twenty-five years in ministerial office in five different departments of state; forty years as MP for no fewer than seven different constituencies (North Wilts, Devizes, Liverpool, Bristol, Dublin, Middlesex and Westminster) – and an apparently immovable fixture in the councils of the Carlton Club. In 1911 he came within an ace of succeeding Balfour himself. And as an Irish Unionist – bafflingly diehard and pragmatic by turns – he played a darkly ambivalent role in the tortuous manoeuvres of 1918–21. He even helped to draft the two-headed Government of Ireland Act (1920).[81]

Apollo's function therefore as a vehicle of ambition at this time scarcely needs stressing. Its roll-call of lawyers – of whom more in Chapter 4 – certainly makes that clear. But among Apollo's late-Victorian grandees perhaps the most memorable example is William Lehman Ashmead Bartlett, master of hypergamy, who entered Apollo in 1872. Born in Plymouth, Massachusetts, he was raised by his widowed mother in Torquay, Devon. She introduced him to the richest heiress in England, Angela Burdett-Coutts. And it was that famously philanthropic baroness who paid for young Bartlett's education. At Keble College, Oxford – then newly founded – he achieved only a third-class degree in Modern History. But by then he was already a member of Apollo and a student at the Inner Temple. Within six years he was not only organizing the disbursement of the Burdett-Coutts fortune, but had actually married his patroness, some thirty-seven years his senior. This '*mad* marriage', as Queen Victoria called it, was curiously successful. Financially, it made much work for lawyers. But at least it seems to have pleased the baroness. It was certainly the making of Bartlett. In the year of his wedding, thanks to the magic of royal licence, he even managed to quadruple his surname:

> For fortune hunting to eternal fame stands
> William Pole Tylney-Long-Wellesley-Tylney-Long's name.
> But he was scarcely fit to lick thy boots
> William Lehman Ashmead Burdett-Coutts-Bartlett-Coutts.[82]

Sir Michael Hicks Beach, 1st Earl St Aldwyn (Apollo, 1856). Twice Lord Salisbury's Chancellor of the Exchequer as well as Disraeli's Colonial Secretary and Chief Secretary for Ireland. 'A firm believer in the Masonic virtues of charity, patriotism and good fellowship.'

Among those whose social position was rather more secure, the responsibilities of Freemasonry were taken on out of a sense of duty, specifically to reinforce the bonds of community. In newly developing urban centres such ties had to be created afresh. But in rural areas the links between classes – through occupation, sport, religion or folk memory – were already there. Here Freemasonry was able to build on local tradition. The career of Sir Michael Hicks Beach supplies a neat example. Apollo Lodge, Cottesmore Lodge, Westminster and Keystone Lodge, Provincial Grand Master of Gloucestershire: all his life Hicks Beach believed firmly in the Masonic virtues of charity, patriotism and good fellowship.

He deemed it well for a countryside that men of all kinds should meet periodically as friends, untroubled by class or creed, by politics or social status. He would spare no trouble to attend such meetings, even in remote country places, and it was a matter of marvel to some of his acquaintances that he should readily endure what they esteemed as boredom if not waste of time. But in truth he was not bored. Deep in his nature was love of the country folk, gentle or simple, among whom he was bred. He was at home among them, ready to exchange jokes with his old acquaintance, and to talk with an ease and friendliness which would have amazed some of those who only knew him in public life.[83]

4 CLERICS AND LAWYERS, 1830s–1880s

(opposite) Oscar Wilde (Apollo, 1875). 'Perfected' into the 18th degree of the Rose Croix, 1876; advanced into the Mark Degree at the University Mark Lodge. 'I have got rather keen on Masonry lately', he noted in 1877; 'I believe in it awfully – in fact would be awfully sorry to have to give it up.' However, he was expelled from Apollo in 1883 for failing to pay his subscription; and his name was later 'erased' from the 'Golden Book' of the Rose Croix Chapter, following an order from the Supreme Council of the 33rd Degree of the Rite.

IN THREE YEARS, BETWEEN 1872 and 1875, no fewer than 27 Magdalen men joined Apollo out of an intake of 218; an influx second only in number to Christ Church with 36. Two of this group became firm friends. Their later careers diverged widely. But the coincidence of their meeting tells us much about later-ninteenth-century Oxford and still more about late-Victorian Apollo. The first of these was David Hunter Blair (later the Rt Revd Sir David Oswald Hunter Blair, 5th Bt, OSB; Abbot of Fort Augustus and titular Abbot of Dunfermline). The second was Oscar Wilde.

Years later, Hunter Blair recalled that when he arrived in Oxford there was a good deal of 'vigorous Masonic propaganda going on' at Magdalen.[84] The vice president of the College (Revd Reginald Bird) was at that point also Deputy Master of Apollo – Deputy, in fact, to the Prince of Wales. Magdalen was a fashionable place to be. Hunter Blair was a handsome Etonian, heir to a baronetcy and to a great estate at Blairquhan in Ayrshire. Oscar was simply Oscar. Hunter Blair went up in 1872 aged 18; Wilde in 1874 aged 20. So they were very close in years. Close too in their fascination with the Middle Ages and with Catholicism. Both were able to attend lectures by John Ruskin and Walter Pater; and Wilde certainly did so.[85] Wilde was already a closet Catholic: as an infant he had been covertly baptised during a holiday in Wicklow. Hunter Blair converted to Catholicism in 1875, and took Wilde with him on a visit to Rome in 1877. There they were received by Pope Pius IX. Wilde was moved to write one of his more evocative pieces, 'On hearing the Dies Irae sung in the Sistine Chapel'.[86]

It was apparently J.E.C. Bodley of Balliol (Apollo, 1874) who introduced Wilde to Apollo. On 21 February 1875 Bodley noted in his diary:

> Went down with W[ilde] to Corpus. Found the Count [W.O. Goldschmidt of Dresden] … we called on [Robert] Williamson [Christ Church; Apollo, 1871], where we had a long talk on Masonry. He produced his properties [Masonic regalia] and Wilde was as much struck by their gorgeousness, as he was amazed at the mystery of our conversation.

Wilde's father had been an active Freemason in Dublin; so Oscar cannot have been wholly unacquainted with life in the lodge. He certainly found it an early forum for his wit. At initiation on 23 February, after learning that the founder of the Order was reputed to be St John the Baptist, he replied: 'I hope we shall emulate his life but not his death – I mean we ought to keep our heads.' Singing Masonic choruses, however, proved rather more difficult than producing epigrams: Wilde's voice was apparently no more than 'a well-meaning but unsteady monotone'. That did not impede his Masonic career in Oxford. In 1875 he joined the nearby Churchill Lodge (then under the mastership of the historian H.O. Wakeman of All Souls); in 1876 he was 'Perfected' into the 18th Degree of the Rose Croix; and in 1877 he was advanced into the Degree of Mark Master Mason at the University Mark Lodge No. 55. 'I have got rather keen on Masonry lately', he wrote to William Ward (Apollo, 1873) in 1877: 'I believe in it awfully – in fact would be awfully sorry to have to give it up.' By 1880, however, his early enthusiasm – and his resources – had diminished; and in 1883 he was expelled

The Rt Revd Sir David Oswald Hunter Blair, 5th Bt, OSB (Apollo, 1872). An Oxford friend of Oscar Wilde. In 1875 he converted to Roman Catholicism and repudiated Freemasonry, later becoming Abbot of Fort Augustus and a privy chamberlain to Pope Pius IX.

from the lodge for failing to pay his subscription. In 1895 – as a mark of final ignominy – his now scandalous name was 'erased' from the Golden Book of the Rose Croix Chapter, following an order from the Supreme Council of the 33rd Degree.[87]

As an undergraduate Wilde had been more than happy to follow Masonic routine. Famously photographed in a variation of the Apollo uniform – knee breeches and tails; white tie, silk stockings and pumps – he looks very much at ease (see p. 70). Certainly when he progressed to the Rose Croix degree in 1876 he had no trouble with the appropriate regalia. Wilde's knee breeches, in fact, would become something of a trademark in Aesthetic circles; just as the panelling in Pater's rooms at Brasenose (1864) – mingling the colours of primrose flower and primrose leaf – became an icon of 'greenery-yallery' taste.

Hunter Blair, however, developed doubts more quickly, and more decisively than Wilde. His memoirs put the matter bluntly.

> Grand Lodge [gave me] a dispensation [as to my age of entry]. This cost several guineas, so did my entrance to the Lodge; so did my annual subscription; so did my dues to the Grand Lodge; so did the purchase of the insignia or regalia of the brotherhood; so did the 'banquets' or suppers which took place after each lodge-meeting; so did one's share in the expenses of annual Masonic balls and other festivities. What did one get by way of *quid pro quo* for all these guineas? [Merely] the privilege of assisting at a good deal of … silly and childish ceremonial; and of listening to long-winded exhortations, expressed in indifferent English, mouthed out in a clerical drone by our reverend Worshipful Master [Revd H. Pickard of Christ Church], and recommending us to the practice of various social and civic virtues, in which, as far as I know, Freemasons had no sort of monopoly, although some of them seemed to think they had.

Reacting to the ceremonies of the lodge, Hunter Blair did not mince words: 'I object to the ritual; I object to the preliminary oath; … And I object very particularly to those un-Christian prayers.' His words caused 'some flutterings in the Masonic dovecotes'. He was directed to consult the Provincial Grand Chaplain (Revd W.F. Short of New College). Short suggested that since Hunter Blair took his religion so seriously he should look beyond Apollo – with its mixed ranks of 'theists and deists' – to the higher 'mysteries of Christian Masonry'; to something infinitely greater; to something beyond mere belief in

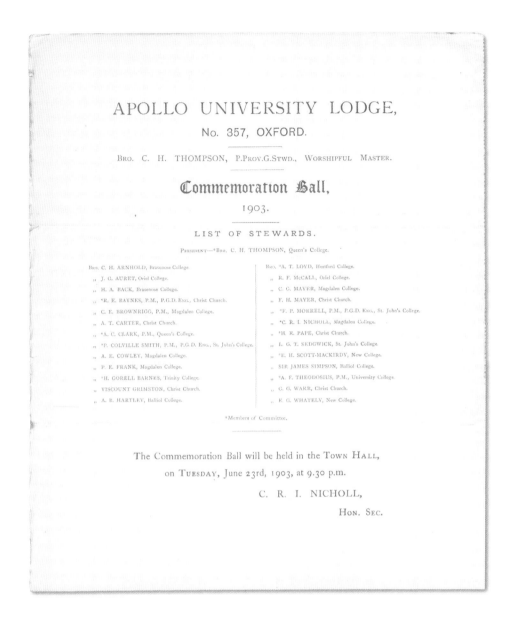

APOLLO UNIVERSITY LODGE,

No. 357, OXFORD.

BRO. C. H. THOMPSON, P.PROV.G.STWD., WORSHIPFUL MASTER.

Commemoration Ball,

1903.

LIST OF STEWARDS.

PRESIDENT—*BRO. C. H. THOMPSON, Queen's College.

Bro. C. H. ARNHOLD, Brasenose College.	Bro. *A. T. LOYD, Hertford College.
„ J. G. AURET, Oriel College.	„ R. F. McCALL, Oriel College.
„ H. A. BACK, Brasenose College.	„ C. G. MAYER, Magdalen College.
„ *R. E. BAYNES, P.M., P.G.D. ENG., Christ Church.	„ F. H. MAYER, Christ Church.
„ C. E. BROWNRIGG, P.M., Magdalen College.	„ *F. P. MORRELL, P.M., P.G.D. ENG., St. John's College.
„ A. T. CARTER, Christ Church.	„ *C. R. I. NICHOLL, Magdalen College.
„ *A. C. CLARK, P.M., Queen's College.	„ *H. R. PAPE, Christ Church.
„ *P. COLVILLE SMITH, P.M., P.G.D. ENG., St. John's College.	„ L. G. T. SEDGWICK, St. John's College.
„ A. E. COWLEY, Magdalen College.	„ *E. H. SCOTT-MACKIRDY, New College.
„ P. E. FRANK, Magdalen College.	„ SIR JAMES SIMPSON, Balliol College.
„ *H. GORELL BARNES, Trinity College.	„ *A. F. THEODOSIUS, P.M., University College.
„ VISCOUNT GRIMSTON, Christ Church.	„ G. G. WARR, Christ Church.
„ A. B. HARTLEY, Balliol College.	„ E. G. WHATELY, New College.

*Members of Committee.

The Commemoration Ball will be held in the TOWN HALL,

on TUESDAY, June 23rd, 1903, at 9.30 p.m.

C. R. I. NICHOLL,

HON. SEC.

'a Grand Architect or a Grand Geometrician of the Universe'. Alas, in doing so Hunter Blair then found that his worst suspicions were confirmed.

> Somewhere back in a quiet square … in the purlieus of Soho, [I was] introduced into a great hall, with a flower-bedecked altar blazing with lights. [Here was] a real secret society, which ordinary Freemasonry can hardly be called, [consisting of a few] quite elderly gentlemen, some of them of foreign name and appearance [engaged in] strange medieval rites. [They were, apparently] members of the Supreme Grand Council of the 33rd Degree. I never got further than the 18th. [It seemed just] an echo, I hope not a travesty, of the deepest Christian mysteries.

(above and opposite) List of stewards and subscription form for an Apollo University Lodge Commemoration Ball in 1903.

Apollo University Lodge

Of Antient, Free, and Accepted Masons, No. 357, Oxford.

COMMEMORATION BALL.

TUESDAY, JUNE 23rd, 1903.

Tickets for the Apollo University Lodge Commemoration Ball will be issued through *the Secretary and Members of the Lodge only* :—

I.   Tickets 21/- each, (after Saturday, June 20th, 26/-).

II.   For the actual issue of Tickets the Committee will sit at the Masonic Hall, Frewen Court, on Friday June 19th, Saturday June 20th, Monday June 22nd, and Tuesday June 23rd, from 12 to 2 p.m., though applications for Tickets may be made at once to the Secretary and the numbers of the tickets required will be reserved.

III.   *The Names and Addresses of those for whom Tickets are required must be given and the Committee reserve to themselves the right of rejecting any application.*

IV.   No Tickets will be issued to Members who are in arrears to the Lodge, nor will any be issued without previous payment.

V.   Cheques and Post Office Orders should be made payable to C. R. I. Nicholl, and crossed "Oxford Old Bank."

                                   C. R. I. NICHOLL, Hon. Sec.

University Masonic Hall,   Magdalen College.
    Frewen Court, Oxford.

To the Hon. Sec.,
           Please issue   *Tickets for the Ladies and Gentlemen undermentioned, for which I*
enclose the sum of £

                        (Signature)

                                        Member of the Apollo University Lodge.

GENTLEMEN.	ADDRESSES.

LADIES.	ADDRESSES.

Thus it was that the future Benedictine abbot conceived an aversion to 'the mummery – as I had reason to think, dangerous mummery – of the whole business'. He concludes with an almost perceptible shudder: 'I cut myself off from it all. But I often wondered what those mysterious old gentlemen did with all my guineas.'[88]

FREEMASONRY AND CATHOLICISM

Hunter Blair's was a very partial account, omitting, for example, all mention of Masonic charity. But it does touch upon a peculiarly sensitive nerve: the relationship between Freemasonry and Catholicism. As his priestly career progressed, Hunter Blair came to the conclusion that Latin Freemasonry – that is, the practice of Masonic lodges in France, Italy and South America – was engaged in 'a perpetual and untiring warfare against the Catholic Church'. Masonic schools in those areas, to take one example, apparently set out to exclude 'every semblance of Christian teaching' from their curricula. These Latin lodges, he concluded, were thus 'not only anti-Christian but Atheistical'. And to a lesser degree so were lodges in Great Britain. Secret Masonic oaths, he decided, were either frivolous – and therefore 'an act of blasphemous irreverence' – or else serious, and therefore 'in the highest degree unlawful, criminal and immoral'.

One Pro Grand Master, Lord Carnarvon, explicitly repudiated any tendency among Freemasons to indulge in revolutionary forms of secular and anti-clerical prejudice. So did Sir Charles Dalrymple Bt, MP (Hunter Blair's brother-in-law), Grand Master of Scottish Freemasons. He maintained that in reality the Masonic motto was: 'Pro Rege, lege, et grege' (For King, Law, and People), and that Freemasons taught and practised religion, loyalty and good citizenship. Yet fraternal relations – perhaps even reciprocal rites – apparently persisted between British and Continental lodges. Anglo-Saxon Freemasonry came to seem irrevocably tarred with Latin Freemasonry's conspiratorial and secularist brush.[89]

Hunter Blair's doubts were, however, part of something much wider. Behind the evolution of Masonic organization – and the development, for example, of Apollo itself – lay a larger and more significant tale: the long story of papal opposition to Freemasonry. This calls for a brief digression.

Pope Clement XII condemned Freemasonry in 1738, Pope Benedict XIV in 1751. It is doubtful whether either actually knew of Anderson's *Constitutions*. The Vatican cared little for English practice. It trained its fire on rather more immediate threats: the political lodges, secret and anti-clerical, of France and Italy. Similarly, when Pope Pius IX condemned Freemasonry in 1846, 1865, 1869 and 1873 he went out of his way to assert the civil jurisdiction of the Vatican in Italy as much as its theological authority worldwide. Again, when Pope Leo XIII condemned Freemasonry in 1884, 1894 and 1902 he had Latin Freemasonry in mind: not only its anti-clerical liberalism but also its philosophical relativism, postulated for example in the 'rationalistic naturalism' of G.E. Lessing's *Philosophy of Freemasonry* (1777–80). Both of these aspects – political and philosophical – seemed to pose an existential threat to papal power. 'Christianity and Freemasonry', Leo XIII concluded, 'are essentially incompatible'.[90] That remained the official view in Rome – renewed by Pope Benedict XV in 1917 – until the great resettlement of attitudes associated with the Second Vatican Council from 1959 onwards. However, any tendencies thereafter to a rather more irenic stance were cut short in 1983–85 by successive declarations from Cardinal Ratzinger, later Pope Benedict XVI. Under his influence, the Sacred Congregation flatly restated its traditional prohibition, lumping together Latin and Anglo-Saxon Freemasonry; Catholic Freemasons were held to be excommunicated.

Needless to say, that was not the end of the story. Individual Catholics, particularly in England – though not, it should be said, Catholic clergy – sometimes contrived to keep a foot in both camps. After all, Grand Lodge had never prohibited Catholic membership. And on the Roman side philosophical defences of Freemasonry as a non-religious philanthropic brotherhood, held together by a secret system of signs and symbols, continued to find occasional support.[91] The Church of England remained – and remains – divided on the matter. Archbishop Geoffrey Fisher, for example – Grand Chaplain in 1937 and 1939 – was an enthusiastic Freemason. And although Rowan Williams, Archbishop of Canterbury 2002–12, whose father was a Freemason, once confessed that Masonic oaths filled him with 'unease', John Habgood, Archbishop of York 1983–95, was content to describe the ceremonial of the lodge as simply 'a rather inoffensive eccentricity'.[92]

The tensions between Freemasonry and Catholicism in Victorian England – never far from the surface – exploded publicly in 1874 during the Grand Mastership of George Frederick Robinson, 1st Marquess of Ripon. Now Ripon was a man of contradictions: a Liberal politician of Cabinet rank, a socialist sympathizer and a considerable landowner, lord of Fountains Abbey in Yorkshire. After the death of the Duke of Sussex in 1843, the Grand Mastership had passed to his deputy, the 2nd Earl of Zetland. When Zetland retired in 1870 Lord Ripon, Zetland's deputy since 1861, was elected in his stead – but within four years he had resigned. Openly he announced his conversion to Rome; he abdicated his Grand Mastership; and he withdrew from Gladstone's Cabinet. The comments of *The Times* – in robustly jingoistic style – tell us the public reaction.

It is notorious that Freemasons are under the especial ban of the Church of Rome. That Church tolerates no secret society, except that of the Jesuits; and the first sacrifice which would be demanded of a convert like Lord Ripon would be his withdrawal from [Freemasonry] … [And so he] has renounced his mental and moral freedom, and has submitted himself to the guidance of the Roman Catholic priesthood. To become a Roman Catholic and remain a thorough Englishman are – it cannot be disguised – almost incompatible conditions … [Ripon's] mind must necessarily have undergone what to Englishmen can only seem a fatal demoralisation. [Thus, after several centuries] … Fountains Abbey passes once more into Roman Catholic hands.[93]

Well, at least Ripon was not an Apollo man.

APOLLO, OXFORD AND THE CHURCH

In Oxford the working alliance between Freemasonry and Anglicanism remained intact. Among nineteenth-century Apollo members, conversions to Roman Catholicism were rare. Before Hunter Blair's 'perversion' in 1875 there were no more than half a dozen; and several of these occurred in circumstances from which no general trend can be drawn. William Monsell, later 1st Baron Emly (Apollo, 1831), for many years Liberal MP for Limerick, went over to Rome in 1850. His motives cannot have been entirely divorced from politics: he was much involved with attempts to ameliorate the Great Famine in Ireland. With others the case is less clear. Lord Charles Thynne (Apollo, 1831), for example, born the seventh son of the 2nd Marquis of Bath, became a Canon of Canterbury in 1845 but seceded to Rome in 1852, only to return in 1886. Three more – W.H. North (Apollo, 1854; later 11th Baron North), Verney Cave-Browne Cave (Apollo, 1855) and G.S. Lane-Fox (Apollo, 1857) – were to join the Roman Communion around this time but their secession created little impact.

Not so the case of Frederick Oakeley (Apollo, 1825). Forgotten now, except as a creator of Victorian Christmas: in 1840 he translated *Adeste Fideles* into English; his career illustrates only too well the mental turmoil – what he described as the 'volcanic' force – of the early Oxford Movement. Oakeley was a shy, overwrought classicist from Christ Church who became first a Chaplain Fellow of Balliol and then priest in charge of Margaret Street Chapel. From that ritualist base – predecessor of All Saints, Margaret Street – he was drawn inexorably into the orbit of John Henry Newman. From 1829 Oakeley had been a member of Newman's select Oxford dining club. From 1839 the fitting up of his chapel in London's West End came close to aping the liturgical precedents of Newman's chapel at Littlemore. His services had a wide following. Gladstone thought them among the most devotional he ever attended. But Oakeley had already begun to test the boundaries of Tractarian principle. 'We are Catholics', he liked to think, 'without being Roman Catholics, and Protestant without protesting against the truth which, with all the corruption, Rome holds.'[94] When in 1841 – and more explicitly in 1845 – he claimed 'the right … of holding (as distinct from teaching) all Roman doctrine, … notwithstanding my subscription to the Thirty-Nine Articles', Bishop Blomfield of London decided that a line had to be drawn. The turbulent priest of Margaret Street was suspended by the Court of Arches.[95] Oakeley's response was to join Newman's community of exiles at Littlemore. In October 1845 – three weeks after his mentor – he was received into the Roman Communion in the obscure chapel of St Clement's, Oxford, just across Magdalen Bridge. Thereafter he became a champion of resurgent Catholicism.

From 1850 until his death in 1880 – as a canon of the new diocese of Westminster – Oakeley served as missionary rector of a poor Irish parish, St John's, Duncan Terrace, Islington. There he was fondly remembered as 'our Father O'Kelly'. 'Limping about the streets of London', Mozley recalled, he seemed a mere 'misshapen fabric of bare bones upon which hung some shabby canonicals. Yet his eye was bright, and his voice, though sorrowful, was kind.'[96] His escape from Balliol's cerebral Broad Churchmanship seemed complete. And yet he remained friendly with his former pupils, notably Archbishop Tait. What part, if any, Freemasonry played in Oakeley's spiritual odyssey is now very difficult to discern. His name was 'taken off the books' of Apollo after only three years. Perhaps his initiation in 1825 can be seen as just a symptom of young Oxford's search for stranger, ritualized forms of commitment, outside the conventions of evangelical Anglicanism.[97]

But before any further speculation, the bare statistics of Apollo's Anglican recruitment must first be set out. The figures are instructive. They demonstrate conclusively that for very many Victorian Anglicans there was in practice no conflict at all between Christianity and Freemasonry.[98] During the first twelve years of Apollo, 1818–30, no fewer than one in three initiates became ordained clergy of the Church of England. During the next two decades, 1831–49, the proportion of prospective clergy remained much the same: one in four. During the 1850s, at a time of rapidly expanding recruitment, Apollo enrolled nearly 200 future clerics, still more than a third of the total intake. That was the high point. The next decade – the 1860s: a time of post-Oxford Movement uncertainty – showed a distinct slowing down of momentum. The figure for the first half of the new decade was just above one in five (63 out of 301); for the second half just above one in eight (34 out of 262). During the 1870s, recruitment of Apollo men into the Anglican Church settled at approximately that figure: rather less than one in eight. It was still a significant number. But the heyday of Apollo Anglicanism had passed. The lodge had begun its slow transition from seminary to chambers. Henceforward Apollo men were to be found more frequently in Law than in the Church.

COLLEGE LIVINGS AND FAMILY BENEFICES

Friendships formed in lodge and common room shaped many a clerical career. Appointments to college and family livings – first moves in an ongoing game of ecclesiastical patronage – were often crucial, and the rewards could be considerable. In 1863, for example, New College appointed Edward Fox (Apollo, 1847) to a College living at Romford, Essex, for which he received £700 p.a., plus a house.[99] As fellow and warden of All Souls – and for a while as vice chancellor of Oxford – Francis Leighton (Apollo, 1827) also enjoyed the Rectory of Lockinge, Berkshire (£450 p.a., plus house), as well as the Rectory of Harpsden, Oxfordshire (£773 p.a., plus house). In some ways Edward Coleridge (Apollo, 1820) did even better. Very much an Eton fellow, he was appointed by his alma mater to the Vicarage at Mapledurham, Oxfordshire (£881 p.a., plus house). He stayed in that agreeable berth for forty years until his death in 1881, becoming a noted philanthropist: he built several churches in Bethnal Green and sold his collection of watercolours to help pay for the refurbishment of St Augustine's, Canterbury. Family influence could be even more pervasive than college patronage. John Horner (Apollo, 1834), for instance, did not have to look far for preferment. Within a year of initiation and graduation he moved into a delectable rectory in the Horner fiefdom of Mells in Somerset (£914 p.a.). That was soon followed by a prebendal stall at Wells. Not surprisingly, he stayed there until his death in 1874. Among the Apollo intakes of 1845–46

Revd G.R. Portal (Apollo, 1848). A key figure in the development of the Grand Lodge of Mark Master Masons and other related degrees or orders.

several moved easily into family benefices and stayed there for the rest of their lives: Walter Marcon at Edgefield, Norfolk; Augustus Haster at Preston All Saints, Cirencester; Francis Tuke at Borden, Kent; and Theophilus Puleston at Worthenbury, Flintshire. All benefited from a system which regarded benefices as a form of heritable property. Similarly, William Beaumont (Apollo, 1850), the younger son of a baronet, inherited the family rectory at coal-rich Coleorton in Leicestershire (£300 p.a., plus house).

Some of these appointments were very profitable indeed. William Ellis (Apollo, 1855), second son of Baron Howard de Walden, owed his career to his relative the 5th Duke of Portland: he became rector of Bothal with Sheepwash at Hebburn, near Morpeth. That was worth £1,477 p.a., plus house. Charles Martyn (Apollo, 1856) was himself both patron and incumbent in the enviable family property of Long Melford, Suffolk. The income was £1,100 p.a., plus house. During his incumbency Martyn served as Deputy Provincial Grand

Master of the Freemasons of Suffolk, and Grand Chaplain to the Freemasons of England. Equally Masonic was the career of W.K.R. Bedford of Westminster and Brasenose College. Within four years of initiation in 1846, he succeeded his uncle as rector of Sutton Coldfield, Warwickshire, and stayed there for forty-two years. He was twice Master of Apollo, as well as Chaplain to Grand Lodge.

The career of George Portal (Apollo, 1848) flew even higher. He went first to St Barnabas, Pimlico – a focus of High Church ritual – and thence to a succession of family benefices. His first patron was his uncle, the banker Henry Drummond MP: he supplied him with a rectory at Albury, Surrey. His second patron was the Earl of Carnarvon: he came up with a rectory at Burghclere, Hampshire. The latter was worth £1,350 p.a., plus house. At the same time Portal became domestic chaplain to both the Earl of Carnarvon and the Duke of Northumberland. Portal took his Freemasonry seriously. His career as Mason, High Churchman and High Tory, was based on conviction. In 1855 he published *Personal Faith, the Only Source of Peace* and in 1867 *Short Prayers etc. for Those Who Have but Little Time to Pray*, which went through seventeen editions.

Such Masonic trajectories could span generations. Charles Holling (Apollo, 1866) succeeded to his father's benefice at Okehampton, Devon, in 1872, and John Brymer (Apollo, 1868) followed his father at Childe Okeford, Dorset, in 1873. The Wigan family expanded their interests and influence even more. William Wigan (Apollo, 1839) – Eton and Christ Church – inherited the family benefice at East Malling, Kent; then compounded his territoriality by marrying the daughter of Aretas Akers of nearby Malling Abbey. A generation later another Aretas Akers, this time of Eton and University College (Apollo, 1871),

Aretas Akers-Douglas, 1st Viscount Chilston (Apollo, 1842). For many years Conservative chief whip in the House of Commons.

with six generations of West India wealth behind him – and from 1875 known as Akers-Douglas, thanks to the inheritance of a Scottish estate – emerged as a celebrated Tory chief whip, the formidable 1st Viscount Chilston.

Just occasionally, scraps of evidence do survive that pin down precisely the timing and manner of Masonic influence. Such evidence can be critically specific. In 1838 W.H.P. Ward of Oriel (Apollo, 1831) became rector of Compton Valence, Wiltshire. He stayed there until 1870. His patron was Robert Williams MP, a banker and Inner Temple lawyer, of Bridehead, Dorset. Williams was also an Oriel man; and he was initiated not only in the same year as Ward, not only in the same month, but on the very same evening, 27 January 1831. The friendship formed that night turned out to carry a lifetime's dividend. Equally long-lasting, and rather more glamorous, was the influence which made possible the career of Robert Collins. Born the son of a Berkshire cleric, Collins moved smoothly from Marlborough to Lincoln College, and thence to Lincoln's Inn. On the way he became tutor to HRH Prince Leopold, and then Comptroller of Household to that same royal prince, by then known as the Duke of Albany. In due course Collins became Comptroller of Household to Prince Leopold's duchess, climbing the ranks of honour as he went, from CB to KCB. Again, Collins had been initiated in Apollo not only in the same year as his patron, the prince, not only in the same month, but on the very same evening, 1 May 1874. Here surely, and on an impressive scale, is a tale of Brother helping Brother. In such details – at the quadruple interface of Freemasonry, Anglicanism, royalty and Toryism – we can see something of the network of influence which radiated outwards, generation after generation, from those comparatively modest premises in Alfred Street and Frewin Court.

The pattern of Apollo patronage did change over time. By the 1870s the course of a clerical career was not quite so straightforward as it once had been. Instead of an easy passage from Apollo to family or college benefice, initiation and graduation might by that date be followed by a couple of years' theological training at Chichester, Durham or Salisbury. Clement Danby (Apollo, 1872), of Radley and Brasenose, for example, spent 1875–77 at Chichester before progressing through half a dozen obscure incumbencies in the Midlands. Lewis Smith (also Apollo, 1872), of The Queen's College, spent 1874 at Cuddesden before ending up at Llanddewi-Ystrad-Ennau in Radnorshire. By that date the *cursus honorum* for a budding Apollo cleric was no longer so predictably easy as it had been half a century before.

The wide range of the lodge's Anglican allegiance in the Victorian period can be nicely measured by the contrasting careers of Weldon Champneys and Walter Kerr Hamilton, Bishop of Salisbury (both Apollo, 1830). In churchmanship they were poles apart. All his life Champneys was a committed evangelical with a heroic capacity for work. As a Brasenose tutor he was known as 'the BNC omnibus' because he took on board so many pupils. As a plain man's parson, he cut his teeth in Oxford's downmarket district of St Ebbe's. Thereafter, in the slums of Whitechapel and St Pancras, he preached to hundreds and laboured for thousands. Ballast heavers, shoeblacks and coal whippers; the sick and the indigent; Champneys cared for them all, in soup kitchens, ragged schools, orphanages and hospitals. Queen Victoria dismissed him as 'an insignificant Low Churchman'. But Gladstone called him 'the most devoted parson and active clergyman who ever existed'. Today he is rightly remembered as 'one of the foremost evangelical slum parsons of his generation'.[100]

Champneys was too Low for Queen Victoria. Hamilton was too High. Hamilton had been Gladstone's schoolfriend and Thomas Arnold's private pupil. He emerged from Eton and Christ Church fired by the ritual symbolism of the Tractarians. Yet he still retained a few hints of his early evangelical fervour. As Bishop of Salisbury he swept aside the conventions of the Georgian cathedral. His sermon in the nave in 1861 was the first for eighty years. By wearing a cassock – then an innovation – he made a statement of his sacramental convictions: the real presence, the eucharistic sacrifice, the power of priestly absolution. At one time Cardinal Manning even thought that Hamilton might secede to Rome. That was never likely. He remained at home in the Church of England, and in local diocesan matters, over many years, could rely on at least one prebendary of Salisbury with a similar Oxford background: Charles Harris (Apollo, 1831), of Oriel, All Souls and the Inner Temple, later Bishop of Gibraltar.

Between these two poles – High and Low – there was ample scope within Apollo for many varieties of Anglican belief. Outside the lodge it was less easy to agree to differ. George Spencer, Bishop of Madras (Apollo, 1821), tried hard to retain an intermediate position, poised between High and Low Church, but he was attacked from both sides of the theological fence, in India and in

England too. In his far-flung diocese he fell foul of both the Society for the Propagation of the Gospel and the Church Missionary Society. At issue was the vexed question of episcopal authority in matters doctrinal. Back in England he crossed swords with the Ven. George Denison, a Tractarian archdeacon of Taunton. This time the battleground was only too well worn: the exact meaning of the real presence.[101]

Spencer's difficulties as Bishop of Madras were as nothing, however, compared with those experienced by the Revd W.K. Macrorie (Apollo, 1854), Bishop of Maritzburg in South Africa. It was Macrorie's fate to be drawn into one of the thorniest theological disputes in the whole history of the Victorian Church. This was the case of Bishop Colenso. Like the fabled Schleswig-Holstein question, the Colenso affair was so prolonged, and so complicated, that before it was over most of those involved had either died or else forgotten its origins.[102] Battle was joined on three interlocking fronts, over a period of nearly four decades: High Church versus Broad Church; ecclesiastical authority versus civil jurisdiction; and Tractarian theology versus Germanic biblical criticism. In 1853 Colenso was appointed Bishop of Natal by royal letters patent. Ten years later he was delated for heresy – he was equivocal on the subject of polygamy – and finally deprived of office. Undeterred, he refused to recognize his deprivation and survived in a kind of schismatic limbo – supported by native Zulus in his diocese – until his death in 1883. Meanwhile Macrorie had been consecrated in his place, not in England but in South Africa. To avoid titular duplication, he was given an alternative honorific within the same diocese: he became a bishop not of Natal but of Maritzburg. As such he was the first colonial bishop not to be appointed by the Crown. Colenso had been a fighting evangelical. Macrorie was an uncompromising High Churchman. In effect there were now two bishops in Natal: a bishop and an anti-bishop. Macrorie struggled on, after the death of Colenso, until his own retirement in 1891. Weary of colonial disputation, he retreated eventually to the quiet of an Ely canonry. He survived until 1905.

SEEMLY CEREMONY AND PRAGMATIC FAITH

Freemasonry's impatience with the niceties of religious belief can be seen in the career of William 'Hang Theology' Rogers (Apollo, 1840). At Eton and Balliol, Rogers had been more interested in rowing than in book learning.

But after some theological training at Durham he found his metier in a poor City parish – St Thomas's, Charterhouse – which he christened Costermongria. There he began his career as a secular-minded educational reformer, establishing a network of schools, first for street children, then for the offspring of clerks and tradesmen. He brooked no opposition. On one occasion in 1866, when various difficulties were raised, he brushed aside all objections: 'hang economy, hang theology. Let us begin'. Hence his memorable nickname. In educational debates he found a staunch ally in Benjamin Jowett. Other Balliol friends whom he found helpful and congenial included Lord Coleridge, Stafford Northcote, Lord Hobhouse, Dean Stanley and Archbishop Temple. They formed a liberally minded, progressive group. And among them Rogers – a lifelong bachelor, humorous and brisk – stood out for his no-nonsense sense of equity. Balliol responded by making him rector of St Botolph's, Bishopsgate. In 1873 he confided to Jowett that over the years he had become rather tired of 'the disguise of a clergyman'. Still, he never doubted his conviction that the established Church, for all its contradictions, was essentially a mechanism for good; in effect a vehicle for spiritualized good manners, for *noblesse oblige*. 'He may be an atheist', remarked one opponent, 'but he is a gentleman.' [103]

The Revd Samuel Reynolds Hole, Dean of Rochester (Apollo, 1842). Grand Chaplain of the United Grand Lodge of England. Priest and landed proprietor; a well-known hunting man and famous rose gardener; a Conservative with Gladstonian sympathies.

If we are looking for an archetypal Apollo clergyman in the mid-Victorian period, we might well settle on Samuel Reynolds Hole, Dean of Rochester (Apollo, 1842). His no-nonsense approach suggests a very English set of attitudes: a fondness for seemly ceremony and an aversion to metaphysics. Hole came from a family of Nottinghamshire gentry with business interests in Manchester and the West Indies. He went up to Brasenose in 1840, intending to read for a First in preparation for the Church. But there he fell in with the hunting and boating set. 'How they loved the river, and the boat', he recalled fifty years later, 'those grand, genial, brave-hearted men! Again I see those eager faces – as they listen for the signal … and eight oars dip and rise as one … "Bravo Brasenose!"' [104]

Within months of joining Apollo he was rusticated for two terms 'for mis-behaviour visiting … the rooms of several undergraduates, and destroying their property'. But in 1845 he seems to have turned over a new leaf. He joined the Ecclesiological Society, and embarked on a clerical career as a moderate High Churchman. At Caunton in Nottinghamshire he was both priest and proprietor, a well-known hunting man and a famous gardener. He grew 400 varieties of roses on his estate; at Rochester there were 135 varieties in his deanery garden. But he never lost his youthful appetite for words. Stainer set his hymns to music. John Leech introduced him to the table at *Punch*. Thackeray put him up for the Garrick and invited him to contribute to the *Cornhill Magazine.* As first president of the National Rose Society, he became an international figure. Tennyson christened him 'the Rose King'. In politics he was a staunch Conservative with Gladstonian sympathies. And as a popular preacher – fluent, plain-spoken, down to earth; playing whist for small stakes, drinking in moderation – he retained a sizeable following in England and in America too. His commanding presence – 6 ft 4 in., with a rasping voice – made him a powerful speaker at St Paul's. And his enthusiasm for good company led on to his appointment as Grand Chaplain.

Hole's religious position was fairly representative of his Oxford generation. By 1840 undergraduates had begun to find the etiolated Anglicanism of college chapel services dispiriting and drab. Many were susceptible to Oxford Movement influence. All his life Dean Hole remained a loyal supporter of the Established Church. When a memorial statue to Cardinal Newman was proposed in Broad Street, he denounced the idea as preposterous: 'the representation of a deserter … in a barrack-yard of the Church Militant'. But he was a lifelong advocate of the 'reunion of Christendom on Catholic principles'; and he could well understand the hunger of his contemporaries for a more sympathetic expression of the Anglican tradition.

> I never heard a note of music in our [Brasenose] college chapel … the University sermons (I do not remember that any were preached in college) failed to impress the undergraduate mind, except when Newman, or Pusey, or Claughton [of Trinity] preached … It was a time in which ugliness and dirt were regarded as bulwarks of the Protestant faith, and beauty and order were 'marks of the beast'. Doctrine was bigotry, reverence was idolatry, and zeal was superstition.[105]

In other words, cut off from both Catholic aesthetics and evangelical fervour, pre-Oxford Movement Anglicanism seemed in danger of shrivelling into monotony. Here was fertile soil for a rather Higher form of churchmanship; perhaps even for the good fellowship and arcane symbolism of Apollo. Here, in Church and lodge, could be found formulations of belief to spark the imagination of a new generation of Oxford men; a generation starved of mystical enthusiasm and hungry for its ritual expression.

Something of the tension inherent in the relationship between Freemasonry and Christianity can certainly be seen in the career of Henry Bellingham (Apollo, 1869), later Sir Henry, 4th Bt, of Castle Bellingham, County Louth. Born in 1846, Bellingham was an Anglo-Irish Harrovian, who would eventually, in 1889, inherit 16,000 acres in Mayo and Louth. In the meantime – accumulating along the way the sort of responsibilities appropriate to his

The Very Revd Arthur Perceval Purey-Cust (Apollo, 1848). Brasenose and All Souls; Grand Chaplain of the United Grand Lodge of England; Canon of Christ Church and Dean of York. Photographed in about 1862 with his wife and two of his younger children. 'Freemasonry', he believed, constitutes 'a mighty engine for the religious, moral and social stability of our nation … The aim of our Craft [is] to fear God and work for righteousness.'

status: MP, JP, DL – he went over to Rome, in 1873. He advertised his change of faith before his neighbours by erecting a shrine to the Virgin Mary in the grounds of Castle Bellingham. Married twice, in 1874 and 1895, on both occasions into old English Catholic families, he compounded his family's rejection of Protestantism – they had fought for King Billy at the Boyne – by becoming private chamberlain to three successive Popes: Pius IX, Leo XIII and Pius X. It was during those three pontificates that the gulf between Freemasonry and Catholicism became apparently irrevocable. Pius IX condemned liberalism; Leo XIII condemned modernism; Pius X condemned both. The Vatican set its face against forces that it considered tainted with secularity and relativist thinking. Among these it certainly counted Freemasonry, in Europe if not in England. Bellingham not only saw these papal policies unfolding, and at close range. He made himself a public witness of their significance. In 1914 he published an apologia: *Reminiscences of an Irish Convert*.

MASONIC VOWS AND BELIEF

When it comes to another debatable area, the strength and persistence of individual Masonic belief, firm evidence is harder to come by, and by its nature tends to emphasize not mere acceptance but the extremities of opinion: either rejection or commitment. No doubt a few Apollo men fell back on an undogmatic, deistic line: in 1860 the lodge contributed 5 guineas towards the erection of a statue in the Oxford Museum in honour of that Great Geometrician, Euclid himself. Equally, others must have pursued their Freemasonry beyond the customary Three Degrees, towards the higher levels of Royal Arch ritual. But in many cases Masonic vows entered into as an undergraduate must have come to mean very little in later years.

That could never be said of Arthur Perceval Purey-Cust (Apollo, 1848), whose whole career was lived in an aura of Anglican Freemasonry. From Brasenose and All Souls, he moved into a family benefice in Buckinghamshire (patron the 1st Earl Brownlow); and thence – via marriage to a daughter of the 5th Earl of Darnley – to a canonry of Christ Church, the deanery of York and the chaplaincy of Grand Lodge. Along the way he published sermons on the ethics of war and on the scriptural context of Freemasonry.

The texts of four of his sermons survive. They reveal a good deal of the rationale – and the mystique – of late Victorian Freemasonry,[106] and they certainly merit quotation.

Freemasonry [constitutes] a mighty engine for the religious, moral and social stability of our nation …[It] is something more than mountebanking in quaint costumes, something more than mere secret conclaves, something more than mere social banquets … The aim of our Craft [is] to fear God and work for righteousness … Christianity alone can help us to attain [its] true ideal … If our 'clothing' is quaint, our diction conventional, our ritual archaic, [such things] simply illustrate those principles of faith, and order, and conduct [that make for righteous living] … Freemasonry does not profess to be a religion… [but its first] Cornerstone [is] the distinct recognition of God … [From this stems the imperative of social action], the relief of the needy, the provision for old age, the education of the young … The Bible [remains our] centre light … No Atheist can obtain admission or consistently occupy a place in our ranks … [For] there must have been a great First Cause … for whom and by whom all things exist … [Neither] invertebrate and jelly-fish Agnosticism … [nor] Captious Positivism … [nor even] pseudo-liberality …[can supply the] centripetal power [that counteracts] the centrifugal force … of [market competition and makes for] better citizens … better members of society … In our social gatherings are known no distinctions of rank. We know nothing of politics. We know nothing of religious differences … [Our members are drawn] from every portion of the habitable globe … from the parish, the bench, the barracks, and the fleet – from the easel, the surgery, and the orchestra – from the anvil and the plough – from the warehouse and the shop – from the mansion (aye, from the palace) and the cottage … [And] the Queen herself is the Patron of our Order, as many of her predecessors, back to the days of Athelstan, have been members of our Society, as are her sons today, our Worshipful Grand Master being even the Heir-apparent of the Crown … Our girdle of fellowship embraces 2,073 British Lodges, containing about 100,000 members … and we are in close communion with Lodges and members of almost every nation under heaven.

At its minimum, therefore, Freemasonry was a vehicle of good citizenship; at its maximum it aspired to communion with the divine. In its English manifestation its theology was perhaps consciously opaque. But whatever its conceptual

Walter Bradford Woodgate (Apollo, 1860), photographed with Weldon Champneys at Henley in 1861. 'Guts' Woodgate (seated left with dog) was the greatest oarsman of his generation and famously handsome: 'The Apollo of Apollo'. Of his year at Brasenose (1859) one-third became members of Apollo University Lodge. Woodgate later joined the Inner Temple and became a successful, if mildly eccentric, barrister.

formulation – Church and King or Crown and Creator – the focus of loyalty which resulted was very much the same: allegiance to the sacralized state.

SPORTING MASONS AND LITERARY TYPES

Mid-Victorian Apollo could never be described in any sense as a pietistic organization. It attracted future Anglican priests in large numbers. Its enthusiasms, however, were social and athletic. The *Reminiscences* of 'Guts' Woodgate catch the flavour of the lodge in this period. Walter Bradford Woodgate (Apollo, 1860) was the son of a clergyman from Worcestershire and he went on to become an Inner Temple lawyer. As an undergraduate, he was able enough to pay his way by writing sermons for idle parsons. And in later years he willingly put on record his own middle-stump Anglicanism: *A Modern Layman's Faith* (1893).[107]

More memorably, he was the greatest oarsman of his generation. He rowed in the winning Oxford crews of 1862 and 1863; he rowed in the Brasenose 1st VIII no fewer than eight years running; at Henley he won the Grand Challenge cup, the Stewards' cup, the Diamond Sculls and the Goblets (five times); he also won the Wingfield Sculls (three times), and became founder and first president of Vincent's, the University's premier sporting club. He even went three rounds with Tom Sayers, and swam in the Channel with Captain Webb.

Woodgate's homespun beliefs were shot through with a puckish sense of fun. In the Stewards' Cup at Henley in 1868 he persuaded a freshman, Fred Weatherly, the Brasenose cox, to jump ship at the start of the race, thus creating in effect the first coxless four. Weatherly, who could not swim, survived this episode and eventually followed Woodgate to the Bar. He later made himself immortal by writing the lyrics to 'Danny Boy' (1912) and 'Roses of Picardy' (1916).[108]

Woodgate's eccentricity was unstudied, in costume, manners and speech. In winter he wore a low-crowned 'John Bull' hat; in summer a white top hat of excessive height. In youth he was notably handsome: 'the Apollo of Apollo'. But during a long life as a literary barrister – fifty years a columnist in *The Field* – he remained an embattled bachelor. He once fled from a train compartment rather than travel alone with a lady; he would 'sooner have a mad dog rather than a single woman in the carriage'.[109]

One–third of 'Guts' Woodgate's year at Brasenose (1859) were members of Apollo; exactly ten out of thirty. Even the Brasenose porter at that time, John Bossum – a mountainous figure weighing 22 stone – was a regular guest in Alfred Street. The influence exerted by Woodgate on Apollo in the 1860s can be measured in the numbers recruited from the College: more than a score in less than a decade, and overwhelmingly sportsmen. Many were members of Vincent's too: W.E. Heap (Apollo, 1861), a crack quarter-miler; T.M. 'Springy' Colmore (Apollo, 1864), a sprinter who could run like the wind – once, for a sizeable bet, he actually raced against a galloping horse; Stonehewer Illingworth (Apollo, 1862), who regularly hunted three days a week with three different packs; Duncan Pocklington (Apollo, 1862), who in three successive years stroked the Oxford VIII, and the BNC VIII as well; Fred Crowder (Apollo, 1864), another Captain of Boats and Master of Foxhounds; and W.C. Crofts (Apollo, 1867), twice winner of the Diamond Sculls. All muscular Masons, not a few of whom went on to be muscular clergy and muscular lawyers too.[110]

Several of these themes – religion, travel, sport, literature – are summed up in the career of Henry Kingsley (Apollo, 1851). Part of a clerical and literary tribe – Charles Kingsley, author of *The Water Babies*, was his elder brother; Mary Kingsley, African explorer, his future niece – Henry Kingsley spent his Oxford days on the river, or else in the company of idlers. He was co-founder of the Fez Club: 'a short-lived nonsensical secret society of fifty undergraduate men dedicated to misogamy, misogyny, and celibate freedom'. They breakfasted and smoked oriental pipes at Dickenson's Hotel and Coffee House in the Turl. Fortified by a timely legacy, Kingsley spent much of the 1850s in the Australian goldfields. He found no gold, but he did manage to stockpile memories for future novels. In later years, in the Franco-Prussian War, he proved to be more talented as a war correspondent than he was as a popular novelist. The *Saturday Review* dismissed his *Oakshott Castle* (1873) as perhaps the 'worst novel ever written'.[111] But he did produce *Ravenshoe* (1862), a work of undoubted literary power. Its plot crystallizes several of the conflicts central to the mid-Victorian psyche: Catholic versus Protestant; old money versus new; misguided heroism (the Crimean War) versus unjustified despair (post-Darwinian doubt). 'No writer of the mid-Victorian age', noted Michael Sadleir, 'had so delicate a sympathy for splendour in decay, so sensitive an admiration for the forlorn present of a noble past. He is the prose-laureate of wasted beauty.'[112]

LAWYERS IN APOLLO

Rectory and manor house, in Joseph Foster's phrase, were Apollo's 'principal *couches sociales*'.[113] That was certainly true for successive cohorts of future lawyers, as much as for those from clerical stock. The figures for barristers emerging from Apollo are revealing.

1818–30: 27 out of 211
1831–49: 43 out of 292
1850–59: 64 out of 365
1860–65: 49 out of 301
1866–71: 69 out of 262
1872–77: 57 out of 275

The later 1860s mark a turning point. After the turmoil of religious doubt associated with *Essays and Reviews* (1860), a clerical vocation must have seemed rather less alluring than a career at the Inns of Court. By the 1870s Apollo had become a nursery for lawyers rather than a training ground for clerics. But it is worth remembering that the numbers for both these categories throughout the Victorian period far outstrip, for example, those for the recruitment of potential soldiers, financiers or civil servants. After 1854 it was no longer necessary for graduates of Oxford to have subscribed to the Thirty-nine Articles. After 1871 the same requirement was no longer a condition of MA and therefore of fellowship status. Until at least World War I, Oxford remained a flagship of Anglicanism. But it no longer produced career clergymen as a matter of course.

These changes inevitably altered the clerical/secular balance of senior common rooms.[114] In 1845 there had been 325 out of 470 Oxford fellows in holy orders. By 1964 there were only 30 out of 586. So the proportion of clerical to secular fellows – and with it the proportion of Masons to non-Masons – steadily declined. The Revd Frederick Bussell (Apollo, 1894), for example, was – in several senses – a rare bird in late-nineteenth- and early-twentieth-century Brasenose. Aesthete, polymath and pluralist, he avidly collected donative benefices; he even joked of his rustication for simony. Still, he was an effective vice principal for seventeen years; and Walter Pater for one believed he had 'a real touch of genius'.[115] In 1900 he became Master of Apollo. He did not retire from Brasenose until 1917. And the list of Masters (see Appendix 1) since Bussell's time underlines the continuity of Apollo loyalties among the University's senior membership. W.C. Costin – historian, president of St John's and Master of the lodge on no fewer than five occasions: 1928, 1937, 1946, 1959 and 1969 – is one notable example.

Despite the dilution of Anglicanism within the University, Apollo continued to retain its Anglican flavour. One intriguing piece of evidence is relevant here. The lodge minutes for 3 December 1841 contain a cryptic note: 'the Election of Mr. Lopes is postponed'. Now Ralph Ludlow Lopes, of Winchester and Christ Church, was the second son of Sir Ralph Lopes, 2nd Bt

The Revd Dr Frederick Bussell (Apollo, 1894); Master, 1900. Aesthete, polymath and pluralist. 'I must confess myself a prig, a pedant and in some ways a poltroon.' His close friend, Walter Pater, however, believed he had 'a real touch of genius'. Portrait by W. Rothenstein.

W.C. Costin. Five times Master of Apollo: in 1928, 1937, 1946, 1959 and 1969. Historian, president of St John's College, and a stalwart of Oxford Freemasonry.

(formerly Franco), of Maristow, Devon. The family was undoubtedly rich: Sir Manasseh Masseh Lopes, 1st Bt, was reported in 1831 to have left £800,000, a colossal sum in those days, deriving from a West India fortune multiplied in the City and consolidated in West Country land. But the family's Anglicanism was as new as its wealth: the 1st Bt had abandoned his Jewish faith in 1802, before he entered Parliament (and before he was convicted of electoral corruption). Whether Apollo looked askance at the family's Jewish origins – or whether it sniffed at such a chequered political record – we shall never know. Perhaps Mr Lopes simply changed his mind. In practice Jewish affiliations were no formal barrier to membership: witness the initiation of Francis and Leonard Montefiore (Apollo, 1880 and 1909), Francis Oppenheimer (Apollo, 1893) and Joseph Sassoon (Apollo, 1907). But, whatever the reason, initiated Lopes was not. The rejection – if that it was – did no harm to his career. He went on to the Inner Temple, ending as Sheriff of Wiltshire and a member of both the Carlton and Conservative Clubs.[116]

Lopes cannot have been short of Oxford connections at the Inner Temple. During the first sixty years of Apollo – out of a total of more than 1,700 initiates – only 3 Apollo men chose to enter Gray's Inn; one of these was an Irishman, and one soon transferred his allegiance to the Middle Temple. Nor was the Middle Temple much more popular: during the same period only 24 Apollo men dined regularly in that noble hall. Lincoln's Inn seems to have had greater attraction, particularly in Apollo's early years; exactly 100 chose to

"That won't do, you know!"

Sir Lewis William Cave

stroll its famous lawns. It was the Inner Temple, however, which consistently topped the list. Generation after generation of Oxford Freemasons followed each other there: at least 180 during the lodge's first sixty years. And the momentum of preference – Inner Temple as against any other Inn – increased as the century progressed. In 1872–77, for example, there were 38 Inner Temple recruits out of 275 Apollo initiates. Numerically – at least as regards distribution – this seemed to emphasize the truth of the old jingle:

> Lincoln's Inn for garden, Gray's Inn for walks.
> The Inner Temple for the rich, and the Middle for the poor.

Few of these recruits went on to the higher reaches of the law. Sir Stephenson Surtees (Apollo, 1825; Inner Temple, 1831),[117] Sir James Marshall (Apollo, 1851; Lincoln's Inn, 1858)[118] and Sir Charles Turner (Apollo, 1856; Lincoln's Inn, 1858)[119] were all knighted after long careers as puisne judge and High Court judge, albeit in the jurisdictions of Mauritius, Gold Coast and Allahabad. But most Apollo lawyers stayed closer to home and seldom aspired to positions of leadership in their profession. 'Guts' Woodgate (Apollo, 1860; Inner Temple, 1872) was rather more typical than Sir Lewis Cave (Apollo, 1852; Inner Temple 1859), a bankruptcy judge in the Queen's Bench Division and editor of *Addison on Contracts* and *Addison on Tort*.[120] One or two – W.G. Ellison-Macartney; W.P. Eversley (both Apollo, 1872) – did reach the higher sanctum of the renowned King's Bench Walk:

> Persuasion tips his tongue whene'er he talks,
> And he has chambers in the King's Bench Walks.[121]

But most gravitated to slightly less prestigious chambers. Partly this was a question of custom. No doubt the familiarity of the Oxford Circuit was often preferable to the responsibilities of the High Court.[122] Still, in sheer numbers, these Apollo lawyers formed a notable cohort. How much they helped each other in their legal careers must now be considered almost certainly unknowable. What is incontestable, however, is the fact that Apollo lawyers – ambitious, prosperous, well-connected, naturally Inner Temple men – occupied a very significant presence in the late Victorian legal profession.

5 SOLDIERS: CRIMEA TO WORLD WAR I, 1850s–1919

VICTORIAN APOLLO PRODUCED FEW professional soldiers. It was an organization peopled by territorial gentry, budding lawyers and prospective clerics. Military matters must have seemed no more than peripheral to their Masonic fellowship. All this changed dramatically with the advent of World War I.

PROFESSIONAL SOLDIERS, GRANDEES AND TERRITORIALS

When we examine the cohorts of lodge members in the mid-nineteenth century we find no more than a sprinkling of career soldiers; they are consistently outnumbered by contingents of local grandees with territorial military connections. A handful of professionals can be found. Three close contemporaries (Apollo, 1852–53), for example, found themselves in the Crimean War: Alexander Adair (Coldstream Guards) and Boscawen Griffith-Boscawen (Royal Welch Fusiliers) took part in the Siege of Sebastopol; and Harry Clarke-Jervoise became a captain with the Coldstream in the same conflict, as well as ADC to General Alrey. Another professional was T.C.P. Colley (Apollo, 1875), a captain in the Life Guards: he served in the Egyptian Campaign of the 1880s, earning a medal, clasp and bronze star. Thomas Shaw-Hellier (Apollo, 1850) was in Egypt at the same time, but with the 4th

(opposite) Exterior of Freemasons' Hall, London.

Dragoon Guards. By 1885 he was colonel of the regiment. In Egypt, too, we encounter the splendidly named Fenwick Bulmer de Sales La Terrière (Eton and Magdalen; Apollo, 1875). He was with the 19th Hussars at Tel-el-Kebir; then married a daughter of Baron Hambro, and ended as a colonel in the Royal Fusiliers Militia. As ever, there were one or two of the grandest military grandees. Two members of Apollo's 1856 intake served simultaneously in high ceremonial command at the end of the 1870s: Cecil Innes as colonel of the Royal Horse Guards and major general of the Blues; Lord Skelmersdale – a key figure in lodge history – as captain of the Yeomen of the Guard.

But all these were unusual. The typical *cursus honorum* for aspiring senior officers at this time involved attendance at Sandhurst rather than Oxford. Wyndham Portal (Apollo, 1849), for instance, was never actually a member of the University: he was initiated but never matriculated. He went straight from school to Sandhurst and then became a captain in the Hampshire Yeomanry Cavalry. William Blacker (Eton and Christ Church; Apollo, 1865), from 'a family of ancient Norwegian extraction', matriculated but never graduated: he entered the 12th Lancers instead. Such a non-academic career path was very much a military convention, and it could lead directly to the very top. The future Earl Haig (Clifton and Brasenose) was most unusual in experiencing both Oxford and Sandhurst. He was a Mason as well, but never a member of Apollo.[123]

Much more typical were Apollo initiates who managed to combine a brief military career with long-term, family-based, territorial responsibilities. Edward Hegan-Kennard (Apollo, 1857), for example, of Dawpool, Cheshire, followed Radley and Balliol with marriage to a Liverpool shipping heiress, then became an MP and a captain in the 8th Hussars as well as ADC to the Lord Lieutenant of Ireland. Similarly Alan Plantagenet Stewart, Viscount Garlies, later 10th Earl of Galloway (Apollo, 1854). For a time a captain in the Royal Horse Guards, he then moved into semi-retirement as a major in the Royal Ayr and Wigton Militia. H.J. Tollemache (Apollo, 1867) of Dorfold Hall, Cheshire, JP and MP was, predictably, a captain in the Cheshire Yeomanry.

Local duties formed the basis of these careers, but status reinforced by politics lay at the heart of the process. Francis Pym (Eton and Christ Church; Apollo, 1868) – coming from a long line of Pyms of Hazells – had just the right profile to take him beyond his native Bedfordshire to a commission in the 1st Life Guards. Sir Robert Hermon-Hodge, 1st Bt (Apollo, 1870), of Wyfold Court, Oxfordshire, JP, DL, MP married an heiress, occupied a safe Tory seat, became a lieutenant

Impression from a copperplate summons, late nineteenth century, the format of which is still used today to summon members to each lodge meeting by email. The code at the bottom of the summons represents the initial letters of the following phrase: 'We Have The Honour To Greet You By The Name Which You Know And To Give You The Honours Which Are Due To You'.

V D B

  We have the honour to inform you that the *Apollo Lodge of Free and accepted Masons. N° 711, will hold their next convention at the*

        P. M. and will immediately march to the pursuit of their mysterious labours. You are particularly invited to be present at this convention, and to assist in enlightening the mysteries by those means which true brethren alone understand; By so doing you will not only reap the advantage of making continued progress in the deep and endless mysteries of our science, which, you well know, can only be attained by constant attention and unwearied perseverance; but you will also have the satisfaction of knowing that you are augmenting amongst us the innumerable pleasures which arise from our fraternal affection.

       W H S H S G Y B S N W Y K.
       A S G Y S H W A D S Y
          W M.

Anno Domini 18
  Architectonicæ 58
            Secretary

in the Oxfordshire Yeomanry Cavalry, then first Baron Wyfold, and belonged to four appropriate clubs: White's, Pratt's, the Carlton and the Cavalry. On the other side of the political fence, Edward Knatchbull-Hugessen, 2nd Baron Brabourne (Apollo, 1877), successfully combined the Coldstream Guards with a career as Liberal MP for Rochester. And Henry Gerard Leigh (Eton and Christ Church; Apollo, 1875), son of a very rich Liverpool solicitor, consolidated his accelerating social trajectory by adding a captaincy in the 1st Life Guards to the inheritance of no less a seat than Luton Hoo in Bedfordshire.

From a Masonic point of view, each of these not only formed a crucial link in the nationwide network of lodges but also broadened Apollo's influence. Richard Fort (Eton and Brasenose; Apollo, 1875), of Reade Hall, Lancashire, JP, DL, for example was MP for Clitheroe, and a stalwart of the 11th Hussars, as well as Master of the Meynell Hounds. Again, the career of James Reade (Harrow and Christ Church; Apollo, 1861) might almost be taken as paradigmatic: lieutenant in the 14th Hussars, captain in the Royal Glamorgan Light Infantry Militia, captain in the Suffolk Yeomanry. A lifelong bachelor, and for a while a barrister at the Middle Temple, he was also a Suffolk JP and a member of no fewer than five clubs: Buck's, Arthur's, White's, the New University and the Bachelors'. When not with his regiment, he appears to have oscillated between his country seat, Crowe Hall near Ipswich, and his London pied-à-terre at 8 Duke Street, St James's. Such careers seem to have suited, too, the circumstances of Irish Freemasons. William Brabazon, 11th Earl of Meath (Apollo, 1823), for example, was a Liberal MP for Dublin, Lord Lieutenant of Co. Wicklow and colonel of the Dublin Militia. Gavin Hamilton (Cheltenham and Univ.; Apollo, 1863), of Killyleagh Castle, near Dundalk, and Shanganagh, near Dublin, the son of a captain in the 5th Dragoon Guards, became a lieutenant in the Royal North Down Militia and then a captain in the 7th Princess Royal's Dragoon Guards. At the same time he was acting as JP and High Sheriff for Co. Down. Or again, James Smith-Barry (Apollo, 1875) of Fota House, near Cork. His regiment was the Grenadier Guards; locally his role was that of JP and High Sheriff for Co. Cork. He even married a daughter of the Earl of Enniskillen.

Such Protestant territorial loyalties can also be traced in Wales. Thomas Jones-Parry (Apollo, 1851), captain in the Royal Anglesey Light Infantry Militia, and MP for Carnarvon; Robert Williams (Apollo, 1868), of Plas Gwyn, Anglesey, JP, DL, High Sheriff and captain in the Anglesey Militia; C.R.W. Tottenham (Apollo, 1865) of Plas Berwyn, Denbighshire, a major in the 3rd Battalion Welsh Fusiliers – all these maintained Apollo's military and territorial traditions.

This was a career path well worn by successive generations of Apollo men, and at the very top its trajectory long remained predictable. James Hamilton, 2nd Marquess and eventually 1st Duke of Abercorn (Apollo, 1830) – Irish Grand Master, no less – combined the Lord Lieutenancy of Donegal with a colonelcy in the Donegal Militia. Over the mid-Victorian years, men like these constituted a significant presence in successive intakes of the Apollo. Despite the presence of an active Officer Training Corps from the 1890s onwards, Oxford never became an antechamber for future soldiers, however, and its military membership was never numerically dominant. Then suddenly, in August 1914, the situation changed.

APOLLO CASUALITIES IN WORLD WAR I

First of all, the raw figures. No fewer than 81 members of Apollo died in World War I (see Appendix 3).[124] By any standard that is a tragic catalogue of loss. But breaking down those figures into some sort of meaningful table is by no means straightforward. Two striking facts are immediately apparent. More than a third of these casualties came from only two schools: Eton and Winchester. More than a third came from only two colleges: New College and Christ Church. Traditional links between Eton and Christ Church, and between Winchester and New College, no doubt explain this pattern of involvement. But other figures are less easily accounted for. Of those killed, only 16 were aged 24 or under; no fewer than 35 were aged over 30; 10 were aged 41 or more: 2 were actually in their fifties. Apollo casualties, therefore, were not conspicuously young. During the war as a whole, the majority of officer casualties belonged to the under-30 generation. The life expectancy of a second lieutenant on the Western Front could be measured in weeks rather than months. In the year of the Somme the percentage of officers killed in action was almost exactly double that of other ranks. At the head of their men – volunteers all of them until 1916 – officers were cruelly vulnerable. But Apollo casualties tended to have joined the war in mid-career, often as barristers, solicitors, or soldiers abroad. Already middle-aged, their recruitment was no youthful impulse. They entered as professionals, either via the territorial reserves or else as the result of a conscious decision to join a younger

generation on the front line. The latter impulse must have been particularly true of the four Anglican clergy from Apollo who died in the course of the war.

Inevitably, it is the records of the youngest casualties that make the saddest reading. Rowland Bowen and Joel Seaverns, for example. Both were at Harrow. They joined Apollo on the same night: 28 October 1913. As lieutenants, newly commissioned, both fought with the same regiment: the City of London Royal Fusiliers. And they died in the same action, at Aubers Ridge in France on 9 May 1915. Bowen was 'willing, cheerful and full of fun'; Seaverns was 'loved [by] the whole Company, officers and men alike … that day [he] was magnificent'. Both were only 22. That was the same age as Reginald Fletcher (Eton and Balliol; Apollo, 1910), son of the best-selling historian C.R.L. Fletcher. The father's *School History of England* (1911) – with poems by Rudyard Kipling – had gloried in the panorama of British supremacy. Having rowed in the Oxford VIII of 1914, it was the son's destiny to die almost at the moment of imperial eclipse, killed in action at Veldhoek in Belgium, within weeks of the outbreak of war.

Only a few months older was Myles Matthews (Univ.; Apollo, 1912). After training with the OTC, he joined the 6th Battalion, the Queen's Own Royal

The interior of Freemasons' Hall, London, with stained-glass war memorial.

West Kent Regiment. The Battalion war diary – factual and understated – for just one day on the Somme makes grim reading.

> Watney Street Trench, 3 July 1916. At 12.15 pm. received orders for the attack.
> … At 3.15 am. assaulted the German trenches … On bombardment ceasing,
> A and C Companies rushed the first line and took them with very little losses.
> B and D Companies [with Matthews leading B] charged past them but only a few
> elements of these two Companies reached the second line. A counter attack by the
> Germans drove back the remnants of the Battalion … Casualties: 3 captains killed,
> 11 subalterns wounded, 5 subalterns missing. Other ranks killed, wounded and
> missing 375. Strength of Battalion going into action 617.

One of those captains killed was Myles Matthews, aged 23. 'He had almost auburn hair', remembered one of his men, 'and looked what he was … a gentleman.' His name is carved upon the arch at Thiepval.

Two more who died young, this time on the first day of the Battle of Loos, were Kenneth Mackenzie (Apollo, 1912) and Norman Mackie (Apollo, 1914). Their backgrounds were rather different: Mackenzie from Wellington and Trinity; Mackie from Bancroft's School and Hertford. But both had promising careers cut short by conflict: Mackenzie as a clerk in the House of Lords; Mackie as a lecturer in law. They were both 24. So was Eric McNair (Charterhouse and Magdalen; Apollo, 1913). As a lieutenant with the Royal Sussex Regiment, he was awarded a VC in March 1916, 'for most conspicuous bravery'. The bald language of the official citation catches very well the heroism of just one soldier in that cruel season on the Somme:

> When the enemy exploded a mine, Lieutenant McNair and many men of two
> platoons were hoisted into the air, and many men were buried. But, though
> much shaken, he at once organised a party with a machine-gun to man the near
> edge of the crater and opened rapid fire on a large party of the enemy, who were
> advancing. The enemy were driven back, leaving many dead. Lieutenant McNair
> then ran back for reinforcements, and sent to another unit for bombs, ammunition
> and tools to replace those buried. The communications trench being blocked, he
> went across the open field under heavy fire and led up the reinforcements the same
> way. His prompt and plucky action and example undoubtedly saved the situation.

McNair survived that episode; he went back to the lodge to receive his Grand Lodge certificate and then returned to the front. He eventually died of dysentery at a military hospital in Genoa.

Such courage was not necessarily memorialized by an award. The name of Harold Rayner (Tonbridge and Corpus; Apollo, 1912) comes down to us simply as a model of unsung heroism. At Tonbridge he had been Captain of School and a prize-winning classicist. At Corpus he combined a First in Mods with presidency of the Boat Club. As a second lieutenant with the Devonshire Regiment, he survived the Battle of Loos in September 1915: he was one of only five officers in his battalion to come through that ordeal unscathed. But the Somme did for him, on 1 July 1916. Afterwards, his company commander wrote to Rayner's wife:

> Harold and I were originally to have gone over the top together. But I was kept back, and Harold led my company instead. He was the first man to get out of the trench. He had reached the third line of German trenches when he was hit by a bullet in the body. One of the men who was with him carried him to a shell hole and laid him there … He was buried with his men and many friends of his and mine in our old first line trench, which he and I used to hold last April. I cannot tell you how much we miss him, especially the men whom he so splendidly led. I cannot tell you what his help has meant to me; he and I have been in so many tight places. But I would like you to know this – that there was no other Battalion in the Army that attacked so magnificently or was so heroically led as the 9th Devons. They went into and through fire that could hardly have been more terrible, and everywhere they won through to their objectives even when the officers were gone. I know that Harold would not have wished to have died otherwise than in leading such men.

As one school friend remembered him: 'He was just steel and gold.'

Charles Mills (Magdalen; Apollo, 1908), from a millionaire banking family, died with the 2nd Battalion, Scots Guards, at Hulluch in France on October 1915, aged just 28. John Pixley (Eton and Merton; Apollo, 1908) was recommended for an MC in 1916, but died under sniper fire on the first day of the Battle of Passchendaele in October 1917, aged 29. These were both predictable heroes, but sometimes the physical bravery of these soldiers almost defies belief. Ferdinand Marsham-Townshend (Eton and Christ Church; Apollo, 1901) was a second lieutenant with the 2nd Battalion, Scots Guards. He was a keen steeplechase rider and owned many racehorses. On 16 May

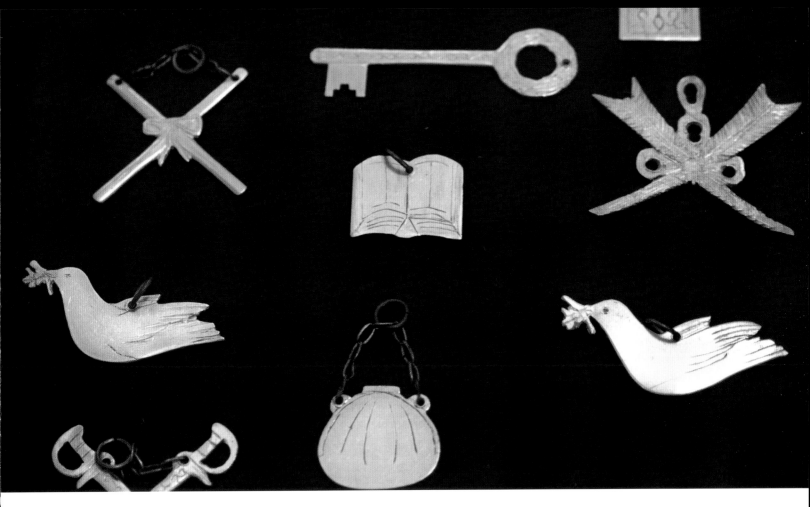

Masonic symbols in tin, made by soldiers of the First World War.

1915, in Rue du Bois, near Festubert, two officers and eighty men of the Scots Guards fought to the last cartridge and the last bayonet, surrounded by heaps of German corpses.

> Soaked by the rain, blackened by the sun, their bodies were not beautiful to look upon; but the [200] German dead spread plentifully around, the empty cartridge cases scattered about, the twisted bayonets and broken rifles showed the price a Scots Guard sets upon his honour. No monarch ever had a finer lying in state than those eighty guardsmen dead amid the long coarse grass of this dreary Flanders plain.

One of those officers was Ferdinand Marsham-Townshend, aged 35.

NOBLE LOSSES AND GALLANT REGULARS

Apollo would not be Apollo had it not included five members of the nobility in its list of casualties. The Hon. Charles Henry Lyell (Eton and New College; Apollo, 1898), heir to the 1st Baron Lyell witnessed the build-up to World War I from the highest governmental level. As MP for South Edinburgh he was parliamentary private secretary to Sir Edward Grey, Foreign Secretary, and to H.H. Asquith, the prime minister. In 1915 he joined the Highland Royal Garrison Artillery and was mentioned in despatches. Then he switched to military diplomacy. In 1917 he became a general staff officer with the rank of major, responsible for liaison with the United States Army. He died of pneumonia in Washington, in October 1918, and rests today in Arlington National Cemetery.

The career of Charles Duncombe, 2nd Earl of Feversham (Eton and Christ Church; Apollo, 1899), was scarcely less elevated. He had been a lieutenant colonel in the Yorkshire Hussars before becoming assistant private secretary to the First Lord of the Admiralty and Conservative MP for Thirsk and Malton, all before inheriting his title in 1915. That was the year he died on the Somme during the Battle of Flers-Courcelette, as Commander of the 21st Battalion, King's Royal Rifle Corps. Similarly, Sir Matthew White Ridley, 2nd Viscount Ridley (Eton and Balliol; Apollo, 1894), had been assistant private secretary to the Chancellor of the Exchequer, and rose to be lieutenant colonel of the 5th Battalion, Northumberland Fusiliers. But his health had never been robust. Duodenal ulcers, rather than military wounds, killed him at the age of 41 in February 1916.

Not so Lord Alexander Thynne, son of the 4th Marquess of Bath (Eton and Balliol; Apollo, 1894). Much decorated in the Boer War, he was twice wounded on the Somme, while commanding battalions first of the Worcestershire then of the Wiltshire regiment, before being killed in action near Bethune, almost at the end of the war in September 1918. Thynne was by then 45 years of age.

By comparison, Henry Parnell, 5th Baron Congleton (Eton and New College; Apollo, 1910) – sportsman, traveller, writer – was still a young man with a bright future before him. He died in action – at Zillebeke in Belgium – at the age of only 24, within a few months of the outbreak of war. Congleton was a second lieutenant in the Grenadier Guards; the first member of the House of Lords to be killed in World War I.

By no means all Apollo casualties were so well connected. John Norwood (Rugby and Exeter; Apollo, 1896) came from a family of Kentish hop merchants. He served with the Dragoon Guards in India, South Africa, Transvaal and Natal before mobilization in 1914 at the age of 38. But he was no ordinary soldier. He had won a VC near Ladysmith in 1899: he rescued a wounded trooper, carrying him on his back for 300 yards under heavy fire, while leading his horse with one hand. He fought at Mons in the second month of World War I and fell at the Battle of the Marne while trying to help a wounded sergeant. His fellow VC winner, John Stanhope Collings-Wells, VC, DSO (Uppingham and Christ Church; Apollo, 1902) was only a little better connected; but his bravery was certainly a match for Norwood's. Beginning as a regular soldier with the Bedfordshire Regiment; badly wounded in 1915; promoted to acting colonel in 1916; he won his DSO in 1917 and his VC in 1918. On the last occasion, with a small body of volunteers, he held up the enemy until the last round of ammunition, while the rest of his battalion withdrew to safety. Later on – at Bouzincourt Ridge, near the Somme – he led a fierce counter-attack until wounded in both arms. He was then carried to a bunker, only to receive a direct hit from a mortar shell. His body was not immediately recognized.

Perhaps 'the most costly single death of the war to mankind generally', as Isaac Asimov noted, was Henry Moseley (Eton, KS and Trinity; Apollo, 1907). A brilliant physicist, a pupil of Rutherford and a potential Nobel prizewinner – discoverer indeed of 'Moseley's Law': decoding the atomic numbers of the periodic table – he died with the Royal Engineers at the Dardanelles, shot in the head near the front line by a Turkish sniper at Seddulbahir on 10 August 1915. Here was 'a young man twenty six years old', wrote Robert Millikan, who 'threw open the windows through which we could glimpse the sub-atomic world with a definition and certainty never dreamt of before'.[125]

The death of Duncan Mackinnon (Rugby and Magdalen; Apollo, 1909) was also a loss but of a rather different kind. Mackinnon was a world-class oarsman. He won a gold medal in the 1908 Olympics; he rowed in the winning Oxford Boat Race crews of 1909, 1910 and 1911; at Henley he won the Stewards' Cup and Visitors' Cup in 1907 and 1908, as well as rowing in the winning crew in the Wyfold Cup and Grand Challenge Cup (twice). The outbreak of war found him serving with the Calcutta Light Horse. He returned to join first the Royal North Devon Yeomanry and then the 1st Battalion, Scots Guards. Gallipoli he survived, but soon his luck ran out. He died at the age of 30 on 9 October 1917, on the first day of the Battle of Poelcappelle.

Not the least remarkable biography of these Apollo men who died in World War I – though in a rather different way – is that of Sir Schomberg McDonnell, fifth son of the 5th Earl of Antrim (Eton and Univ.; Apollo, 1880). 'Pom' McDonnell served as principal private secretary to Lord Salisbury during his time as prime minister, before becoming Secretary to the Office of Works in 1902–12. During those years he was responsible for organizing the funeral

of Edward VII, the coronation of George V and the investiture of the Prince of Wales, as well as the maintenance and construction of a whole series of Edwardian public buildings.[126] At court he was a very stylish figure. But his career was cut short in 1912 thanks to his involvement in a celebrated divorce case. Two years later, after a brief period in intelligence, he joined the Queen's Own Cameron Highlanders and was soon promoted to major. He died in Belgium, fighting in the trenches at the advanced age of 56.[127]

Among those who saw service in World War I a number were decorated with the DSO and the MC. Holders of the DSO included Arthur Gilbert

Ceiling of the Grand Temple at Freemasons' Hall, London.

Master (1867–1942; Apollo, 1899), who was taken prisoner at Mafeking in the Boer War, but escaped before the relief. He won his DSO in 1915 and was mentioned in dispatches seven times. He went on to have a distinguished career in the East India Company, mainly in India.

Several Apollonians had their war service recognized with the award of the Military Cross. The Hon. George St Vincent Harris (1889–1984), later 5th Baron Harris of Seringapatam and Mysore, served as a captain with the Royal East Kent Yeomanry, was mentioned in dispatches and wounded before the award of his MC. Colonel A. Dennis Burnett Brown was the Apollo's Junior Warden in 1918. The Rt Hon. John Jestyn Llewellin, Lord Llewellin (1893–1957), an officer in the Royal Garrison Artillery, was wounded in the war before going up to University College and on to the Inner Temple. As an MP for Middlesex from 1929 to 1945 Llewellin held several government appointments including Lord of the Admiralty (1932–38) and, during the Second World War, Minister of Aircraft Production (in which capacity he served on the Combined Policy Committee set up by the British and United States governments to oversee the construction of the atomic bomb) and Minister of Food (1943–45).

After being injured in the war, Lt Col. George Douglas Amery (Brasenose; Apollo, 1931) returned to Oxford to complete his degree, and subsequently became a University demonstrator and lecturer in the history and economics of agriculture. Amery was appointed Master of Apollo in 1933; then Provincial Grand Secretary and Provincial Grand Master (1948–55). Thomas Dewar Weldon (1896–1958; Magdalen; WM 1934) was awarded the MC and bar. Appointed lecturer in Philosophy at Magdalen in 1922 and a fellow and tutor there from 1923 to 1958, Weldon was the Apollo's Master in 1934 before becoming one of its Trustees in 1938. During the Second World War Weldon became the personal assistant to Arthur 'Bomber' Harris at Bomber Command.

W. Conrad Costin was awarded his MC while a captain in the Royal Gloucestershire Regiment.

CLERGYMEN AND THE END OF THE WAR

One unexpected aspect of Apollo's contribution to the war deserves separate mention. Four of the lodge's casualties were also Anglican clergymen. Arthur Steward (Wellington and Magdalen; Apollo, 1909) had served with the Norfolk

Regiment in South Africa, before taking holy orders in Yorkshire in 1913. He joined the Royal Artillery in 1915, only to die near Ypres in October 1917, aged 35. Percy Beresford (Magdalen; Apollo, 1896), once a priest at St Mary's, Westerham, Kent, was awarded the DSO 'for conspicuous gallantry and ability' in command of his battalion of the Royal Fusiliers: 'holding on to an almost impossible position'. He died of wounds in West-Vlaanderen, Belgium, in October 1917, aged 42. His brother-in-law, Oswald Holden (Exeter; Apollo, 1897), vicar of Penn, Staffordshire, became a chaplain to the 60th Infantry Brigade in 1917. He was killed outright, between Cambrai and Péronne, 'whilst going to help the wounded'. By comparison Philip Blakeway (Malvern and Magdalen; Apollo, 1884), vicar of Walberton, Sussex, had a rather more lengthy career. He had served in India with the 8th Hussars before joining the Chaplains' Department. At the outbreak of war, although already in his late forties, he applied to go to the front, and went out to Egypt with one of the first drafts of troops. He died of heatstroke in Ismalia, on 15 June 1915, at the age of 50. The thermometer that day registered 118 degrees Fahrenheit.

Not all the stories of Apollo in World War I are tales of undoubting bravery. Misfortune and uncertainty must often have played a part. The life of Arthur Mackworth supplies a cautionary corrective. The son of Sir Arthur Mackworth, 6th Bt, and Alice Cubitt, he went up to Magdalen in 1906; joined the Wellesley Lodge at Sandhurst while working as a tutor at Wellington; and then became a fellow of Magdalen in 1913, having been initiated in Apollo in 1912. With the war scarcely begun, his brother Captain Francis Mackworth was killed on active service with the Royal Field Artillery. Meanwhile Arthur Mackworth started with the Rifle Brigade, but soon transferred – perhaps on medical grounds – to the Intelligence Department of the War Office. He committed suicide on 25 November 1917, at the age of 31. He rests today not in France or Belgium, but in the north-east corner of Holywell Cemetery, Oxford.

With the end of hostilities, memorials of the Great War were erected in towns and cities across the land. London was naturally the central focus of Masonic tribute. And in the capital, Apollo, with its metropolitan and royal connections, had an obvious role to play. In March 1924 architects were invited to submit plans for a Masonic Peace Memorial Building close to the historic site of Freemasons' Tavern. On 8 August 1925 a Special Festival of fund-raising – the Masonic Peace Memorial Fund – was held at Olympia. No fewer than 7,000 Brethren attended; and a total of £826,014. 16s. 8d. was collected. Plans were accepted in June 1926. And on 14 July 1927, in the presence of 8,000 Brethren, the foundation stone was laid 'by electrical connection'; that is, via radio link from the Albert Hall in South Kensington to Great Queen Street in Holborn. Work began the following year; building was completed in 1931. And in 1933 the new Grand Temple was at last dedicated by the Grand Master, the Duke of Connaught. The future King Edward VIII was in attendance.

Had that dedication taken place a decade previously – when plans were in fact drawn up – critics might have hailed the Grand Temple as an exercise in abstracted neoclassicism. Had the competition been truly open, the result might well have been a triumph: a Grand Temple by Lutyens or Norman Shaw might even have justified the million-pound outlay. Instead the design turned out to be, aesthetically speaking, a disappointment: its style was too literal, too late. The firm employed – H.V. Ashley and F.W. Newman of Hampstead – were no more than competent practitioners. Still, the imagery – particularly in the Great Hall – is appropriately Masonic: *beaux arts* with more than a dash of symbolism. The vestibule contains a striking memorial shrine with a roll of honour recording all the Masons who died in World War I. The roll of honour lists the many hundreds of Masonic war dead. All Oxford Freemasons will know that pride of place on this roll goes to the Apollo University Lodge, where 79 of the members who perished are recorded.

The interior sculpture in the Great Hall sums up the founding spirit of Grand Lodge in all its Hanoverian dignity: a colossal figure of the deistic Duke of Sussex; as well as busts, among others, of two Anglican Monarchs, George IV and William IV. As a composition the Grand Temple looks inwards, ignoring the language of the Modern Movement; ignoring indeed the world beyond its own walls. *The Buildings of England* dismisses its structure as 'bewilderingly self-possessed'.[128] But then neither fashion nor advertisement entered into the architects' brief. Secrecy, and a shared code of symbolic imagery, have always been part of the Freemason's armoury. In its timing, Freemasons' Hall was a private expression of corporate grief. In its confidence and stature, it was a monumental commentary on two centuries of Masonic achievement. In the context of this narrative, it was a fitting epitaph on two centuries of Grand Lodge, and on one century of Apollo.

6 APOLLO'S CENTENARY, 1919

IN NOVEMBER 1919, HAVING barely survived the war, and despite the loss of so many of its members, Apollo celebrated its centenary in ample form. From the lodge's records and the press reports (see below) it would seem that the event was orchestrated by Philip Colville Smith (St John's; Apollo, 1886), who had succeeded Sir Edward Letchworth as Grand Secretary of the UGLE in 1917. So proud was the lodge of its Secretary that it presented him with a silver cup and a cheque for £55 'as a token of the gratification which the members of his Mother Lodge felt at the honour conferred upon a friend and a brother, as well as upon the Lodge itself', and elected him to be its Master for its centenary year.

Earlier that year, on 27 June, Pro Grand Master Arthur Oliver Villiers Russell (New College; Apollo, 1890), the 2nd Baron Ampthill, had presided over an Especial Grand Lodge of over 8,000 Freemasons held at the Royal Albert Hall to celebrate the end of the war. Ampthill had already been the Provincial Grand Master of Bedfordshire (1891–1935), Governor of Madras (1900–04), the District Grand Master of the UGLE's lodges in Madras (1901–05), Pro Grand Master to Prince Arthur, Duke of Connaught, since 1908 and seen war service in France as a battalion commander. He was also a renowned oarsman: he had rowed in two winning eights against Cambridge, presided over the OUBC in 1891 while also president of the Oxford Union, twice won in the Silver Goblets and once in a Grand Challenge crew

(opposite) Portrait of Lord Ampthill, 1905.

at Henley – and been an original member of the International Olympic Committee in 1894.[129] It was Ampthill who came back to Oxford to install Colville Smith as the Apollo's Master at its Centenary Anniversary Meeting in the Assembly Room of the Town Hall.

LODGE MEETINGS IN WORLD WAR I

Apollo University Lodge held five meetings between January 1914 and the outbreak of the war. The minutes give no hint of the war's approach, let alone of the deaths of more than eighty of its members on active service. Indeed, the minutes of the first of its two meetings in February 1914 show as healthy a lodge as it is today: sixty members and twenty-five visitors came to the University Masonic Hall at 5 p.m. to attend the initiation of seven men and the installation of Arthur Ernest Cowley (Magdalen; Apollo, 1899) as the Master for the year, before proceeding to dinner, probably at the Clarendon Hotel.

Born in 1861, Cowley, one of seventeen children of a south London customs house agent, had been Master twice before, in 1905 and 1911, and was again in that chair when the war broke out. By the time of this third period as Master he was a leading Semitic scholar, a sub-librarian at the Bodleian Library, a fellow of Magdalen College, a D.Litt. and a recent Senior Grand Deacon in Grand Lodge (1911). He was appointed Librarian of the Bodleian in 1919 and died in 1931, leaving the bulk of his estate to the University for use by the Bodleian.

The visitors at his installation in 1914 included a delegation from the Isaac Newton University Lodge (INUL), Cambridge – Apollo's much younger 'sister', it having been founded as recently as 1861. At the outset of the year Apollo had £160 in the bank (a staggering £13,710 in today's money), and the ball held on the Wednesday of Commemoration week in May 1914 made a healthy enough profit for the cost of repairs and improvements to the Hall in the following months to be met by a gift of £60 from the ball account.

By October 1914, however, much had already changed. The Masonic Hall at 50A High Street, owned by Alfred Lodge and Bertie Lodge, had been requistioned to become the '3rd Southern General Hospital' and Apollo had granted the town lodges' request to meet at the University Masonic Hall, Frewin Court, for the duration of the war.[130] The private secretary to the Prince of Wales sent a telegram to the lodge's Secretary, Philip Colville Smith, annnouncing that His Royal Highness had set up a National Relief Fund 'to

alleviate the acute distress which must inevitably occur on account of the
war. Your Masonic Lodge has been suggested by the Committee to his Royal
Highness as a body from whom a subscription may be expected'; the lodge
dutifully subscribed £21.[131] The minutes of 27 October are the first to mention
by name a member's death in the combat: Second Lieutenant Edward Fenwick
Boyd (University College), who was killed at the Battle of the Aisne on 20
September 1914. He was a member of Vincent's and had played football for
Blackheath and for the Army & Navy XI.[132]

Meetings continued to be held throughout the war – 22 in all beween
October 1914 and November 1919 – but they were unusual in several respects.
Often fewer than a dozen men attended (including visitors), only one initiation
was conducted and no other degree ceremonies were performed.

Other appointments were made necessarily in the appointees' absence on
active service. For instance, J.C.B. Gamlen (see below), who was first installed
as Master of the Apollo in 1915 and re-elected in February 1916 while he was

absent 'on military service'. In November that year he again sent his apologies, this time 'from the Front in France'. Major Frank Grégoire Proudfoot, MD, RAMC, attached to the Queen's Own Oxfordshire Hussars, took over in December 1917 as Master after 2/Lt Arthur Mackworth, his predecessor, committed suicide after only nine months in office (see p. 112), but his installation was delayed until well into 1918 by 'military exigencies'. Unusually, Proudfoot appointed his officers for the year while he was still away, including the 8th Earl of Jersey and Colonel A.D. Burnett Brown MC as his wardens.

APOLLO'S CORE TEAM DURING WORLD WAR I

That the lodge continued to meet at all was due to the efforts not only of its Secretary, Philip Colville Smith, and the Master at the outbreak of war, Arthur Cowley (see above), but also of the Revd Thomas Trotter Blockley (Magdalen) and the lodge's three treasurers during World War I: Brothers Baynes, Cronshaw and Gamlen. Colville Smith, known to his Masonic contemporaries as 'PC', had been Master of the Bicester Hounds while still an undergraduate, and was also at one time the treasurer of both the Bullingdon Club and Vincent's; Sir James Stubbs describes him in the lodge as 'a splendid figure, supported by his two sticks, and with an accompanying stammer that made him all the more impressive, he dominated the scene.'[133]

The Revd Thomas Trotter Blockley (Magdalen) had been the Master of the lodge in 1910 and was appointed as Grand Chaplain in the UGLE in 1918. Re-elected Master in 1920 he was then appointed as the lodge's chaplain and continued in that office until shortly before his death in 1950, regularly attending its meetings even after he became the Provincial Grand Master for Oxfordshire (1935–48).

Robert Edward Baynes (Christ Church), Apollo's Master in 1886 and a stalwart of the lodge throughout the latter half of the Victorian period, was its Treasurer until 1915, when he resigned, and then held the office of Deputy Provincial Grand Master until his death in 1921.[134] The Revd George Bernard Cronshaw (1872–1928) was elected Treasurer in 1915 and re-elected annually until his death in 1928. Cronshaw had already served twice as Master (in 1910 and 1912) and went on to become the UGLE's Grand Chaplain in 1921. He easily combined his Freemasonry with careers in the University, the city of Oxford, and the Anglican Church. Cronshaw took a First in chemistry while at The Queen's College and was then ordained in Leeds before returning to Oxford in 1898 on being appointed Chaplain at The Queen's (a post he filled for thirty years) and curate at St Cross Church, Holywell, until 1900 when he was appointed lecturer in Chemistry. Cronshaw gave up his teaching responsibilities when in 1912 he was promoted from junior to senior bursar and then served as chairman and secretary of the Committee of College Bursars. Uniquely, Cronshaw was also treasurer of St Hugh's College and oversaw its move to Banbury Road. A member of the Hebdomadal Council from 1911 until 1923, he was in addition a Visitor to the Museum, Acting Curator of the Schools and a member of the boards of Natural History and Medicine. As chairman and treasurer of the committee for the Radcliffe Infirmary (1910–28) Cronshaw helped to establish its throat and ear, maternity and electrical departments. Cronshaw's last appointment was as the principal of St Edmund Hall in 1928 but he died the same year.

John Charles Blagden Gamlen (Balliol) succeeded Cronshaw as Treasurer in 1928. He was the only son of W.B. Gamlen, the secretary to the curators of the University Chest. He lived in Banbury Road. Master of Apollo in 1915 and 1916 (see above) and Treasurer from 1928 until 1946, he was reinstalled as Master in 1949 and then filled the office of Lodge Almoner until his death in 1952.

Lodge dining presented some difficulties during this period, and while the record is by no means complete, it would appear that with such small numbers attending, the lodge was able to dine in college Common Rooms, such as Magdalen's in 1915 (as the guests of A.E. Cowley) and The Queen's the following year, presumably as Cronshaw's guests. Not that the lodge's finances were a problem: in 1916 the Treasurer was able to report that the lodge held £19 in cash, £50 on deposit, £755 in Consols and £400 Canada 3 per cent, about £60,000 in today's terms. Its operating loss of £13.10s.0d in 1918 was 'considered satisfactory considering the circumstances'.[135] And the lodge continued its charitable giving throughout the war, including fourteen guineas to Masonic charities and ten to the Radcliffe Hospital.

THE CENTENARY CELEBRATION

The two press reports of the centenary in the *Oxford Chronicle*, filed in the Minutes Book, give us a taste of the occasion and include a photograph of Colville Smith. In the principal report in the main section of the newspaper,

(opposite) Newspaper report on the centenary celebrations, November 1919, filed in an Apollo Minutes Book.

Oxford Chronicle

Apollo University Lodge.

(NO. 357.)

CENTENARY CELEBRATION

BANQUET LAST NIGHT.

An event of great Masonic and University interest was celebrated at the Town Hall yesterday, when the Apollo University Lodge of Freemasons, No. 357 on the register of the United Grand Lodge of England celebrated the centenary of its foundation, and Mr. P. Colville Smith, Grand Secretary of England, was installed for the fourth time as Worshipful Master of the Lodge.

Yesterday's function also partook of the nature of a re-union, as owing to the absence of so many members on active or other war service, the work of the Lodge since 1914 has of necessity been confined to formal meetings, but yesterday's gathering afforded a fitting opportunity of welcoming back the absent members, as well as remembering in honour and gratitude those who had laid down their lives for their country.

Mr. P. Colville Smith presided at the banquet which followed, which was held in the Town Hall.

THE INSTALLATION.

In proposing the toast of the Grand Master, the W.M. read a letter received from H.R.H. the Duke of Connaught, in which he congratulated the Lodge upon the celebration of its centenary, adding, "I grieve with you in the loss of your 59 members."

Lord Amphill, Pro Grand Master, installed Mr. P. Colville Smith as W.M., being assisted by Mr. C. E. Keyser, P.G.W., as S.W.; Rev. C. E. Robbrts, P.G.C., as J.W.; and Mr. H. Passmore Edwards, P.G.D., as I.G. The following officers were appointed and invested: Dr. F. G. Proudfoot, P.P.G.W., I.P.M.; Dr. C. G. Douglas, M.A., P.P.G.P. S.W.; A. D. Burnett-Brown, M.C., P.P.G.A. Sec., J.W.; Rev. T. T. Blockley, M.A., P.G.C., Chaplain; Rev. G. B. Cronshaw, M.A., P.P.G.C., Treasurer; J. C. B. Gamlen, M.A., P.P.G.D.C., Secretary; C. H. Thompson, M.A., P.P.G.Reg. D.C.; J. A. Tawney, M.A., P.P.G.W., S.D.; Rev. A. G. Parham, M.A., J.D.; H. T. Tizard, M.A., A.D.C.; C. E. Brownrigg, M.A., P.P.G.W., Almoner; Dr. John Ivimey, P.G.O., Organist; H. A. B. Whitelocke, M.A., I.G.; H. B. Hartley, M.A., P.P.G.Std., and Dr. H. C. Bazett, Stewards; T. Stilgoe, Tyler.

THE FALLEN.

After a short history of the Lodge had been read, the names of fifty-nine past members of the Lodge who had fallen in the war were read out, all the members and visitors standing.

Lord Amphill, in responding to the toast of the Grand Lodge Officers, said he was indebted to the Apollo Lodge for admitting him to a phase of life which had been full of happiness and good fortune.

Mr. H. B. Hartley proposed the toast of the Provincial Grand Lodge Officers, to which Mr. R. E. Baynes, P.G.D., Deputy Provincial Grand Master, responded. He paid a high tribute to the work done for the Province by Viscount Valentia, the Provincial Grand Master, whose compulsory absence from that gathering they all deplored.

Sir Alfred Robbins, President of the Board of General Purposes, proposed the toast of the Apollo University Lodge. The Lodge, he said, had done, was doing, and would do a great work in Freemasonry. It was in a Lodge like the Apollo that the morrow was being manufactured. That Lodge was continually bringing into existence some of the finest characters the Craft could possibly boast.

Mr. P. Colville Smith, in responding to the toast, said that of the 3,000 members initiated in the Lodge during its hundred years' history, he had in a membership of 33 years initiated 155. He had never been out of office during that time, and he had only missed attendance at five regular meetings.

AFTER 59 YEARS.

The Right Hon. T. F. Halsey, Deputy Grand Master, who also responded to the toast, said his only claim for being included was that he was initiated in the Lodge 59 years ago. His father had been initiated in the Lodge, and all his sons who had been at Oxford had been initiated there.

Dr. A. E. Cowley, P.G.D. (Bodley's Librarian), proposed the toast of the Sister Lodges. All university lodges had, he said, during the last few years suffered most terrible losses, but that should not deprive them of the determination to go on and do what they had done.

The W.M.'s of the Isaac Newton University Lodge and of the Oxford and Cambridge University Lodge responded.

The Rev. G. B. Cronshaw, Provincial Grand Secretary, proposed the toast of the Guests, to which the W.M. of the Alfred Lodge, No. 340, Oxford, responded.

During the evening several songs were rendered by the Magdalen Glee Singers.

An interesting feature of the gathering was an official visit from the Isaac Newton University Lodge, Cambridge.

Among those present, taking the names in alphabetical order, and in addition to those whose names have already been mentioned, were Lord Aldenham, P.G.W.; Major W. Alston, Mr. W. J. Armitage, P.G.D., Rev. Dr. Rosslyn Bruce, Mr. W. T. Beeston, Sir Robert Buckell, Mr. A. Burnett-Brown, P.G.D., Grand Supt. of Works; Rev. J. E. Cardigan-Williams, Mr. E. H. Cartwright, P.G.D., Mr. C. A. Cochrane, P.G.D., Mr. A. Ransford Collett, D.G.D.C., Rev. Dr. H. R. Cooper-Smith, P.G.C., Mr. Dudley Cory-Wright, P.G.D., Dr. A. E. Cowley, P.G.D., Sir Lionell Darell, Bart., Rev. Dr. T. H. Davies, Hon. R. C. Devereaux, Dr. G. Claridge Druce, Mr. W. Reskury Few, P.A.G.D.C., Rev. A. W. G. Giffard, Rev. F. J. O. Gillmor, P.A.G.C., Sir Park Goff, M.P., Mr. J. S. Granville Grenfell, G.D.C., Hon. G. St. V. Harris, Mr. A. D. Hansell, P.G.D., Rev. G. Halsey, Lieut.-Col. G. H. Hoare, Rev. O. M. Holden, P.A.G.C., Mr. H. Dixon Kimber, Grand Treasurer; Rev. W. W. G. Lloyd, Major R. L. Loyd, Mr. Percy G. Mallory, P.A.G.D.C., Capt. S. A. Mavrojani, Mr. L. Mieville, P.G.St., Mr. J. T. Morland, Prov. G.M., Berks; Rev. M. W. Myres, Major F. P. Nunneley, Mr. A. B. Nutter, P.A.G.D.C., Mr. Mostyn Pigott, P.A.G.Reg., Archdeacon Southwell, Mr. W. Lascelles Southwell, P.G.D., Mr. J. E. K. Studd, P.G.D., Mr. C. H. Taphouse, Mr. J. E. Terry, P.G.D., Mr. A. F. Thedosius, Mr. G. E. Underhill, Mr. S. A. White, P.G.St.B., Rev. C. E. L. Wright, P.G.D., and Dudley Wright.

Viscount Valentia, the Provincial Grand Master for Oxfordshire, was unable to attend in consequence of his duties as Lord-in-Waiting, and the Earl of Donoughmore, P.G.W., Grand Master of Ireland, was detained in a Committee of the House of Lords.

The catering arrangements for the banquet were in the hands of Messrs. Weeks and Co.

(An article on the past history of the Apollo Lodge appears in our University Pages, Topics, page II.).

under the heading 'Centenary Celebration', the newspaper's correspondent
describes the event as one of 'great Masonic and University interest', which
had provided 'a fitting opportunity of welcoming back the absent members,
as well as remembering with honour and gratitude those who had laid down
their lives for their country.' According to this report, Colville Smith – at the

banquet, before reading the provisional list of the fallen – read out a letter
from the Duke of Connaught in which he as Grand Master congratulated the
lodge upon its centenary but added 'I grieve with you in the loss of your 59 [*sic*]
members'.[136] In proposing the health of the lodge, the President of the UGLE's
Board of General Purposes, Sir Alfred Robbins, said:

> The Lodge had done, was doing and would do a great work in Freemasonry. It was
> in a Lodge like the Apollo that the morrow was being manufactured. That Lodge
> was continually bringing into existence some of the finest characters the Craft
> could possibly boast.

In his response, Colville Smith said that 3,000 members of the University
had been initated in the lodge since 1819, adding that he had been a member
for thirty-three years, never been out of office and missed only five meetings.
The UGLE's Deputy Grand Master (1903–26) and its Provincial Grand Master
for Hertfordshire (1873–1923), the Rt Hon. Thomas Frederick Halsey (Christ
Church; Apollo, 1861), also replied to the toast, saying that some fifty-nine
years earlier he too had been initiated in the lodge, adding with some pride
that he had also been followed into the lodge by the three of his four sons who
went to Oxford.[137] Halsey had rowed in the losing eight against Cambridge
in 1860 and sat as a Conservative MP for Hertfordshire from 1874 until 1906,
by when he had been elected chairman of the House of Commons Standing
Orders Committee and been sworn to the Privy Council. He was created
a baronet in 1920. 'Dr A E Cowley, PGD [Past Grand Deacon], Bodley's
Librarian', proposed the toast to the Apollo's sister lodges, and the Masters of
the Isaac Newton Lodge and the Oxford and Cambridge Lodge responded.
During all this, several songs were rendered by the Magdalen Glee Singers.

The second report, on the paper's 'University Pages', consists of a brief
history of the lodge. It ends with the claim that

> Few Lodges, if indeed any … have on its membership roll so many distinguished
> names in ecclesiastical, political, legal, military, naval, or literary circles as the
> Apollo University Lodge; certainly none can have so many distinguished initiates.

7 APOLLO BETWEEN THE WARS, 1918–38

BETWEEN THE TWO WORLD wars Apollo became less prominent in Oxford and less exclusive. Some drifting away from early loyalties was only to have been expected among Apollo men at this time. In a shifting, sceptical world the familiar certainties of Oxford before 1914 had begun to fade. And there would never be another grand Eights Week Masonic Garden Party. Many of the social certainties had evaporated. What surely remained, however, well into the twentieth century, was a familiar network of relationships; a certain sense of entitlement, of belonging to a supra-generational elite.

Membership was still an object of ambition. Each year star undergraduates were recruited in significant numbers. The confidence, the camaraderie, were still there. During the years of World War I recruitment had been at a standstill: only one initiate in 1917; only three in 1919. But in 1920 there was a bumper intake, with no fewer than fifty-one recruits. At least seven of these became major public figures: Geoffrey Faber, fellow of All Souls, creator of Faber & Faber, 'the godfather of modern English poetry'; Gerald Gardiner, the future Baron Gardiner, radical law reformer and Labour Lord Chancellor; Douglas Jardine, ice-cold captain of the English 'bodyline' cricket tour of Australia in 1932–33; Frederick Barrington-Ward, fellow of All Souls (brother of Robert Barrington-Ward, editor of *The Times*); Godfrey Elton, 1st Baron Elton – for many years a celebrated don at The Queen's; Roger Lumley, 11th Earl of Scarbrough, Lord Chamberlain of the Royal Household, 48th Grand

Master of the UGLE (1951–67); and, finally, J.C. Masterman, a formidable Modern History tutor (Hugh Trevor-Roper was one of his pupils in later years), wartime intelligence officer, Oxford vice chancellor, master-networker and author of that arch bible of collegiate intrigue *To Teach the Senators Wisdom* (1952).

Six very different men; all of them Apollo initiates of 1920. Not every year could match 1920, but during the following decade Apollo continued to attract talent and ambition. Roger Makins, for example – later Lord Sherfield, diplomat and mandarin – joined the lodge in 1924. A year later he was awarded a congratulatory First, the following year a fellowship at All Souls. His career was now on a very fast track for Washington, the City and the House of Lords. By comparison, another fellow of All Souls, Charles Harris, who joined Apollo in 1925, seems to have led a rather sequestered life: he was an authority on *Duns Scotus* (1927) and wrote a study of *Germany's Foreign Indebtedness* (1935). In all, between the two world wars six current or future fellows of All Souls entered Apollo University Lodge, but Ernest Swinton (in 1926) was to be the last.

One evening in January 1926, two undergraduates were admitted who would play a considerable – and progressive – part in imperial affairs: Alan Lennox-Boyd (Christ Church), later Viscount Boyd of Merton, and Evelyn Baring, later Baron Howick. Lennox-Boyd turned out to be a future Colonial Secretary, a genial, larger-than-life figure who married a Guinness heiress. Baring – 'the last pro-consul' – son of the 1st Earl of Cromer, became a notable colonial governor and Commonwealth diplomat. The careers of both men were curiously intertwined. Both for example – along with another Apollo recruit of 1931, Carruthers Melville ('Monkey') Johnstone – were involved in Kenya's ill-fated Mau Mau rebellion of the 1950s. All his life Baring retained the staunch Christianity of his Apollo years. Lennox-Boyd became rather more of a politique, though distantly loyal to Masonic ideals.

In some ways Apollo's collective discretion increased after 1914, but its social net was now more widely cast. On 24 November 1928 one notable double election records the names of Peter Cazalet, a future racehorse trainer to royalty, and William Harcourt, 2nd Viscount, a future merchant banker to

Hugh Trevor-Roper, Lord Dacre (Apollo, 1936). Regius Professor of Modern History at Oxford and Master of Peterhouse. By 1942 he had rejected Freemasonry. 'It won't do', he noted in his diary. 'I have been initiated into the mysteries, I have been a Freemason and a member of the Secret Service, and I have had enough of esoteric societies.'

Sir Osbert Lancaster (Apollo, 1928). Cartoonist and wit. 'A veritable caricature of one of his own amusing caricatures ... it is hard to believe he took his Masonic vows too seriously.'

the great and good. Whatever their avocation, the Establishment potential of Apollo recruits around this date seems indisputable. It is hard to believe, however, that Sir Osbert Lancaster (Apollo, 1928) – a veritable caricature of one of his own caricatures – took his obligations too seriously. But in other instances, it can be presumed, Apollo loyalties may well have lasted a lifetime.

Two years – 1927–28 – saw the initiation of three members who certainly left a formidable mark on public life. Duncan Sandys, Winston Churchill's son-in-law, held a series of key posts in successive Tory Cabinets. Best known today for setting up the European Movement in 1947, as Housing Minister he introduced the Clean Air Act (1956) and Green Belts (1955).[138] Harold Caccia, Baron Caccia – in some ways the ultimate panjandrum – became both ambassador to Washington and provost of Eton, as well as chairman of several banks, and even chairman of the MCC. Frank Pakenham, eventually 7th Earl of Longford and 1st Baron Pakenham, created for himself a unique persona: philosopher, socialist, religious commentator, Cabinet minister, philanthropist and saintly clown (see below, pp. 136–7). How far he strayed from the Masonic ideals of his youth is now impossible to ascertain. But it is hard to believe – despite his later Catholicism – that Apollo faded entirely from his consciousness.

Throughout the 1920s and 1930s, Apollo remained distinctly smart, but that phase in its history – Apollo as a nursery of Oxford's *jeunesse dorée* – was coming to an end. Talent was now more likely to be prized than birth. Though sometimes both elements – and good looks too – might still be combined. What was certain, however, was that as the 1930s progressed, and even more so with the coming of World War II, Apollo began to reflect the changing demography of Oxford. Links with famous schools would continue, but as the balance between private and state education shifted, so the lodge began to assimilate different kinds of recruit: products first of grammar schools, then of comprehensive schools. The elitist image was fading.

8 FROM FREWIN COURT TO THE HIGH, 1920s–1930s

APOLLO PROSPERED IN THE 1920s. Its members donated £3 per head to the 1925 Masonic Peace Memorial Fund (see above, p. 112), a total of £700 (with a purchasing power of about £30,000 today). Its Secretary, P. Colville Smith, as Grand Secretary of the English Craft, was knighted (KCVO) and the lodge began dining at the Randolph Hotel. By an odd coincidence, an aptly named county court judge, Joseph Randolph Randolph [sic] rejoined the lodge while chairman of the Wiltshire Quarter Sessions. Randolph had graduated from Magdalen to the Inner Temple in the 1890s. He became a King's Counsel during the war and served as a county court judge in Oxfordshire from 1924 until his death in 1936. The 'Judge Randolph Dinners' are still held at Magdalen.

The lodge's numbers swelled again, not only with initiates but also with former members renewing memberships that had ceased during the war and other University men who had started their Masonic careers elsewhere. While English Freemasonry as a whole saw a significant increase in lodge memberships, few lodges if any matched the speed and size of Apollo's expansion.[139] Nearly sixty men were initiated in 1920 alone – among them John Molesworth-St Aubyn, a collateral descendant of one of the founders of the lodge in 1818, William St Aubyn[140] – and to deal with the demand the lodge often had to perform two degree ceremonies on the same evening and then meet again the following day.

Members and visitors who attended the lodge's meetings between the end of World War I and 1940 were lucky enough to hear the renowned composer and organist Haldane Campbell Stewart DMus playing the lodge's organ during the ceremonies. Stewart had sung as a chorister in the chapel

Sir Philip Colville Smith (Apollo, 1886). Master of Apollo five times over, in 1891, 1893, 1896, 1919 and 1935–36.

of Magdalen College under Walter Parratt, also of Apollo (see above), and went on to become the College's organist and choirmaster. The youngest son of the Scottish 6th Baron Appin, he played county cricket for Kent and was appointed Grand Organist in 1929. His son created the television show *Top of the Pops*.[141]

It was during Stewart's mastership, in 1926, that the lodge had to find new premises, at apparently short notice. Colville Smith announced at the second meeting in January that 'the tenancy of the lodge in the present building', the University Masonic Hall at Frewin Court, had been terminated 'on 25 March inst and could not be renewed as the Trust Houses Limited, who were the owners of the Clarendon Hotel, had determined to build additional bedrooms on the site.'[142] The lodge left Frewin Court 'with the deepest regret'; as Colville Smith recorded in his minutes of the last meeting held there:

> its foundation stone … had been laid with Masonic honours on Aug 4th 1864 and [it] had been the home of the Lodge since Feb 26th 1865 … [and] over 2000 Masons had been initiated in that Hall during the last 61 years … The last proceeding in this Lodge Room was the singing of one verse of the National Anthem.[143]

The two meetings in the summer term had to be held in the Assembly Room at the Town Hall, but after a change in the lodge's by-laws enabling it to meet on Saturdays the Apollo moved into the Masonic Hall on the High Street, where it remained as a tenant until after World War II.

LEADERS OF THE CRAFT AT HOME AND ABROAD

Several of the initiates during this period would become leaders of the Craft. (Lawrence) Roger Lumley (Magdalen), later the 11th Earl of Scarbrough, is the only Grand Master of the UGLE that Apollo has produced. After serving with the 11th Hussars in France in World War I, he completed his degree at Oxford and was initiated in Apollo in 1920. After two spells in the House of Commons as a Conservative MP (Hull East 1922–29; York 1931–37), Lumley went to India as the governor of Bombay and in 1940 he became the UGLE's District Grand Master there. As governor it fell to Lumley to execute the viceroy's order to arrest Gandhi and the other leaders of the All-India Congress Party in Bombay in 1942. Returning to England in 1943 he succeeded to the earldom

in 1945 and was made a Knight of the Garter. In his Masonic career Lord Scarbrough then served as the UGLE's Deputy Grand Master to the 10th Duke of Devonshire KG (1947–51) and was elected an honorary member of Apollo in 1949. He succeeded Devonshire as Grand Master in 1951. Three years later Scarbrough witnessed the initiation of his own son in the University lodge. While Lord Chamberlain (1952–63) and chancellor of the University of Durham (1958–69) Scarbrough materially assisted the formation of the Grand Lodge of India in 1961. He installed HRH the Duke of Kent as Grand Master at the celebration of the UGLE's 250th anniversary in 1967 in the Royal Albert Hall and died in office as his Pro Grand Master just two years later. The strapline to his obituary in *The Times* read 'Politician, freemason and former Lord Chamberlain'.[144]

The Masonic Hall in Frewin Court, Oxford in 1899. Headquarters of Apollo University Lodge from 1865 to 1926; designed by Brother E.G. Bruton of Alfred Lodge. Here as many as 2,000 undergraduates were initiated. This view shows Masons and their guests photographed for the Masonic Ball of 1899. Prince Meerza, son of the Nawab of Bengal, is standing top right. Dr. Bussell (Master 1900) is sitting in the second row, eighth from the left.

Scarbrough is not, however, the only Apollonian to have been elected as a Grand Master: four others have filled that office in other countries' Grand Lodges, namely the Lords Bledisloe, Donoughmore, Montgomerie and Porritt.

Charles Bathurst rejoined Apollo in 1920 as Baron Bledisloe KBE MP,[145] and was both Governor General of New Zealand and Grand Master of the Grand Lodge of New Zealand (1930–35). While in New Zealand Bledisloe not only presented the Bledisloe Cup, to be competed for by the national rugby teams of New Zealand and Australia; he also purchased the site where the Treaty of Waitangi had been signed and then presented it to the nation as a memorial. On his return to England Bledisloe was created the 1st Viscount Bledisloe, received an honorary doctorate from the University and was made a fellow of University College. He died in 1958.

John Michael Henry Hely-Hutchinson, Viscount Suirdale, later the 7th Earl of Donoughmore (Apollo, 1923), sat in the Commons as the MP for Peterborough (1943–45), succeeded his father as Lord Donoughmore in 1948 and eventually became the Grand Master of Ireland (1964–81), following in his father's footsteps.[146] Apollo made him an honorary member in 1968 and he attended the lodge to receive the honour. Uniquely, as a peer, Grand Master of Ireland and member of Apollo, Donoughmore was kidnapped by the IRA in 1974, but was released a week later.

Archibald William Alexander, Lord Montgomerie, later the 17th Earl of Eglinton and 5th Earl of Winton, was initiated in 1936 and served as the Grand Master Mason of Scotland from 1957 to 1961.

Arthur Espie Porritt, who achieved great distinction in sport, medicine, colonial administration, the Establishment and Freemasonry, came up to Magdalen from Otago University, New Zealand, on a Rhodes Scholarship, and succeeded Charles Bathurst as both Governor General of New Zealand and Grand Master of the Grand Lodge of New Zealand. He won the first of his four Blues in athletics in 1923, and in the summer Olympics of 1924 in Paris he captained the New Zealand team and won the bronze medal in the 100 metres dash, the race immortalized in the film *Chariots of Fire*.[147] The cricketer and president of the University Athletics Club (OUAC), E.P. Hewetson (Pembroke), a member of Apollo and later its Master (in 1929 and 1930), proposed Porritt for initiation in June 1925 and also assisted in the ceremony.[148] Porritt succeeded Hewetson as president of the OUAC and eventually became a member of the International Olympics Committee. Porritt began his medical career in 1926 as a house surgeon at St Mary's Hospital, London, where he joined the hospital lodge, Sancta Maria Lodge, No. 2682. A fellow of the Royal College of Surgeons, he was also appointed Surgeon to the Royal Household, which at the time included three Provincial Grand Masters, two future kings of England and a future Grand Master.[149] After World War II,[150] he resumed active membership of Sancta Maria Lodge, becoming its Master in 1947 and then running the lodge as Secretary from 1949 to 1967. By the time he was appointed Governor General of New Zealand (1967–72) he had been president of the Royal College of Surgeons (1960–63), the British Medical Association (1960–61) and the Royal Society of Medicine (1966–67), created a baronet, and promoted as a Knight Grand Cross in the Royal Victorian Order and the Order of St Michael and St George. In the UGLE he had been its Junior Grand Warden (1964) and joined the Grand Master's personal lodge, Royal Alpha Lodge, No. 16. The Freemasons of New Zealand, who had formed their own Grand Lodge in 1890, promptly elected Sir Arthur Porritt as their Grand Master, the first native-born New Zealander to hold that office (1967–72). Porritt returned to England thereafter and received further honours: he was created a life peer in 1973 and, on behalf of the Grand Master of the UGLE, HRH the Duke of Kent, he was invested by the 7th Earl Cadogan in Royal Alpha Lodge with the Grand Master's Order of Service to Masonry (OSM), the rarest of Masonic distinctions. Apollo's invitation to become an honorary member of the University lodge was received with pleasure, and a portion of Porritt's letter of acceptance is worth quoting here:

> I have always felt that I owe to 'Apollo' a very significant part of my life – & only regret that my active membership was relatively so brief. At the time, membership of two Lodges was an extravagance I could not afford – & my hospital Lodge 'Sancta Maria' gave me more opportunity to carry on the good work that 'Apollo' had begun.[151]

While not quite in the same league, two Apollo initiates in this period went on to become Provincial Grand Masters. The Hon. William Ralph Seymour Bathurst (Apollo, 1927), the second son of the 7th Earl Bathurst, became Master of Apollo in 1931 and then Provincial Grand Master of Gloucestershire from 1950 until his death in a car accident in 1970. The Earl of Stradbroke, the

Provincial Grand Master for Suffolk (1902–47), attended Apollo in October 1929 to witness the initiation of his son, Anthony Alexander Rous, Viscount Dunwich, who succeeded him as 4th Earl and Provincial Grand Master in 1947.

FUTURE POLITICIANS

A bumper crop of future politicians entered Apollo over the next few years, mostly, it has to be said, of the conservative persuasion. Three would eventually be made Companions of Honour (CH): Alan Lennox-Boyd (Christ Church; CH 1960), later the 1st Viscount Boyd of Merton, and Duncan Sandys (Magdalen, CH 1973), both for their achievements in the colonial service (see above, pp. 126–7); and Harry Crookshank. Harry Frederick Comfort Crookshank (Magdalen) joined the diplomatic service after the war and was posted to Washington DC until 1924, when he was elected as the Conservative MP for Gainsborough. He returned to Apollo and attended regularly from 1928 until 1959. As an MP, Crookshank held ministerial office under several prime ministers (including Chamberlain, Churchill and Eden) and became Leader of the House of Commons, Minister of Health and later the Lord Privy Seal (1951–55). On retiring from the Commons he was made a CH and in 1956 raised to the peerage as the 1st Viscount Crookshank of Gainsborough in the County of Lincoln, the Masonic province over which he had served as the Provincial Grand Master since 1954.

Two Balliol men, initiated together on 2 May 1931, demonstrate Apollo's ability to attract men of quite different political hues: Charles Edward Mott-Radclyffe and John Faithful Fortescue Platts-Mills. Mott-Radclyffe, of Barningham Hall, Norfolk, sat as the Conservative Member for Windsor from 1942 until he retired in 1970. Generally on the right wing of the party, he was, according to his obituarist, 'one of the most engaging figures in the House of Commons … immensely jovial; a splendid raconteur … [with] a shrewd and intelligent mind and a formidable capacity for hard work'. He was knighted during his time as chairman of the Conservative backbench Foreigh Affairs Committee (1951–59). A quintessential 'knight of the shires', Sir Charles Mott-Radclyffe was also a high sheriff and deputy lieutenant for Nofolk.[152]

Platts-Mills came up to Balliol in 1929 on a Rhodes Scholarship from the University of Wellington in New Zealand with a double First in Law and having 'proved himself an outstanding track athlete, boxer and oarsman'. He took another First at Balliol and was called to the Bar from the Inner Temple in 1932. Platts-Mills joined the Labour Party in 1936 and, after war service in the RAF and then as a miner, was elected as the MP for Finsbury (London) in the 1945 general election. 'An unshakable apologist in the Commons for Josef Stalin', he was expelled from the Labour Party in 1948 and lost his parliamentary seat in 1950. His legal career was rather more successful: he took silk in 1964 and became 'recognised as an outstanding leader of the Criminal Bar over three decades', during which time he defended, among others, the Great Train Robbers and the Kray twins. 'A master of courtroom theatre ... his clashes with the Bench entered into legal legend.'[153]

But not all this period's Apollonians who went into politics can be so easily classified. John Angus Macnab (Christ Church; Apollo, 1926) converted to Catholicism and trained as a schoolteacher. In London he shared a flat with his friend, William Joyce, and joined the British Union of Fascists. Thrown out of the BUF by Oswald Mosley, Macnab and Joyce founded the pro-Nazi National Socialist League and visited Germany. Unlike Joyce, however, Macnab returned to the UK from Germany when war broke out and served as an ambulance driver until he was detained on account of his previous Nazi sympathies. Nevertheless, Macnab is said to have been the first one to identify Joyce as 'Lord Haw-Haw'.

Richard Thomas Dyke Acland (Balliol; Apollo, 1927), later the 15th Baronet, qualified as a barrister at the Inner Temple and was elected as the Liberal MP for Barnstaple in 1935. He broke away from the Liberals in 1942 and formed the socialist British Common Wealth Party, giving his family seat, Killerton House in Devon, to the National Trust in 1943. Acland lost his parliamentary seat in 1945 and joined the Labour Party. He resigned in 1955 over the Party's nuclear policy and was one of the founders of the Campaign for Nuclear Disarmament.

Francis Aungier Pakenham (1905–2001), later the 7th Earl of Longford KG and the 1st Baron Pakenham of Cowley, was initiated on 4 February 1928 – during the only meeting at which the vice chancellor of the University was also present.[154] He then missed several meetings before taking his Second Degree and it is not clear from the minutes whether he was ever raised to the Third. Pakenham began his life as a Protestant and joined the Conservative Party after graduation, but he then converted to Catholicism and transferred his allegiance to the Labour Party in 1945. As Lord Longford he then held several ministerial posts while in the House of Lords and died in 2001 at the age of

95 as its oldest serving member.[155] A social reformer described by the *New York Times* as a 'Champion of Eccentric Causes', Longford also supported the decriminalization of homosexuality when the Wolfenden Report was debated in the House in 1956.[156] Whether he remembered that its author was also a member of Apollo is unknown.[157]

PEERS AND THE CLERGY

While the social elitism of the lodge was now beginning to be diluted, in 1930 alone a trio of youthful peers was recruited: the 4th Marquess of Dufferin and Ava; the 9th Earl of Jersey; and Viscount Furneaux. Basil Sheridan Hamilton-Temple-Blackwood, the 4th Marquess of Dufferin and Ava (Balliol) , sat on the Conservative benches in the House of Lords, becoming a Lord-in-Waiting to King George VI (1936–37), then the Under-Secretary of State for the Colonies (1937–40). He was killed when serving with the Indian Broadcasting Unit in Burma in 1945.

George Francis Child-Villiers, the 9th Earl of Jersey, came from a long line of Apollo men. His father, the 8th Earl, had been Senior Warden in 1918/19, and his grandfather, the 7th Earl, the Provincial Grand Master for Oxfordshire 1885–1915. It was the 9th Earl who gave Osterley Park to the National Trust after the war.

Viscount Furneaux (Christ Church), proposed for initiation by Viscount Harcourt, eventually succeeded Dufferin and Ava as a Lord-in-Waiting to the King (1938–40 and 1951–52) and then to the Queen (1952–55). Furneaux (1907–1975), the son of F.E. Smith, the 1st Earl of Birkenhead, succeeded as the 2nd Earl on the death of his father in 1930. A historian, he joined the Foreign Office's Political Intelligence Department during the war and saw action in Croatia with Randolph Churchill and Evelyn Waugh.

The Hon. John Seymour Berry was initiated at the same meeting as Furneaux and married his sister. Berry became the deputy chairman of the *Daily Telegraph* (1939–87) and vice chairman of the Amalgamated Press (1942–59). He sat in the House of Commons as the Conservative Member for Hitchin 1941–45 and succeeded to his father's title as the 2nd Viscount Camrose in 1954.

Several other peers joined the lodge in those years before World War II, among them Lord George Nigel Douglas-Hamilton (Apollo, 1927), later the

10th Earl of Selkirk KT,[158] who was to be a key figure in World War II as Fighter Command's chief intelligence officer and the personal assistant to Air Chief Marshal Dowding, and then, in the mid- to late 1950s, a Conservative minister in the Lords.[159] Like Furneaux, he was a Lord-in-Waiting to King George VI (1951–52) and then to the Queen (1952–53). He went on to serve as the British high commissioner for Singapore and commissioner general for South East Asia from 1959 to 1963.

There were also, as noted, fewer clergy in the University – and in Apollo – after World War I. The most notable of those to make their mark in the lodge at this time was the Revd Philip Thomas Byard ('Tubby') Clayton, who took a First in Theology and was initiated in Apollo while up at Exeter before the war. Ordained in the Anglican Church he served as an army chaplain in France and Flanders. In 1915, he and the Revd Neville Talbot opened 'Talbot House', a rest house for soldiers, at Poperinge, Belgium. It became known as 'Toc H' and marked the foundation of the Toc H Movement, with houses in London, Manchester and Southampton. In 1928, as the vicar of All Hallows by the Tower in Tower Hamlets (1922–62), Clayton rejoined Apollo and remained in touch with the lodge until 1970 when he sent a letter of apology for non-attendance; this included a quotation from Homer and drew the comment that it was 'correct as to every accent and breathing' from the Secretary (John Griffith, the University's Public Orator). Clayton was made a Companion of Honour in 1933.

Other clergymen who appear in the minutes during this period include the Revd Thomas Blockley, who having been re-elected Master in 1920 was then appointed the lodge's chaplain, continuing in that office until shortly before his death in 1950, and the Revd Cronshaw, Treasurer (1915–28), whom we have already met (see above, p. 119). The Revd R.W.M. Pope DD, who had been Grand Chaplain in 1888, died in 1923, by when he was 'the senior Past Master of the Lodge'.[160] The Rt Revd Henry Kemble Southwell CMG DD, Bishop of Lewes (1920–26), had been Grand Chaplain in 1913, and when he attended the lodge in 1930 was congratulated on reaching the fiftieth anniversary of his initiation while up at Magdalen. Seventieth anniversaries of initiation in Apollo are still quite rare, but the Revd Osmund Humberston Skipwith (New College), initiated at the last meeting in Frewin Court in 1926, celebrated his at a meeting of Reading Lodge of Union, in Wokingham, on 20 February 1996.[161] New initiates included David Rokeby Maddock (1937), later appointed

Bishop of Dunwich (1967–76),[162] and the Revd Walter Thomas Wardle, later Archdeacon of Gloucester, who rejoined the lodge in 1939.

FELLOWS AND OTHER SENIOR ACADEMICS IN THE 1930S

Several Apollo initiates who were fellows of colleges of the University between the two world wars have already featured above; for example, Cowley and Weldon (Magdalen), and Cronshaw (The Queen's).[163] Among the others who also deserve mention is Maj.-Gen. Sir Ernest Dunlop Swinton KBE CB DSO, who was initiated in 1926 when he was already a fellow of All Souls (1925–39) and the Chichele Professor of Military History. He became an official historian of the Russo-Japanese War (1904–05) and in World War I was appointed as the official British war correspondent on the Western Front. In 1915 he suggested to the Secretary of the Committee of Imperial Defence the construction of a bulletproof tracked vehicle that could destroy enemy machine guns and later created the first tactical instructions for armoured warfare: his last military office was Colonel Commandant of the Royal Tank Corps (1934–38).[164]

John Cecil Masterman (see also above) is to date only the second vice chancellor of the University to have been a member of Apollo. Having read Modern History at Worcester, he was continuing his studies at Freiburg in 1914 when war broke out. He was consequently interned as an enemy alien in a detention camp in Ruhleben. After the war he returned to Oxford as a tutor of Modern History at Christ Church and was initiated in Apollo in 1920. Masterman eventually became provost of Worcester College (1946–61) and vice chancellor (1957–58). He was knighted for his services in 1959.[165]

Two brothers Barrington-Ward were initiated at the same meeting as Masterman in 1920: Frederick Temple KC (All Souls) had taken silk in 1915 and became London's Metropolitan Magistrate; John Grosvenor (Christ Church) became the deputy to the University's Public Orator and was described as 'one of the best Latin prose tutors in Oxford'.[166] William Drummond Macdonald Paton (New College; Apollo, 1938) became a leading pharmacologist, being made a fellow of the Royal Society in 1956 and the University Professor of Pharmacology, and a fellow of Balliol College from 1959 to 1984. Knighted in 1979 he became a Rhodes trustee, a Wellcome trustee and the honorary director of the Wellcome Institute for the History of Medicine (1983–87).

Patrick Johnson (Magdalen) is the only Blue and president of the OUBC to have been appointed a fellow of Magdalen College. Initiated in Apollo in the early 1920s while an undergraduate at Magdalen, he was soon appointed the lodge's DC and, despite serving twice as Master (in 1932 and 1936), he effectively filled or managed that office until 1938 when he took over as Secretary. An oarsman, Johnson gained his Blue in the eight that lost to Cambridge in 1926, was treasurer of the OU Boat Club and then coached the 1933 crew. Described by his obituarist as an all-rounder and an 'avuncular bachelor', Johnson was a fellow and lecturer in Natural Science at Magdalen from 1927 to 1947, its dean from 1934 to 1938 and vice president in 1946/7.[167] His time there and in Apollo was interrupted by war service, for which he was awarded an OBE in 1945. On leaving Oxford he became the director of studies at RAF College, Cranwell, then headed the Institute of Armament Studies in Poona (1952–55) and ended his distinguished scientific career as an assistant scientific adviser to SHAPE.

Gerald Brett (Apollo, 1934), an archaeologist, was seconded to the commandos in 1940 and was awarded the MC for his participation in the

Hogarth's *The Mystery of Masonry brought to Light by ye Gormagons*, 1724.

attack on St Nazaire on 28 March 1942, in which he was wounded. Brett emigrated to Canada to take up appointments as an associate professor in the Department of Arts and Archaeology at the University of Toronto and director of the Royal Ontario Museum of Archaeology. Despite his residence in Canada he was appointed as the UGLE's Prestonian Lecturer for 1961, choosing as his subject 'King Solomon', but in the event he was not well enough to deliver it himself.[168] After Professor Brett died in Canada in 1968, his brother Sir Lionel Brett presented to Apollo 'a Hogarth print, as interesting as it was amusing, showing a travesty of a Craft ceremony, depicting a donkey and other grotesquities', which Gerald had owned and which his widow had brought back to England.[169]

Lionel Brett had been initiated in Apollo in 1931, before his brother. After war service and having been called to the Bar at the Inner Temple, Brett renewed his membership of Apollo in 1950, joined the Colonial Legal Service, became a justice on the Federal Supreme Court of Nigeria in 1958 and was the District Grand Master of Nigeria from 1959 to 1968. Knighted for his service in Nigeria, he died in 1990.[170]

9 APOLLO IN WORLD WAR II, 1939–45

THE OUTBREAK OF WORLD WAR II stopped Apollo University Lodge in its tracks.[171] The lodge met as usual on 3 June 1939, but the next meeting could not be held until 3 March 1940. This was partly because the High Street Masonic Hall had again been requisitioned as a hospital and it presumably took Apollo some time to find an alternative meeting place. (Eventually it met first at the Congregational Church on Cowley Road and then at Magdalen.)

APOLLO'S CORE TEAM DURING WORLD WAR II

It was only because of the dedication of a core team of office-bearers and a few other senior members still able to attend that the lodge was able to meet at all and that from 1941 it again had candidates for initiation. The core team comprised three members already mentioned – Patrick Johnson (who, it will be recalled, had taken over as Secretary in 1938), the Revd Thomas Blockley (Chaplain, and by then the Provincial Grand Master) and J.C.B. Gamlen (Treasurer) – plus Clive Saxton (the Assistant Secretary who covered as Secretary while Johnson was away from Oxford on active service), Sir Miles Irving, two recent recruits (Jack Gauntlett and Wimburn Horlock) and John Griffith.

Clifford Clive Saxton (Magdalen) had joined Apollo from Thames Lodge in 1937, the year in which Colville Smith, its long-serving former Secretary, died. Although Saxton was but a Master Mason at the time (i.e. he had yet to be the

Master of a lodge) and was not formally appointed as Secretary until 1945, he was its Secretary in all but title until illness struck him in 1957.[172] He saw the lodge through the war years and was also its Master in 1941 and 1942.[173]

Sir Miles Irving OBE had retired to England in 1934 from the Punjab, where he had been the financial commissioner, and was knighted in the same year. Promoted to Senior Grand Deacon in the UGLE in 1935, he regularly attended Apollo during the war, often filling one of the Wardens' chairs.

J.M.D. 'Jack' Gauntlett (New College) had joined Apollo from his London lodge in 1931. Another 'avuncular bachelor', he was Apollo's Master in 1944, 1961 and 1962, and its DC in 1942–44 and 1958–62. Gauntlett was for many years a teacher at St Edward's School in Oxford. Henry Wimburn Sweetapple Horlock (Pembroke), later the sheriff of London (1972–73), had been initiated in Apollo in 1937 and was its Master in 1943. He installed Gauntlett as his successor in 1944 and was then installed again by Gauntlett in 1945.[174]

John Gordon Griffith (Jesus; Apollo, 1932), was already a fellow and tutor of Classics at Jesus when he first reached the Master's chair in 1938, and remained in office as either Master, Treasurer or Secretary until 1985. Remarkably, he continued as Master for three successive years (1938–40) – until a lorry ran over his legs, causing injuries from which he suffered great pain until his death in 1993.[175] At the war's end Griffith took over as Treasurer until his appointment as Secretary in 1958, an office he filled for a total of twenty-four years, interrupted only by a sabbatical year. Griffith's minutes are more informative than his predecessors' and are the first to comment on the quality of the officers' performance, as a kindly tutor would on an undergraduate's early essays. Surprisingly, however, Griffith records without comment the facts that one of his sons was initiated in Apollo in 1970 and that two meetings later the then Master vacated the Master's chair so that Griffith himself could perform the ceremony of raising his son to the Third Degree. In 1973 Congregation honoured Griffith by appointing him as the Public Orator and in that office his ability to apply Latin to the modern world became legendary, as did his wry sense of humour. His minutes include '*nem. con., sed non sine risu*' and the correction of a '*lapsus calami*'.[176]

Among the few senior members of the lodge who were not in office but could regularly attend were W.C. Costin and G.D. Amery (see below) and two members of the Myres family: A.T.M. Myres and Professor John Linton

Myres (Magdalen), the Wykeham Professor of Ancient History (1910–39), later knighted and in 1944 promoted as a Junior Grand Deacon in the UGLE.[177]

MEETINGS 1940–42

How Apollo came to hold its first eight meetings during the war in the schoolroom of the Congregational Church on Cowley Road is unknown. While it met twice there in both 1940 and 1941 it did not conduct any degree ceremonies in those two years; at both its meetings in 1940 the ten or so members are recorded simply as having discussed how best to keep the lodge going during the war. The minutes of November 1940 also record the deaths of two members: Peter Spilsbury (a junior doctor at St Thomas's Hospital in Lambeth, killed in the Blitz) and E.G.C. Poole (Trinity), the Master of Apollo in 1924 and a fellow and Mathematics tutor of New College since 1929. The lodge was obviously unaware that another of its members, Charles Patrick Norton, the 2nd Baron Rathcreedan, of Bellehatch Park in the County of Oxford and the future Provincial Grand Master, had been taken prisoner at Dunkirk. Rathcreedan was later quoted as saying that 'after his years at school in Wellington College, five years as a POW in Germany held no terrors'.[178] Rathcreedan, or Norton as he then was, had been initiated in Apollo in 1925. He rejoined the lodge in 1955 shortly before taking up his appointment as Provincial Grand Master, an office he held for thirty years. He regularly attended Apollo's meetings and to mark the sixtieth anniversary of his initiation he was elected to honorary membership, shortly before his death in 1990. The lodge contributed to a portrait of him, which was then hung in the Rathcreedan Temple of the Masonic Hall at 333 Banbury Road, Oxford.

Among the six men initiated in 1942, while the lodge was still meeting in the schoolroom at the Congregational Church, two names stand out: C. John Mandleberg and 'Bobby' Milburn. Called away from Apollo for military service before he could take office in the lodge, Mandleberg pursued his Masonic career elsewhere after the war in Oxford, London and Cheshire, wrote extensively about Freemasonry and rejoined Apollo in 2002. He was promoted to the rank of Past Grand Sword Bearer in Grand Lodge and earned a full obituary in *The Times* which mentioned his scientific work, his love of beagling and his support of his local church.[179]

The Revd Robert Leslie Pollington Milburn, a Cambridge graduate, was already an Anglican priest and a fellow of Worcester College (1935–57) by the time of his initiation. The UGLE quickly marked his card, for in 1947 he was presented as Master-Elect by the Grand Director of Ceremonies (Lt Col. Philip C. Bull, DSO) and installed as Master, not by the outgoing Master, Costin, but by the Grand Secretary himself, Sydney White (later Sir Sydney White, KCVO) despite the fact that neither Bull nor White was a member of Apollo.[180] Milburn stayed in office for a second year and attended the lodge regularly until 1957. He was then appointed as the dean of Worcester Cathedral, an office he filled until 1968 in some style, cycling around the city in gaiters and a frock coat; *The Times* called him the 'gaitered dean whose eloquent sermons gave pleasure even to agnostics'.[181] Milburn last attended Apollo in May 1970 when he was Master of the Temple Church (1968–80).

MEETINGS AT MAGDALEN COLLEGE 1942–46

The lodge's links with Magdalen College are of long standing, and the names of some of Apollo's Magdalen men have been highlighted above – Blockley, Cowley, Crookshank, Johnson, Porritt, Scarbrough, Weldon and Wolfenden, for example – but Magdalen's connection with Apollo during World War II is especially remarkable because the lodge met there from October 1942 until 1946.

Perhaps Blockley and J.L. Myres eased the way, but the fact that both the president of the college and the steward of the senior common room (SCR) were Freemasons might also have helped. The president, Sir Henry T. Tizard, KCB FRS, had been the rector of Imperial College, London, where he had joined its lodge and been its Master. Originally an Apollo initiate, he rejoined Apollo in 1942 and was promoted as a Past Grand Deacon of the UGLE in 1943. A chemist and inventor, Tizard is credited with developing the octane rating for the classification of petrol, assisting with the development of radar in World War II and with the first serious studies of UFOs. The SCR's steward was A.C. Chamberlain, a Past Master of Isis Lodge, Oxford.[182]

One of the first men initiated when Apollo began meeting at Magdalen was the 18-year-old Montague Robert Vere Eliot (Christ Church), who, as the younger son of the 8th Earl of St Germans, had been one of the pages to bear the train of King George VI at his coronation in 1937. His father, the 8th Earl, had been appointed as the Provincial Grand Master for Cornwall in 1940 and the Hon. M.R.V. Eliot eventually followed him into the same office in 1979. Eliot's membership of and regular attendance at Apollo was interrupted in 1962 by a brief sojourn in Morocco, but he rejoined in 1964 when he was the Master of Letchworth Lodge in Gibraltar. While based in Morocco he also served for a year as the Master of his family lodge, Eliot Lodge, in Cornwall, and at a dinner in October 1992, the fiftieth aniversary of his initiation, he told the lodge that in that year he had travelled 36,000 miles to attend all twelve of its monthly meetings. Before his unexpected death in 1994 Eliot also served as the Founding Master of both Aedes Christi Lodge (Oxford) and Robert Eliot Lodge (Cornwall).

Five other men were initiated while the lodge was meeting at Magdalen, three of them at the same meeting in January 1943: John Chalmer Stebbings, Charles Edward Leighton Thompson and John Godolphin Quicke. Stebbings, later Sir John Stebbings, became president of the Law Society in 1979 and was president of the UGLE's Grand Charity for ten years from 1985 before handing over the reins of the latter to another Apollonian, Sir John Welch (see below). Thompson, later the Revd Prebendary Leighton Thompson, vicar of Chelsea Old Church, became the Third Grand Principal in the Royal Arch (an integral part of 'pure ancient Freemasonry' as defined by the UGLE in 1813) and was the Chaplain of Westminster and Keystone Lodge, London, for many years.

Quicke, whose estate at Newton St Cyres, Devon, had been in his family from pre-Conquest times, studied agriculture at Oxford on his return from war service in Burma, having originally read Chemistry at New College. He presided over the Country Landowners' Association from 1975 to 1977, created national collections of magnolias, azaleas and berberis, and was awarded the Royal Agricultural Society's Bledisloe Gold Medal for Landowners in 1987, an award instituted in 1958 by Lord Bledisloe, whom we have previously encountered as the Grand Master of New Zealand. Quicke was knighted in 1988 for his services to agriculture. According to his obituarist, Sir John 'took delivery of a book on quantum physics' on the day of his death.[183]

Robert Amos Griffiths FRCP (Apollo, 1944) read Medicine at University College before serving as a regimental medical officer in the Grenadier Guards. After the war he became the first senior registrar in geriatric medicine at Cowley Road Hospital, Oxford, a consultant physician in geriatric medicine to the United Oxford Hospitals, and clinical lecturer in the University. After two years as Master of Apollo (1976 and 1977), the second year while also in the chair of Westminster and Keystone Lodge in London, Griffiths was appointed as the Assistant Provincial Grand Master for Oxfordshire and as a Past Senior Grand Deacon in the UGLE. The Masonic province's Amos Griffiths Bursary, administered by the University, is named after him.

(opposite) Minute Book from 1943, detailing the visit of the Grand Master.

APOLLO'S CONTRIBUTION IS RECOGNIZED, 1943–44

Apollo's health continued to improve from 1942 onwards, with a few initiates in each year and a growing number of members and visitors attending its meetings. The 1943–44 period was the most significant, as it was then that the lodge's outstanding contribution to the English Craft in difficult times was recognized by the UGLE in two ways.

First, four of its members were appointed to senior national rank: Henry Tizard and John Myres (whom we have already mentioned), Frank Edwin Newson-Smith and Lionel Leonard Cohen. Second, the Grand Master himself, the Rt Hon. Henry, 6th Earl of Harewood, KG GCVO DSO, son-in-law of King George V, made an official visit to the lodge in 1943.[184]

Sir Frank Newson-Smith Bt, a holder of Grand rank in the UGLE and a former sheriff of the City of London (1939–40), first visited Apollo in February 1943 as a Past Master of Guildhall Lodge, London. He had been knighted in 1941, the year in which he was awarded the honorary degree of Master of Arts by the University. That honorary degree seems to have qualified him for membership of Apollo for he was elected to joining membership in 1943, by which time he was the Lord Mayor of London. The Grand Master then made him the Junior Grand Warden of the UGLE in 1944 and 1945. Newson-Smith was created the 1st Baronet Newson-Smith, of Totteridge, Hertfordshire, in December 1944 and the University awarded him with the honorary degree of Doctor of Civil Law.

Lionel Leonard Cohen (Apollo, 1908) first achieved national Masonic rank in 1939. Knighted in 1943, he was promoted to Past Junior Grand Warden the following year. He had taken Firsts in History and Law while up at New College before World War I, and been called to the Bar at the Inner Temple in 1913, taking silk in 1929. He was sworn to the Privy Council in 1946 and eventually became a Lord of Appeal in Ordinary (1951–60), with a life peerage as Baron Cohen of Walmer in Kent. As a member of a prominent Jewish family, Cohen was vice president of the Board of Deputies (1934–39) and president of the

16th October 1943 — A Regular Meeting of the Lodge was held (by Dispensation) at Magdalen College Oxford at 2.30 p.m.

Present.

M.W. Bro. Rt. Hon. the Earl of Harewood, K.G. G.C.V.O. D.S.O
Most Worshipful Grand Master.

W. Bro.	C. Clive Saxton	W.M.
" "	W. C. Costin	as I.P.M
" "	Sir Miles Irving	S.W.
" "	A.W.W.S. Horlock	J.W.
R. " "	Rev. J. J. Blockley	Chaplain
" "	J. C. B. Gamlen	Treasurer.
" "	Patrick Johnson	Secretary.
" "	J. M. S. Gauntlett	D.C.
" "	D.R. Boult	S.D.
" "	Rev. R. L. P. Milburn	J.D.
" "	Rev. R. R. Martin	I.G.
" "	J.F. Boothby	Steward.

Past Masters. W. Bros. C.H. Thompson. H.A.B Whitelocke

Bros. K. N Irvine. L.A Bruce. J.C. Tebbing

C. E.L. Thomson. D.W. Shenton J.L. Reeves

B.G. H. Rowley J.F. Fenwick F.A. de Hamel

D. Leigh.

Honorary Members: W. Bro. Lt. Col. M. E. G. R. Wingfield P.G.D.
Deputy Provincial Grand Master.
V.W. Bro. Sydney White, M.V.O. Grand Secretary.

Visitors. W. Bro. Sir Frank Newson-Smith P.A.G.D.C

W. Bros. L. Ward Bennett. A.G.Ch. Wm. Lodge P.A.G.D.C J.F. Vincent P.G.S.B

... S. King P.G.W.B. L. V. Murphy P.G.St.B. H.C Edwards P.G.S.B

... Sir William Shenton, P.G.S.W. J.M Eldridge P.R.G.W. L. Windmarsh P.R.G.Reg.

... J.C.B Ellis P.R.G.D. E. Hope P.R.G.S.Wks. J.W. Taylor. P.R.G.S.B.

Bros. G.H.Hobby H.M.Best (478)

Jewish Board of Guardians (1940–47). He seems not to have visited the lodge after 1948 but the lodge mourned his death when it met in 1973.

For the visit of the Grand Master on 16 October 1943, the lodge opened at the exceptionally early time of 2.30 p.m., passed two brethren to the Second Degree and was then 'called off' for refreshment. After the meeting resumed at 4.45 the Grand Master, accompanied by a numerous retinue of Grand Officers, demanded admission and was formally received. The Grand Master then witnessed the raising of two members to the Third Degree as well as the passing of two more to the Second Degree. At 'the supper which followed', the Grand Master, 'In a gracious speech … expressed the great pleasure it gave him to be present at a meeting of this Lodge and to see it at work, despite wartime difficulties, bringing the light of Freemasonry to undergraduate members of the University.'

NOTABLE DEATHS AND DISTINCTIONS

All the while the war was continuing, yet there is little mention of it in the minutes. Few deaths are recorded, but two who did get a mention are Hubert Dainton 'Trilby' Freakes and Sir Archibald Philip Hope, 17th Baronet of Craighall.

Freakes (Apollo, 1937) was born and raised in South Africa and came up to Magdalen in 1936 on a Rhodes Scholarship. He captained the University's rugby team against Cambridge in 1938/39, played for Harlequins and was capped three times for England. He joined the Royal Air Force Volunteer Reserve before the war started and was killed when the plane he was delivering from across the Atlantic crashed in England in 1942. Hope was a luckier airman. Initiated in 1933 while reading Modern History at Balliol, he was called to active service with 601 Squadron in August 1939 and was first shot down over Bapaume (France) on 16 May 1940. He was shot down again on 27 May, this time between Calais and Dunkirk, but managed to get back to base in England still carrying his parachute. His record for four days in August 1940 reads like something out of *Boys' Own*: on 11 August he claimed two probable Ju 87s; on the 13th two probable Me 110s and damaged another, shared one probable Ju 88 and damaged another; on the 15th shared a Ju 88 and damaged another; and on the 16th destroyed a Me 110 and a probable Ju 87, and damaged another. Hope was promoted to acting squadron leader on 19 August and then took command of the squadron. He was awarded the DFC later that year and ended the war as the group captain commanding RAF Peterhead.[185] His wartime exploits, and his death in 1987, went unnoted by Apollo.

Several other current or later members of the lodge had remarkable war careers, three of whom were awarded the Military Cross.[186] William John St Clair Anstruther-Gray, Baron Kilmany (Apollo, 1926), Unionist MP for North Lanarkshire from 1931 until 1945, won his MC in May 1943. Seconded as a major to the Coldstream Guards he led his squadron to take the town of Hammam-Lif and the Bey of Tunis's palace, until then held by the Hermann Goering Division, destroying the enemy's 88 mm gun and forcing its tanks to withdraw. Re-elected to the House of Commons in 1950, he was created a baronet in 1956, appointed a privy counsellor in 1962 and served as the Lord Lieutenant of Fife 1975–80.

John Anthony Kershaw (Balliol; Apollo, 1938), was called to the Bar at the Inner Temple in 1939. As a temporary captain in Head Quarters 26 Armoured Brigade he was awarded the MC for his conduct during an action north of the Kasserine Gap, in Tunisia, in February 1943. 'After the wireless in the brigade's scout car failed, Kershaw ran between his own tank and his brigadier's to take orders for transmission from his own radio, all the time under intense shell and machine-gun fire.'[187] He later commanded the Royal Gloucestershire Hussars.[188]

Geoffrey William Hugo Lampe (Exeter; Apollo, 1947) took Firsts in Lit. Hum. and in Theology in 1935 and 1936, and served as a chaplain to 34 Armoured Brigade. The Revd Captain Lampe won his MC for bravery when rescuing injured troops under fire.[189] He was later appointed Professor of Theology at Birmingham (1953–60) and Professor of Divinity at Cambridge (1960–79).

Space does not allow the wartime careers of all the Apollonians engaged on active service to be noted here, but we must mention two special warriors and two key players in the intelligence field. John Norman Stuart Buchan (Brasenose; Apollo, 1932), later the 2nd Baron Tweedsmuir, travelled to Canada in 1936 to join his father, John Buchan, the novelist and by then the Governor General of the dominion. When the war began in 1939 Buchan junior joined the Governor General's Foot Guards and reached England with them that December. As Lord Tweedsmuir (his father had died in 1940) he was in temporary command of a battalion of the Hastings and Prince Edward Regiment in Sicily when the regiment's advance was halted by the Germans' well-fortified position high above it in Assoro. An infantryman and historian in the same regiment later described Tweedsmuir's role in the ensuing action:

> Barely thirty years of age, soft-spoken, kindly, with a slight tendency to stutter, he was a tall fair-haired English romantic out of another age … Going forward on his own reconnaissance that afternoon … Tweedsmuir looked up at the towering colossus of Assoro with the visionary eye of a Lawrence of Arabia, and saw that the only way to accomplish the impossible was to attempt the impossible. He thereupon decided that the battalion would make a right flank march by night across the intervening trackless gullies to the foot of the great cliff, scale that precipitous wall and, just at dawn, take the summit by surprise.[190]

The operation succeeded. Later Tweedsmuir led scientific expeditions to Libya and St Ninian's Isle and presided over the British Schools Exploring Society for two decades.

Arthur Douglas Dodds-Parker (Magdalen; Apollo, 1929) was in the elite Sudan Political Service and the Grenadier Guards before he joined the Special Operations Executive (SOE) and Orde Wingate's Gideon Force operating against the Italians in Ethiopia. Dodds-Parker later played leading roles in the SOE's European operations.[191] He ended the war with the rank of colonel in the Supreme Headquarters of the Allied Expeditionary Force (SHAEF) in Paris and was awarded the Légion d'honneur and Croix de Guerre. After the war he was elected to Parliament as the MP for Banbury (1945-59) and served as a junior minister in the Foreign Office during the disastrous Anglo-French attack on the Suez Canal in 1956. Dropped by Macmillan the following year, he was re-elected (this time for Cheltenham) in 1964 and was vice chairman of the Conservative Party until 1970. Dodds-Parker was knighted in 1973 and retired from the House of Commons and the European Parliament in 1974 and 1975 respectively.[192]

During the war Hugh Alexander Dunn joined the 1st Australian Specialist Intelligence Personnel Group and he served under General Douglas MacArthur in West Papua and the Philippines. Dunn then completed his B.A. at the University of Queensland, came to Oxford on a Rhodes Scholarship, was initiated in Apollo in 1950 and took a First in Chinese. After a distinguished career in the Australian diplomatic service, during which he served as the ambassador to China (1980–84), he held professorships in Asian Studies and

Modern History at Griffith University and the University of Queensland. His obituary in the the *Sydney Morning Herald* in 2005 bore the intriguing headline 'Scholar spy shined light on China'.[193]

Roger Fleetwood-Hesketh (Christ Church; Apollo, 1924) had already reached the rank of major in the Duke of Lancaster's Own Yeomanry when he was transferred to the Royal Artillery in 1940. Later, as a lieutenant-colonel, he was the mastermind behind Operation Fortitude, the SHAEF's deception plan covering the Allied invasion of Normandy in 1944, called by Kim Philby 'one of the most creative intelligence operations of all time'. After the war Fleetwood-Hesketh returned to Lancashire and rebuilt his family's ancient home, Meols Hall, at Southport. Described as 'the beau ideal of an English country squire', he served as high sheriff of the county in 1947 and then as a deputy lieutenant (1950–72) and the MP for Southport (1952–59).[194] In 1952 Fleetwood-Hesketh married the eldest daughter of the 11th Earl of Scarbrough, another Apollonian, who had become the Grand Master in 1951 (see above).[195]

This chapter ends with the name of an Apollonian who was interned as a PoW in Germany (1941–45) and then served on the War Crimes Commission: Lt Col. John Leighton Byrne Leicester-Warren (Apollo, 1926). On his release from the camp, his father, Major C. Leicester-Warren, the Provincial Grand Master for Cheshire (1925–49) – who had attended his son's initiation in 1926 – founded the Lodge of Gratitude, in Knutsford, Cheshire, in gratitude for his safe return.[196]

10 THE LODGE IN TIMES OF SOCIAL AND ECONOMIC CHANGE, 1946–69

FREEMASONRY IN OXFORD AND, indeed, the whole of the 'Craft' in England not only survived World War II but came through relatively unscathed, despite the death of many of its members in the war, the paucity of candidates, the reduction in the number of meetings and for some lodges, like Apollo University Lodge, their removal to temporary accommodation. Once the war ended, Apollo left its temporary lodgings in Magdalen College and eventually, on 1 February 1947, moved back to the Masonic Hall on the High Street – after brief stopovers at the Congregational Church on the Cowley Road for the meeting on 1 May 1946 and the Randoph Hotel for the three other meetings that year.

The 'great and the good' were still well represented in the Craft's membership. King George VI had been Grand Master of the Grand Lodge of Scotland and was a Past Grand Master of the UGLE; the 6th Earl of Harewood (the UGLE's Grand Master 1942–47) was succeeded by two other Knights of the Garter, namely the 10th Duke of Devonshire (1947–50) and the 11th Earl of Scarbrough (1951–67). Lord Scarbrough (Magdalen; Apollo, 1920) resigned from that office in 1967 in favour of HRH the Duke of Kent, KG, the present Grand Master, whom he then served as Pro Grand Master. In addition to Lord Scarbrough the University lodge had other members in the upper echelons of Grand Lodge too, including its Grand Wardens in 1946 and 1947 (Lord Llewellin and Viscount Crookshank respectively), the President of the Board of General

(opposite) Sir James Stubbs (Apollo, 1930). Grand Secretary of the United Grand Lodge of England. Grandson of Regius Professor William Stubbs, later Bishop of Oxford.

Purposes from 1946 until 1958 (Sir Ernest Cooper),[197] and, from 1948, James Stubbs (Brasenose; Apollo, 1930), who went on to become the Grand Secretary (1958–80) and died in 2003 as Sir James Stubbs, KCVO, OSM.

Several Provincial and District Grand Masters were also members of Apollo, including the Provincial Grand Master for Oxfordshire, the Revd Thomas T. Blockley, who was to be followed by another Apollonian, Lt Col. George Amery in 1948. The latter's 'foresight and enthusiasm was largely responsible for settling the lodges of Oxford, including Apollo, in a new home in North Oxford' in the late 1950s, and one of the meeting rooms at Freemasons' Hall at 333 Banbury Road (see below) was named after him.[198]

Several college fellows were also members of Apollo, as we have seen. One, W.C. Costin, soon to be the president of St John's College, was Apollo's *éminence grise* from the end of the war until the 1960s, and the day-to-day running of the lodge remained in the safe and experienced hands of members such as Saxton, Griffith and Gauntlett. During this period the lodge met twice a term and only in four of those meetings was just one degree ceremony worked rather than the usual two (or one plus the annual Installation cermony).[199]

With its finances also in good order, and with a steadily increasing membership again, all seemed set fair for Apollo. But Britain was changing quickly and its economic circumstances would soon begin to affect the lodge, as would the retreat of the landed gentry from public office, the increasing pace of the Empire's dissolution and the questioning of 'the Establishment' and of institutions such as Freemasonry. Greater ethnic and cultural diversity, membership of the European Union and the impact of Butler's Education Act would slowly be reflected in the composition of the lodge's membership. The United Grand Lodge of England would successfully celebrate its 250th anniversary in 1967, and the University lodge its 150th in 1969, but the quarter of a century from 1946 would test the lodge's ability to withstand new pressures, both from within the Craft and without.

IMPERIAL AND AMERICAN CONNECTIONS

The period 1946–69 also saw a significant number of men from the former British Empire coming to Oxford and being initiated in or joining the University lodge. Some were British expatriates withdrawing to their native land and/or whose overseas lodge had either been removed to England or ceased to function altogether, but the majority were to return overseas after their time at the University. The independence of India and Cyprus probably explains why several members of the UGLE's lodges there joined Apollo in 1947 and 1948, including John Rawdon Dashwood from Ceylon, who had been made a Past Grand Deacon of the UGLE in 1945 and who became Apollo's Master in 1950. A few other examples must suffice. Rasiah Sri Ramakrishna was initiated in 1961 and died in 2002 as the head of Chemistry at the University of Colombo, Sri Lanka. Krishnan Srinivasan (Christ Church) began his membership of the lodge on 8 June 1957, went through the three degrees, returned to India and then rejoined the lodge in March 1968. He became India's Foreign Secretary and the deputy secretary-general of the Commonwealth of Nations, and wrote *The Rise, Decline and Future of the British Commonwealth* (2005). In June 1962, at the request of the recently founded Grand Lodge of India, 'Bro Nawabzada Saleem Abid Ali Khan', an initiate of the Lodge of East and West in New Delhi, was passed to the Second Degree in Apollo. He was the third son of Maj.-Gen. His Highness the Nawab of Rampur, who had been promoted to the rank of Past Junior Grand Warden of the UGLE in 1952.

Thomas Ellis Robins (Christ Church), later the 1st Baron Robins, was a Rhodes Scholar from the University of Pennsylvania who became a British citizen in 1912 and fought with the City of London Yeomanry in Egypt, Gallipoli and Palestine. He was then appointed as the general manager and later as a director of the British South Africa Company (founded by another Apollonian, Cecil Rhodes) in Rhodesia. During World War II he commanded the 1st Regiment of the Rhodesia Regiment. Knighted in 1946, he occasionally resurfaced at Apollo meetings as the District Grand Master for Southern Rhodesia, a post he held from 1937 to 1957. He was raised to the peerage as Baron Robins of Rhodesia and Chelsea in 1958 in recognition of his public services in Rhodesia.

Ralph Telford O'Neal was already a member of the UGLE's Harmonic Lodge in St Thomas in the US Virgin Islands when he joined Apollo in May 1968 while at Trinity. In 2015 he was the longest serving MP in the English-speaking Caribbean and had thrice served as chief minister or premier of the British Virgin Islands. In 1994 he wrote to Apollo enclosing a copy of the *History of Freemasonry in the Virgin Islands*.[200]

Roger Hollinrake, the son of the dean of the Music Faculty at Auckland University College, New Zealand, was made a Mason in the UGLE's Te

Awamutu Lodge there, but joined Apollo in 1960 when he came up to Merton to continue his study of music. He became Master of the lodge in 1972 and is still remembered as its greatest organist since Walter Parratt (see above, p. 42). Though he often played for the lodge, he was not formally appointed as its organist until 1995, by which time Grand Lodge had promoted him to Past Grand Organist (1988) and then to Past Junior Grand Deacon. His magisterial work, *Nietzsche, Wagner and the Philosophy of Pessimism* (1982), is already in its eighteenth edition. His monograph *The Masonic Life and Times of W.Bro. Sir Walter Parratt, K.C.V.O., Master of the Music, Grand Organist* (2001) presents an entertaining account of University life in the second half of the nineteenth century, including a vignette of Parratt's 'antics at the Sheldonian Theatre when Apollo men had played up during the Honorary degree Ceremony for W.H. Smith' – Smith being the First Lord of the Admiralty who never went to sea; Parratt played music from *HMS Pinafore* during his investiture.[201] Hollinrake, a shy and diffident man to the end, died in 2010.

Hollinrake's predecessor as the lodge's organist was Basil Burwood-Taylor, an 'English eccentric, colourful, choleric, comedic and clever',[202] who joined Apollo in February 1967 while working in the Sudan, where he also held office in the UGLE's District Grand Lodge. As British Honorary Consul in Asmara he was kidnapped by the Eritrean Liberation Front in October 1975, but was released in Khartoum in May 1976. A gifted jazz pianist, Burwood-Taylor once played with Humphrey Lyttelton, and when Louis Armstrong visited Khartoum Burwood-Taylor accompanied him at the piano. Burwood-Taylor devoted much of his retirement in Oxford to Freemasonry and achieved distinction in many Masonic orders. A bastion of University Masonry he was Apollo's Master in 1994 and was elected to honorary membership of the lodge shortly before his death in 2011.

Four American Freemasons joined or rejoined Apollo while they were at Oxford at this time, including Leonard George Bradford (Christ Church). He had first joined the lodge in February 1923 when he was a member of Bethlehem Lodge, Brookline, Massachusetts. A career diplomat, Bradford then served in Sweden, Italy, Budapest, Turkey and France before rejoining Apollo in October 1955 when he was the Master of the Lacydon Lodge in Marseilles, France, and was described in the minutes as 'Consul of the USA, rtd.'

CLERGYMEN AND MEDICS

Among others who joined or were initiated in Apollo in this period, two groups are notable: clergymen and medics. One clergyman went on to make a national name for himself though more for his life outside the Church. Timothy Wentworth Beaumont (Christ Church), later the Revd Lord Beaumont of Whitley, seems to have disappeared from Masonic view after he joined the lodge in 1950. He managed to get a Fourth in Agriculture while still up at Christ Church before being ordained as an Anglican priest in Hong Kong, and being appointed vicar of Kowloon. Beaumont inherited a substantial fortune and returned to London where he 'was prominent in the radical reforming movement in the Church' (1960–65) until he applied his energy to the Liberal Party, becoming its chairman in 1967 and its president in 1969, during which time he was made a life peer (1967). He resigned his orders in 1973 but, having exhausted his fortune, he resumed them in 1984 and served as the priest-in-charge of a church in Kew for five years before returning to politics, first as a member of the Liberal Party's policy committee and then as the Green Party's spokesman on agriculture.[203]

Unlike Beaumont, most of Apollo's clergymen who joined at this time remained active Freemasons and were appointed to national rank within Grand Lodge. A few examples must suffice here. Arthur William Stowell Brown (Apollo, 1948), became the UGLE's Deputy Grand Chaplain in 1988, as did Sydney John Bryant in 1991 (Apollo, 1951). John Weaver, later the Venerable Canon Weaver (Apollo, 1954), worked for more than forty years as a missionary in Natal, South Africa, where he was active in many Masonic units; he was appointed to Grand rank in 1996. The Revd Thomas Brian Williams (St John's; Apollo, 1947) served as Apollo's Master in both 1954 and 1955. The Revd Arthur Evelyn Armstrong eventually retired from active Masonic office as the District Grand Master of Barbados in 1957. And the Revd Richard C.D.V. Martin, the UGLE's Assistant Grand Chaplain in 2009, was initiated in 1961 and served as Apollo's Chaplain for many years until 2015.

As for the medics who became members in this post-war period, the names of four stand out: John Howell Evans, FRCS (St Catherine's), joined Apollo in 1947 from Westminster and Keystone Lodge. He had served as a surgeon in the Boer War and World War I, and been a Hunterian Professor (in 1907, 1915

and 1927) and a University examiner in surgery. Like Porritt, Howell Evans was made a member of the Grand Master's OSM.

Thomas Pomfret Kilner, FRCS, the renowned plastic surgeon, joined Apollo at the same meeting as Howell Evans. A Past Master of Rahere Lodge (a medical lodge in London), he was the first Nuffield Professor of Plastic Surgery at Oxford (1944–57) and a fellow of St John's. After serving as a surgeon in the RAMC in World War I, he was appointed as a plastic surgeon at Queen Mary's Hospital for Face and Jaw Injuries, Sidcup, the base from which plastic surgery was established in the UK. Kilner continued to attend Apollo until shortly before his death in 1964.

Henry Renwick Vickers, FRCP, joined Apollo in 1954 from a lodge in Sheffield. After service in the Royal Navy as its first official dermatologist, Vickers moved to Oxford in 1957 to set up the department of dermatology and later became chairman of the University's medicine board. Vickers was also the president of the British Association of Dermatology as well as chairman of the Bach Choir.

John Michael Kenneth Spalding, DM FRCP (New College; Apollo, 1951), was a distinguished neurologist, who became the lodge's Master in 1956 before taking over the treasurership from Griffith in 1958. With his successor, Bryan Pierce (see below), Spalding managed the lodge's financial affairs through the years of high inflation. After twenty-four years as Treasurer and before retiring away from Oxfordshire, Dr Spalding presented the Lodge with 'some fine silver former Lodge cutlery', bearing members' initials and '711', the lodge's original number.[204]

GRAND LODGE OFFICERS

There was also an unusually high proportion of new members who went on to hold senior executive positions in English Freemasonry.

Perhaps the most distinguished member initiated in this 1946–69 period was John Reader Welch, today Sir John Welch, Bt, PSGW OSM, who was initiated in 1955 with four others. (His father, Sir Cullum Welch, Bt, President of the UGLE's Board of Benevolence (1954–68), waited until his son's Second Degree before visiting the lodge.) The UGLE's Grand Treasurer in 1979 and the president of its Grand Charity for ten years from 1985, Sir John was honoured in 2010 with the award of membership of the Grand Master's OSM.

Like Welch, half a dozen more of Apollo's initiates between 1946 and 1969 have taken senior office within Grand Lodge without becoming Master of the University lodge. Geoffrey Michael Redman-Brown (Apollo, 1961) became a senior figure in the banking world, and Master of several lodges in London. He succeeded Lord Rathcreedan as the Provincial Grand Master for Oxfordshire (1985–2001) and had the main temple in the extension to 333 Banbury Road named after him.

James ('Jim') Wallace Daniel (Brasenose; Apollo, 1961), Grand Secretary of the UGLE (1998–2002) and now a Past Senior Grand Warden, is still in office as the lodge's senior Steward. Daniel was recruited into the 'Masonic civil service' in 1989 when he was the cultural attaché in the British Embassy in Washington DC by Sir James Stubbs (see above). David Bennett-Rees (St John's) and Stuart Hampson, aged 18 and 19 respectively, were initiated together in 1966, both products of the Royal Masonic School for Boys.

Bennett-Rees, whose father was the Chaplain to the UGLE's District Grand Lodge of East Africa, is an actuary and has recently been promoted to Past Grand Sword Bearer after a quarter of a century's assistance to Grand Lodge in pension and employment matters. Hampson was knighted while chairman of the John Lewis Partnership and has recently retired as chairman of the Crown Estate, for which service he was awarded a CVO. He served as the UGLE's Senior Grand Warden for three years rather than the normal two (2014–16) and once appeared at an Apollo meeting in full shrieval attire while high sheriff of Buckinghamshire.

Three others, Richard Michael Hone, Malcolm R. Aish and Michael L. Ward, were initiated together in 1968. Hone, now His Honour Judge Richard Hone QC, was the president of the UGLE's Grand Charity from 2012 until 2016 when the four central Masonic charities – The Freemasons' Grand Charity, the Royal Masonic Trust for Girls and Boys, the Masonic Samaritan Fund and the Royal Masonic Benevolent Institution – were amalgamated into the Masonic Charity Foundation, of which he became the first president. (Hone's father, Maj.-Gen. Sir Ralph Hone, KC, attended his son's initiation while he was a Past Grand Warden of the UGLE, a rank in which his son now also stands.)

Dr Malcolm Aish, managing director of N.M. Rothschild & Sons Limited (1974–2003), is now the President of the Committee of General Purposes of the Royal Arch and is a Past Senior Grand Warden. Michael Ward, the Deputy Metropolitan Grand Master (London) from 2009, was promoted to Past Senior Grand Warden in 2016. David Charles Law also achieved high active rank in the UGLE, but he was not an Apollo initiate. Law came up to Brasenose in 1949 to read Law. He got his Blue as a miler and was elected a joining member of Apollo in 1952, the year in which he had been initiated in Sheffield by his father. He represented England on the athletics track in Europe and North America, setting the Commonwealth record for 4×1 mile with Bannister, Brasher and Chataway, and then as a member of the world record-breaking quartet in the 4×1500 metres relay. Practising as a solicitor in Sheffield, he became the Provincial Grand Master of Derbyshire (1994–2005) and once brought a group of twenty Past Masters from Derbyshire to visit Apollo.

Two significant members of the 1959 cohort who still regularly attend Apollo are Thomas Bryan Pierce (St Peter's Hall), who was Master in 1963, Treasurer 1982–2005, elected to Honorary Membership and promoted to Past

Junior Grand Deacon in 2009; and Hillier B.A. Wise of St Catherine's, who has often acted as the lodge's organist.

Finally, Denis H. Merry of St Catherine's College joined the lodge from Churchill Lodge in 1966 while working as an assistant librarian at the Bodleian. He was installed as the Master of Apollo in 1971, became the Provincial Grand Secretary the following year and eventually served as the Province's Deputy Grand Master for five years from 1987. Only from the eulogy Paul Atyeo (Master, 1968 and 1970) delivered in 2006 did Apollo's members learn that Merry had spent most of World War II as a prisoner of war.

OTHER EMINENT APOLLONIANS

Initiates in the 1950s included Ian Campbell, 11th Duke of Argyll (Christ Church; Apollo, 1957), at the age of 54, and Richard Aldred, Viscount Lumley. 'Dickon' Lumley (Magdalen; Apollo, 1955) was initiated in the presence of his father, Lord Scarbrough, the Grand Master. He inherited his father's title in 1969 and died in 2004 as the Lord Lieutenant for South Yorkshire. Ronald Gordon Honeycombe (Apollo, 1959) was an ITN newscaster from 1965 until 1977, and then on *TV-am* before he emigrated to and died in Australia.

The Hon. John Francis Harcourt Baring, now the 7th Baron Ashburton, KG KCVO, was born in 1928 and initiated in Apollo in 1949. Lord Ashburton was a merchant banker and former chairman of British Petroleum (BP). Dr Bertram Maurice Hobby, a specialist in insect biology, was elected as a joining member in 1956. He edited the *Entomologist's Monthly Magazine* and succeeded Dr Costin (see above) as Deputy Provincial Grand Master in 1971 after serving as Provincial Grand Secretary for many years. In 1957 Hobby proposed a chemist, Dr Harry Munroe Napier Hetherington Irving, a Past Master of Churchill Lodge and the vice principal of St Edmund Hall, for joining membership. Irving started his academic careeer as a lecturer and demonstrator at the University, and went on to hold professorial chairs at Leeds and Cape Town.

One initiate during this period deserves special mention: Geoffrey Bownas (The Queen's; Apollo, 1950), the lodge's DC for several years, and its Master in 1957 and 1958. Bownas came up to Oxford after the outbreak of the Second World War, but after a year studying Greats he was transferred to Bletchley Park to help break Japanese military codes and then to India in the Intelligence

Corps. Returning to Oxford after the war to complete his degree, Bownas took Firsts in Greats and in Chinese. After several years in China and Japan, he then set up the department of Japanese Studies in the University in 1954 and became a research fellow at St Antony's before moving to Sheffield to establish a Japanese Department there. His CBE in 2003 recognized his lifetime's contribution to 'education, scholarship and the improvement of Anglo-Japanese relations in commercial and cultural fields'.[205]

Dr Philip Glazer (1913–2004) joined Apollo in 1963 during his twenty-eight years as a consultant anaesthetist at the Radcliffe Infirmary. The son of a Polish immigrant, he had qualified as a doctor in 1935 and served in Iraq, Egypt and India with the RAMC, ending the war with the rank of major.

Flatware presented by Dr John Spalding, showing Apollo engraving.

Glazer was also an expert woodworker and cabinetmaker, and a councillor on Oxford City Council.

APOLLO'S FINANCES AND CHARITABLE WORK

No doubt the flow of new members assisted the lodge's finances during this period. The full accounts were distributed to members once a year and a copy was usually entered in the Minutes Book. From these sources we can see that in November 1952 the lodge voted to increase the annual subscription to 1 guinea and the joining fee (including the annual subscription) to 5 guineas (about £20 and £100 in today's money). The initiation fee was 8 guineas (£160 today) while the dining fee of about £1 (approx. £20 today) which included jugs of beer was waived for initiates. Thus the 'up-front cost' for initiates was 9 guineas (£180 today). In January 1960 members were confident enough of the lodge's financial position to decide 'that the cost of entertainment of Lodge guests at dinner be borne by Lodge funds, in order to keep the cost of dining to members as low as reasonably possible', and that in general 'it was held to be desirable to invite the Master of each Lodge meeting in the City once during his year of office and the Secretary of each such Lodge as often as was reasonably convenient.' In May 1964, however, costs had already risen and 'It was agreed that beer be no longer provided at dinner, but that all drinks be purchased by those dining.'

The lodge's ability to keep its fees relatively low during this period was assisted by a generous legacy of £2,000 (approx. £40,000 today) received in 1961 from the estate of Ernest Henry Cartwright, DM (Exeter; Apollo, 1888). Cartwright had been a subscribing member until his death in 1953, by which time he had been its senior member for many years. He was a physician and surgeon but in his retirement he compiled *The English Ritual of Craft Masonry* (1936) a ritual still used by many lodges today and wrote his *Commentary on the Freemasonic Ritual* (1947).[206]

On the other side of the balance sheet it is clear that the lodge's charitable work was minimal for the first decade after World War II. True, 10 guineas and 5 guineas (about £200 and £100 today) were donated to the Royal Masonic Institution for Boys and the Royal Masonic Hospital in 1948, and 10 guineas to the Royal Masonic Institution for Girls in 1951, but in proposing a grant of £100 to the Royal Masonic Benevolent Institution (RMBI) in May

1958, Dr Costin, the Deputy Provincial Grand Master and a Past Master of the lodge was prompted to observe 'that for many years no appeal for charity had been made in the Lodge because most of the undergraduate members were recipients of grants'.

Saxton, the Secretary, was openly critical of the lodge's record in this respect. He reported that despite the RMBI's appeal for individual donations, which he had included on the summons for the meeting in October 1957, 'the result was zero'. Moreover, in his opinion many of the large number of undergraduates initiated into Freemasonry in the lodge had gone down from Oxford knowing nothing of charity, described in the ritual as 'the distinguishing characteristic of a Freemason's heart'. The 'Charity Box', he added, which used to be circulated at dinner, 'had been ordered to be put away and it was safely lodged in the Muniment Room at Jesus College'.[207] He therefore proposed that in addition to the 100 guineas proposed by Dr Costin, each member present should be invited

Apollo University Lodge firing glasses and candle snuffer.

there and then to make an individual donation and that the lodge should match their donations with a further contribution not exceeding 50 guineas. However, after 'a suitable interval of silence had elapsed, there being no seconder forthcoming, the amendment failed and was not put to the meeting' and the original proposition was carried.

The 'charity box' was reintroduced in February 1960 and there has been a charity collection at Apollo's dinners ever since, the amount collected often still including what is now known as 'the traditional Apollo halfpenny'.[208] Occasional donations to the UGLE's central Masonic charities continued to be made from lodge funds in later years (over £3,000 was covenanted to the RMIG in 1967, for example), and from its foundation in 1980 the Grand Charity also received an annual donation from each member of each lodge, rising from £1 in 1981 to £17 in 2016. All members of the English Craft also contributed to the trust fund established to celebrate the UGLE's 250th anniversary in 1967; this appeal (which included £75 from Apollo's funds in 1966) raised nearly £600,000 by the time it closed in 1970, the interest from which is used for the benefit of surgical research under the direction of the Royal College of Surgeons.[209]

FREEMASONRY'S PUBLIC PROFILE

The English Craft's support of the Royal College of Surgeons found approval in *The Times* of 13 June 1967. In fact, the British broadsheets had generally looked favourably on Freemasonry since the end of the war, without any attempt by the UGLE to advertise itself. (Under the rule of Lord Scarbrough, Grand Master and the Lord Chamberlain, supported by Stubbs, his Grand Secretary, the English Craft deliberately kept itself out of the spotlight.) *The Times* had given quite full accounts of some of Grand Lodge's 'Quarterly Communications', such as the one in June 1948 when, under the headline 'Dominion Grand Lodges', the Grand Master is reported to have mentioned 'requests from some of the Grand Lodges of the British Dominions asking to be informed of any Masons emigrating from this country to the Dominions in order that these Dominion Grand Lodges might extend a suitable welcome and assist in making these Masons feel at home in their new surroundings'.[210] A week after his death in February 1952, King George VI's 'close attachment' to Freemasonry was highlighted by *The Times* in an article 'The King as a Freemason'.[211] *The Times* also published a full obituary of Lord Scarbrough the 'politician, freemason and former Lord Chamberlain' in June 1969.

Other voices were already more critical of Freemasonry, however. *The Times* in 1951 carried a small advertisement for an article entitled 'Should a Christian be a Freemason?', which prompted the Church Assembly to set up a commission to examine the statements made therein.[212] The ensuing discussion was not confined to England, for in 1957 the Transvaal Synod of the Dutch Reformed Church was reported not only to have banned Father Christmas, but also to have ruled that 'no Freemason should hold office in the Church'. And in 1965 the General Assembly of the Church of Scotland held a heated debate on the subject but remained 'uncommitted'.[213]

In sections of some Christian churches the compatibility of Freemasonry with Christianity is still debated today, but at the time of Apollo's sesquicentenary (1969) its rumblings might already have been enough to threaten Grand Lodge's public composure. Freemasonry's compatibility with not just Christianity but also with the armed forces, some professions and even public service in general was to feature more prominently in the following decades. In the next chapter we shall see what effect these challenges had on the University lodge in particular.

APOLLO'S REMOVAL TO 333 BANBURY ROAD AND THE OMHC

The story of Apollo's removal to 333 Banbury Road in 1961, once the Hall on the High Street closed, throws further light on the lodge at that time and its relationship with the Masonic Province. In the 1950s and 1960s the greatest call on Apollo's funds came not from running costs or charities but from the Provincial Grand Lodge of Oxfordshire and in particular from its subsidiary, the Oxford Masonic Hall Company. While Apollo had contributed £5 towards the expenses of the formation of the proposed company in 1942 and provided two of its first directors, it had also set up its own building fund, presumably with the intention of finding its own premises, and members were invited to contribute to it. Saxton, the lodge Secretary, personally donated £105, for example, and in May 1951 the lodge voted to transfer to its building fund 'the sum of £316.13.9 standing to the credit of the "Ball" Account'. But in the same year the Provincial Grand Lodge opened its appeal to buy the large house at 333 Banbury Road, Oxford.

The lodge set up a committee to consider the proposal and in May 1954 it recommended that the lodge transfer its building fund to the Province's.[214] Past Master the Revd Robert Milburn recommended the adoption of the report but Saxton, who had already resigned as director of the company in 1953, opposed this, arguing that the proposed transfer would be premature and that the committee's report should be 'left on the table' for three years. Stubbs, then the UGLE's Assistant Grand Secretary, and with whom few ever dared to argue, stated that the lodge 'must accept the Report of the Committee, whether they liked it or not, otherwise it would show a complete want of confidence in the Master and the other signatories of the Report'. Some more junior members objected to the way the matter was being handled and one, now an emeritus professor elsewhere, had the temerity to suggest 'that in dealing with a purely business matter the members of the lodge should use their judgement on the facts and should not be swayed by authority or concerned in any way with the persons involved in the scheme'. According to the minutes there had never been such a strongly expressed or so long a debate in the lodge since at least 1914. In the event, the report was adopted and Saxton was the only member to withdraw his donation from the lodge's building fund before it was transferred, preferring to donate his money to Masonic charities.

The Oxford Masonic Hall Company Ltd bought 333 Banbury Road in 1954 in the midst of the post-war economic boom. By June 1960 Apollo had managed to contribute £3,500 (£72,000 in today's money) towards the adaptation and initial extension of the property for Masonic purposes. After fifteen years at the Masonic Hall on 'the High' Apollo moved to the new hall in time for its meeting on 1 December 1961. It remained there until the building was sold in 2014.[215]

11 TESTING TIMES, 1969–99

APOLLO UNIVERSITY LODGE HELD its 150th annual festival at 333
Banbury Road on 29 November 1969. Four men were initiated and W. Conrad
Costin, president of St John's and the Deputy Provincial Grand Master,
was installed as Master (for his fifth and final time) by the Grand Secretary
(Stubbs), indications that the lodge was still in good standing. Costin had
taken a First in History at St John's, eventually becoming one of its fellows and
its president in 1957. He had been awarded the MC while a captain in the Royal
Gloucestershire Regiment in World War I. In 1969, Costin was promoted to the
rank of Past Grand Sword Bearer.

The sesquicentennial celebrations proper, over which Costin presided,[216]
were held on 8 May 1970, when more members and Masonic visitors attended
the meeting upstairs than the dining facilities on the ground floor could
accommodate. The meeting included the initiation of six men (of whom four
were 'Lewises' – that is, sons of Freemasons) and the dedication of a lodge
banner by the Very Revd Robert Milburn (see above) with an oration on the
theme of Apollo, the Ancient Greek god of light, depicted on the banner 'and
the words DOMINUS ILLUMINATIO MEA, also embroidered on it'.[217]

In comparison with the lodge's centenary meeting (see Chapter 6), the
celebration of the lodge's 150th anniversary was a relatively low-key affair:
whereas in 1919 the Pro Grand Master had attended in person and the Grand
Master had sent a message of congratulations to the lodge, none of the 'high

(opposite) Apollo University
Lodge Banner.

rulers' attended in May 1970 and there seems to have been no press coverage. Nevertheless, the lodge's future looked bright and there was no hint in 1970 of the problems that would arise before the end of the century to threaten both the ability of the lodge to create and nurture young Freemasons and the entire reputation and standing of Freemasonry in England. No one foresaw the external financial pressures that would cause Apollo's membership to fall from about 400 in the 1970s to about 120 by the turn of the century, nor the effects of the sensational reporting in the media of ill-founded attacks on Freemasonry by a few – sometimes wilfully ignorant – individuals or groups within government (national and local), the churches, the armed forces and the professions, particularly between 1995 and 2005. On the other hand, in the midst of those crises, no one imagined that by 2015 Apollo would be happily re-established in the Randolph Hotel, initiating as many men as ever before, with an effective website, a programme of extra-curricular activities, including visits to other lodges at home and abroad, and a membership drawn from an even wider variety of backgrounds. How all this came about is the burden of this chapter.

FINANCIAL PRESSURES AND THEIR EFFECT ON MEMBERSHIP

The lodge's finances from 1970 until the turn of the century have to be considered in some detail as they are crucial to an understanding of the context in which the lodge had to operate. Apollo had always tried to keep its subscription and fees as low as possible in order to keep lodge membership affordable to undergraduates, but its ability to maintain that tradition now came under threat. However economically the lodge administered itself, it had to meet and dine somewhere and to pay dues annually to its Provincial Grand Lodge and to the UGLE, the amounts of which were beyond its control.

In October 1976 the lodge was forced to raise its annual subscription from £1.90 (about £24 in today's money) to £7.50, having hesitated for some time for fear of losing members.[218] The OMHC wanted (or perhaps already needed) to extend 333 Banbury Road to accommodate non-Masonic events from which it could raise additional revenue and the Province also set itself the target of raising £500,000 for the UGLE's Grand Charity by 1989. Griffith, the Secretary, had told the lodge in June that year that 'the gravity of the situation in the case of a large lodge with scattered membership was obvious and was regarded by those responsible for running the lodge as one of inspissated gloom.'[219]

By October 1982 membership had dropped from 400 to about 300, but the subscription was no longer keeping pace with rising costs and, more particularly, the cost to the lodge of initiating a new member had risen to about £22 (as compared with the lodge's actual charge to the initiate of £9.50).[220] In August 1983 the subscription had to be raised again, to £13, in the knowledge that this further hike would lose another fifty or so members. That rate held until February 1991 when it was increased to £25, but it had to be raised to £40 (about £65 today) just a year later to meet the higher annual dues introduced by Grand Lodge and, more especially, the ever-increasing costs of meeting and dining at 333 Banbury Road. Initiates no longer dined at the lodge's expense, the joining fee rose to £50 (or £20 for students in residence) and the maximum cost for dinner went up to £11.50.

These increases took their toll on the membership: in October 1992 alone the Treasurer reported the loss of 74 members (25 resignations and 49 exclusions for falling more than two years in arrears with subscriptions). Yet the number of initiates showed but a slight decrease over the decade (110 in the 1980s compared with 117 in the 1970s) and the lodge still felt confident enough of the longer-term future to invest £5,000 in ten £500 bonds with an attractive annual interest rate of 11 per cent, which the OMHC issued to finance the proposed extension to 333.[221] Moreover – and in addition to the annual charitable donation from each member that Grand Lodge collected via the lodge – Apollo subscribed £36,814 to the UGLE's Grand Charity between its launch in 1974 and the end of its 'festival' (i.e. its appeal) in 1989, and continued to donate smaller amounts to other Masonic and non-Masonic charities.[222]

Apollo's financial health remained relatively stable during the rest of the 1990s, despite the reduction from 11 per cent to 8 per cent in the interest paid on its £5,000 loan to the OMHC in 1996 and the rising cost of meeting at 333 Banbury Road. Though few realized it at the time, these were symptoms of a deeper malaise. Although by 1995 60 per cent of the company's rental income was generated from non-Masonic letting, the cost of the mortgage the company had taken out to finance the extension and improvements was such that it had to raise more money from the lodges than it had intended, a problem which finally brought matters to a head in 2012, as we shall see later.

The only beneficial outcome of the external financial pressures under which Apollo had to operate in the last decades of the twentieth century was the foundation of the Apollo Association in 1994.[223] Its founders, the Secretary, John Cockin (see also below) and the Treasurer, Bryan Pierce, realized that it was careless to lose touch with members of the lodge once they left the University, particularly if they were still willing to contribute to the cost of Apollo's activities. Subscribing members of the lodge were immediately made members of the association at no additional cost; former members of the lodge wishing to join the association would be charged an annual fee of £13.50, receive a newsletter and be welcomed at lodge meetings and at its social events. Any surplus their fees provided would enable the lodge to keep its initiation fee down and assist it in other ways. (As will be shown, the Association really came into its own after the year 2000 when Apollo's ability to attract and then retain contact with young members became of interest to the English Craft as a whole.)

AN EXCEPTIONAL INTAKE (1970–2000)

It is unlikely that any other of the UGLE's several thousand lodges has produced so many 'Grand Officers' (in other words, officers of the Grand Lodge itself) from its intake of members between 1970 and 2000.

Among those who joined Apollo from other lodges during that period was Alan Englefield in 1976 when, as a police inspector, he was reading Law at Worcester. During his long career in the police and later at the Ministry of Defence he also served as the Master of Apollo (in 1981) and was its Director of Ceremonies for several years. After retiring from public service Englefield became the Provincial Grand Master for Oxfordshire (2002–07) and then the UGLE's first Grand Chancellor (2007–11) when responsibility for its international relations was devolved from the Grand Secretary's office.[224] Also joining Apollo in 1976 was Robert A.H. Morrow (Hertford), a banker, who succeeded Jim Daniel as the UGLE's Grand Secretary, and held that office from 2002 until 2006.[225] John Cockin FRCS, Apollo's Secretary from 1987 until shortly before his death and the first Secretary to produce the minutes on and from his computer (in 1988), joined Apollo from Churchill Lodge in 1977 and remained an active member until his death in 1999. A surgeon, Cockin had been a Fulbright Scholar and Teaching Fellow at Harvard and was a Fellow of Hertford College. A distinguished member of the medical profession, with a senior position at the Radcliffe Hospital, Cockin also rose to prominence in the Craft: in the Masonic Province he served as its Secretary from 1982 and then as the Deputy Provincial Grand Master from 1992; Grand Lodge rewarded him with the high national rank of Past Grand Sword Bearer and he also served as a member of its Board of General Purposes.[226]

A good number of Apollo's own 275 or so initiates in the the 1980s and 1990s have also flourished masonically. James Robert Guy Hilditch (St John's; Apollo, 1984), for example, became Apollo's Master just three years after his initiation. A senior member of a major firm of accountants, Hilditch was well suited to succeed Pierce as Treasurer in 2010 but after only four years in that office he was appointed as the Provincial Grand Master for Oxfordshire, an office he still holds. Jonathan Spence (Trinity; Apollo, 1986) is the highest ranking member Apollo has produced since Grand Master Lord Scarbrough (see above, p. 131). During his first career, as a banker, Spence was appointed to high ceremonial offices in Grand Lodge and eventually became its Grand DC in 2003. He retired as the chief executive of his London bank in 2006 to take up his present appointment as the Senior Bursar of Queens' College, Cambridge. Since March 2009 he has been the Deputy Grand Master of the UGLE, under HRH the Duke of Kent, and is thus a successor to two other members of Apollo who held that office: Sir Thomas Frederick Halsey (see above, p. 123) and the Hon. Edward Lathom Baillieu (Brasenose) who was proposed as a joining member but elected as an honorary member in 1989 at the age of seventy.

Jonathan Mark Richard Baker (St John's; Apollo, 1986), now the Rt Revd Jonathan Baker, Bishop of Fulham, was Apollo's Master in 1989. After ordination as an Anglican priest he eventually returned to Oxford as the Principal of Pusey House (2003). Baker's appointment as the UGLE's Deputy Grand Chaplain in 2010 did not impede his appointment to episcopal office in 2011, but when his translation in 2013 to the See of Fulham caused some members within the hierarchy of the Church of England to question the appointment of a Freemason to hold that office, Baker chose to withdraw from his Masonic activities rather than have his Freemasonry used, mistakenly, to criticise his work as a priest.

On the other hand the Revd Robert Maxwell Sweeney (Christ Church; Apollo, 1989) was already an Anglican priest when he was initiated at the age of fifty. He served as Master of the lodge in 1993 and then became its Chaplain, an office he held until his retirement. Sweeney was not only an excellent ritualist but also an accomplished organist, managing somehow to include versions of Mussorgsky's *Pictures at an Exhibition* and Alfred Hitchcock's signature tune during one of the meetings. Ever keen to promote a better understanding of Freemasonry within academe and the Anglican Church, Sweeney was delighted to obtain permission to hold a service in Christ Church Cathedral in 2002 as part of the UGLE's promotion of 'Freemasonry in the Community'.[227] He was made a Past Assistant Grand Chaplain of the UGLE in 2005. Again, the Revd Timothy John Nicholas L'Estrange (Apollo, 1990), took holy orders after leaving Oxford and is now the vicar of a large parish in West London. He was appointed the Deputy Grand Chaplain of the UGLE in 2015.

Geoffrey Dennis Bourne-Taylor was the Bursar and a Fellow of St Edmund Hall when he joined Apollo in 1989. Master in 1995/96, he succeeded Cockin as the lodge's Secretary in 1998, an office he held until 2011. Bourne-Taylor's previous career as a senior police officer and his role as a bursar, in daily contact with the student body, enabled him firmly but sensitively to interview undergraduate candidates for initiation, and, once admitted, help them to enjoy the status, traditions and fellowship of the lodge. In keeping with a less deferential age Bourne-Taylor's minutes and his informal 'glosses' display not only his affection for the lodge but also the often acerbic wit he applied to its members' appearance and their performance of the traditional Masonic ritual, whatever their rank or fortune.[228] For his services to Apollo and his efforts to keep the Craft available and attractive to younger members (see below) he was promoted to the office of Senior Grand Deacon of the UGLE.[229]

Several other Apollonians have gone on to hold active office in the UGLE, among them three Deputy Grand Directors of Ceremonies: Sebastian Charles Edward Amadeus Madden (Keble; Apollo, 1995, Master in 1999) in 2008–10; Dr Giles Robert Evelyn Shilson (Balliol; Apollo, 1995) in 2013–16; and Dr David Staples (Magdalen; Apollo, 1997), who was first appointed as DepGDC in 2016.[230] Stephen John Tucker (Trinity; Apollo, 1987, Master in 1990 and now the Professor of Biophysics) served as Senior Grand Deacon in 2014 (see also below). James William Ashton Sanders (Exeter; Apollo, 1987), who became Master in 1991, and Richard Forster (Trinity; Apollo, 1996), Master in 2005, were Assistant Grand Directors of Ceremonies in 2004 and 2010 respectively, while Richard J. Hopkinson-Woolley (Pembroke; Apollo, 1989) was appointed as the Assistant Grand Registrar in 2014 and Dr Simon J. Borwick (Brasenose; Apollo, 1999, Master 2002 and now Apollo's DC) as the Grand Pursuivant in 2016.

Among the members of the lodge appointed or promoted to 'Past' (i.e. non-active or honorary) Grand Rank in the UGLE the name of one of

(above) Silver inkstand, presented to Geoffrey Bourne-Taylor, inscribed 'Secretary Emeritus Tuus iam regnat Apollo' ('Your own Apollo is now king!' – a quotation from Virgil's *Eclogues*).

Apollo's initiates during this period stands out: George Robert Boys-Stones (St John's; Apollo, 1993, Master in 1997) who was invested as a Past Assistant Grand Director of Ceremonies in 2010.[231] Boys-Stones is now a professor in the department of Classics and Ancient History at Durham and has played a significant part in the (Masonic) Universities Scheme (see below).[232]

If it were possible to publish a list of Apollo's exceptional intake between 1970 and 2000 it would be seen to include many other men – including several from the USA, West Africa and two Rhodes Scholars from Australia – who on going down from Oxford have distinguished themselves in the worlds of finance, science, the humanities and, in a few cases, politics. Perhaps surprisingly, when compared with earlier periods in the lodge's history, Apollo produced only two British MPs from this intake: Peter Butler and Adrian Flook, both Conservatives. Butler (Apollo, 1988), despite being elected as the MP for North East Milton Keynes in the 1992 general election, served as Apollo's Master that same year, an unusual departure from Apollo's normal practice of restricting the mastership of the lodge to members 'in residence'.[233] Butler lost his seat to Labour in 1997. Flook (Apollo, 1982) left Oxford before he could take the Master's chair but, later, as Master of Westminster and Keystone Lodge in London, led a procession of its members when they visited Apollo. He was elected to represent Taunton in the House of Commons in 2001 but the Liberal Democrats regained the seat by one percentage point in 2005 and Flook now advises internationally on strategic communications.

But perhaps 'Tony' Marchington had the most colourful career. Dr Anthony Frank Marchington (Brasenose, and later a benefactor and honorary Fellow of St Edmund Hall) was raised on the family farm in the Peak District. Initiated in 1992 at the age of 36, he was elected Master of Apollo in 1996. Already a successful biotechnology entrepreneur, energetic businessman and generous philanthropist his future looked even brighter. He made headlines and was dubbed 'the Fat Controller' when he bought and restored the famous steam locomotive *The Flying Scotsman* for about £2.5m. Quickly becoming popular throughout the Province, Marchington was soon made its Assistant Provincial Grand Master, with the prospect of further promotion. Yet a clash of personalities caused him to withdraw from Freemasonry after a short period in that office, and although one of his companies, Oxford Molecular, was once valued at £450 million, he was declared bankrupt in 2003 and died eight years later.[234]

Glass tankard presented to all members of the lodge who attended the Installation of Tony Marchington as W. Master in 1996, showing an image of the Flying Scotsman.

THE CRAFT UNDER ATTACK

Meanwhile, 'Freemasonry' undefined was being sniped at from points within government, the professions and the Church. When questions arose in the General Synod of the Church of England about the compatibility of 'Freemasonry' and 'Christianity' (again undefined), the UGLE responded in considerable detail with a 57-page submission in April 1986. The UGLE also took pains to answer questions put to it by a Home Affairs Select Committee of the House of Commons in the late 1990s and argued that demands to disclose membership of Masonic organizations were unwarranted and constituted unfair discrimination. The seriousness of the situation was brought home to Apollo when, in November 1999, one of its members, a serving officer in the armed forces, resigned from the Craft 'following pressure from the Ministry of Defence through Defence Council Instructions that "membership of Freemasonry was incompatible with Military Command"'.[235] The minutes record that there were 'murmurs of indignation … and the Grand Secretary [Daniel] spoke briefly of the concern being felt at Grand Lodge that such documents were not only unacceptable, but were insulting to the Grand Master, Field Marshal, the Duke of Kent'. The UGLE protested, took leading counsel's advice on the matter and decided it would have to bring the matter before the High Court.

The publicity afforded to 'Freemasonry' through the media by its critics in the 1980s and 1990s and the UGLE's increasing willingness to answer them publicly may well partly explain the continuing attraction of Apollo to such a variety and to so many members of the University. But other factors must surely be taken into account, including the enjoyment evinced by younger members of the lodge at its meetings and its many social occasions to which partners and potential members are warmly invited – from 'Ladies' Nights' in the 1970s to 'Guest Nights' in the 1990s.[236] Apollo further raised its public profile with a website containing a brief history of the lodge and a contact for those wishing to pursue any interest in the lodge it aroused; the first candidate stated in the minutes to have been attracted by this medium was initiated in June 1996. While the 'gown' lodge rarely visited its counterparts in the 'town' (though it always invited their representatives to its annual installation meetings), many Freemasons from the Province visit the lodge. Indeed, it is not unusual that Apollo receives 'coach parties' from further afield.[237]

All things considered, Apollo University lodge reached the turn of the century in reasonable shape. It had survived financial pressures from without (though it lost many non-resident members as a result) and still had about £28,000 in the bank. More importantly, the lodge had faced the challenges of a quickly changing social context and still managed to initiate 114 men in the final decade alone.

12 APOLLO FLOURISHES, 2000–2016

IN 2000 LESS WAS heard from those worried about the compatibility of Freemasonry with Christianity, and the Home Affairs Select Committee's investigation into Freemasonry was running into the sand. Members of Apollo privately greeted these developments with some relief, but when in November 2000 the 'Grand Secretary [Daniel] reported that Grand Lodge had been successful in obliging the Secretary of State for Defence to withdraw the Defence Council Instruction that had been found so offensive to many brethren serving in the armed forces' his announcement 'was received with acclaim, particularly from a number of uniformed officers who were present'.[238]

In fact, members of Apollo had already demonstrated what they thought of the Instruction when in June 2000 one member of the lodge attended in full mess kit as a second lieutenant in the army, and a midshipman in the Royal Navy was initiated. Among members who have returned from the wars in Bosnia, Iraq, Syria and Afghanistan one soldier stands out: Robin Edwin Geoffrey Bourne-Taylor initiated in 2001 when just 20. As a captain in the Life Guards in Afghanistan, he was one of the first members of the British armed forces to receive the Conspicuous Gallantry Cross (CGC), the country's second highest gallantry award, in recognition of which the lodge presented him with a silver wine stand. (Not that the CGC was his only distinction: he also rowed in three winning Oxford eights, became president of the OUBC and twice rowed for Great Britain in the Olympic Games.)

(opposite) Portrait of the Rt Hon. the Earl Cadogan, KBE, DL, by Richard Stone.

DRESS

Since 2000 the summons to each meeting has encouraged members so entitled to wear their military uniform and a number have done so, including a lieutenant colonel. While other members of Apollo and most of their guests wear dinner jackets at Apollo meetings, the lodge officers wear 'court dress' – that is to say, 'white tie', knee breeches and buckled 'court shoes'. The minutes since 1914 do not prove that this has always been the case, though Oscar Wilde seems to be wearing that rig in the photograph elsewhere in this history. What they do reveal, however, is that in 1960 the lodge spent £25 on five pairs of breeches and £300 in 1989 to replenish the stock; a generous member supplied the kit for the lodge Deacons in 2002, while in 2003 the Secretary, from a 'sale

Captain Robin Bourne-Taylor, the Life Guards (double Olympian and three times winner of the Oxford–Cambridge Boat Race), at his investiture with the Conspicuous Gallantry Cross, 16 November 2010.

of judicial impedimenta', obtained for the lodge 'a number of pairs of breeches and court shoes'. Even the Tyler of the lodge, the officer who guards the entrance and prepares the candidates for degree ceremonies, has been fitted out with 'court dress' since 2005. The sartorial elegance of the lodge has been further increased by the addition of a lodge tie, cufflinks and studs embellished with an image of Apollo, and even a lodge blazer – all sold to members at a slight profit to raise funds for the lodge's bicentennial celebrations in 2018/19.

APOLLO'S LEAD IS FOLLOWED BY OTHERS

The year 2000 saw the highest number of initiates in Apollo for more than a century: twenty-eight in all, split over the four meetings when the initiation ceremony was worked. In fact, the 'noughties' produced by far the most initiates in any decade of Apollo's history, a remarkable total of 162.

The lodge's success in attracting large numbers of new members at a time when the English Craft as a whole was noticing a significant decline in membership aroused great interest at headquarters. Members of the UGLE's Board of General Purposes (BGP) attended Apollo in January 2000; the Assistant Grand Master (the Marquess of Northampton) visited in January 2001; and in November that year the 8th Earl Cadogan (Magdalen) headed another group of visitors from the BGP. When Northampton was promoted to Pro Grand Master he charged his successor (David Williamson, a member of Isaac Newton University Lodge, Cambridge) with finding a way to encourage more undergraduates and recent graduates to join the Craft, at home and overseas.

Apollo, the first 'university lodge', had demonstrated that a lodge could recruit and enthuse young university men by offering, for example, a reduced charge for initiates and joining members in full-time education, swift promotion into office, meetings so well choreographed that two degree ceremonies with multiple candidates in each are comfortably worked between 4.15 p.m. and 7.30 p.m. (even with a twenty-minute interlude), dinners that normally end by 10 p.m., and frequent social events. Petitioned by Apollo, Grand Lodge announced its intention to reduce its fees by 50 per cent for members under the age of 25 and in 2005 the Assistant Grand Master, inspired by the examples set by Apollo and the Isaac Newton University Lodges, set up the UGLE's Universities Scheme 'to establish and/or enhance arrangements

and opportunities for undergraduates and other university members to enjoy Freemasonry'.[239] Professor Boys-Stones (St John's; Apollo, 1993) has played a significant part in the Scheme, to which nearly sixty lodges now belong. A criticism levelled against Apollo for initiating more than two candidates at a time (the maximum normally allowed by Grand Lodge), however, is that new

Portrait of James Daniel by William Ashley Hold, showing his chain of office as Grand Secretary of the United Grand Lodge of England.

members soon disappear from the lodge's sight, and often quietly drop out of active membership of the Craft.[240] They have been doing so since 1818, of course, but now Apollo answers the criticism not just by putting greater effort into finding other lodges for them to join, nearer their homes or business addresses, but by recruiting them into the Apollo Association (see above), members of which receive summonses to meetings of the lodge, invitations to social events and newsletters, all made so much easier by email and social media. The proliferation of lodges under the Universities Scheme should also help the Craft to make best use of new members after they leave university. It certainly helped to ensure the success of the Universities Ball which was held at the home of the Honorable Artillery Company in London in November 2013.

Apollo has also led the field in its creation of the Apollo Bursary Scheme, for which Professor Stephen Tucker is largely responsible. The Scheme, funded by the lodge but administered at arm's length by the University, has been granting four bursaries of £1,000 a year to needy outstanding second-year undergraduates since 2008, whatever their gender or nationality. The Masonic Province of Oxfordshire followed suit with its Amos Griffiths Bursary, also administered by the University.

FROM 333 BANBURY ROAD BACK TO THE RANDOLPH

It would be inappropriate to highlight any more of the names of the many other University men who became members of Apollo after the turn of the century. Suffice it to say that the intake has been more diverse than ever. All candidates for initiation have professed their belief in God, and several whose mother tongue is not English have distinguished themselves by excellent renditions of the traditional ritual. 'In many ways', said the Secretary, (Geoffrey) Bourne-Taylor, in his valedictory paper for the lodge committee in October 2011, Apollo 'seems to match the 1870s: we have similar recruitment, thanks now to the evangelism that blisters through our junior members; the Stewards' Dinners have become our proud outreach; rarely does a regular meeting of the lodge attract less than 70 diners … What a joy it still is to be an Apollo man.'

Meanwhile, however, the problem of 333 Banbury Road continued. By 2003 it was costing the lodge about £6,000 a year for its six meetings there, based on a per capita charge per member plus dining costs. Apollo, by far the largest

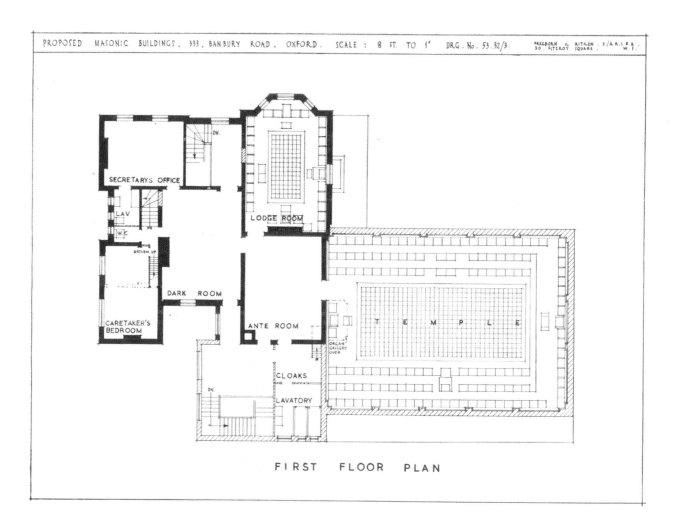

PROPOSED MASONIC BUILDINGS. 333, BANBURY ROAD, OXFORD. SCALE: 8 FT. TO 1'. DRG. No. 53.32/3. FREEBORN & AITKEN. F/A.R.I.B.A. 30. FITZROY SQUARE. W.1.

SECRETARYS OFFICE

LAV

W.C

LODGE ROOM

BATHRM UP

DARK ROOM

CARETAKER'S BEDROOM

ANTE ROOM

ORGAN GALLERY OVER

TEMPLE

DN

CLOAKS

LAVATORY

FIRST FLOOR PLAN

lodge in the Province and thus the most valuable customer of the Oxford Masonic Hall Company, protested on the ground that most of its members could never attend once they left Oxford, but the appeal was rejected. In consequence, the lodge's subscription had to be doubled to £80 in 2004/05 and raised further to £140 in 2008. These increases caused nearly 60 members to resign and the total membership to fall to about 120, which in turn reduced the lodge's payments to the OMHC to about £4,000 a year. The OMHC's income from Masonic and non-Masonic business declined. Unable to pay the mortgage interest, let alone pay off the capital, the company closed 333 Banbury Road in 2012.

At short notice, Apollo had to find a new home. The Provincial Grand lodge and the OMHC found temporary accommodation for the city lodges, but this could not accommodate Apollo, given the much larger attendance at its meetings and dinners, and the fact that it meets on Saturdays to suit its members 'in residence'. The new Secretary, Christopher Noon (Christ Church), initiated as recently as 2006 and already its Master in 2008, met the challenge and arranged for the lodge to meet at the Randolph Hotel just in time for its meeting in October 2012. With but one exception, it has met in the ballroom there ever since.[241] In June 2015, when the ballroom could not be made available, Apollo met in the debating chamber of the Oxford Union Society. The meeting began early enough for a garden party to be held there after the lodge closed. Not to be outdone by the elegance of their partners and other guests at the party, the members wore lounge suits or blazers to the meeting and several bravely sported red trousers.

Apollo's vibrancy was well illustrated at its Annual Festival in December 2016. Three undergraduates, three postgraduates and a senior research fellow were initiated; £4,000 was donated to the University for distribution as bursaries for needy undergraduates; the 140 diners were entertained by the Apollo choir's rendition of the 'The Enter'd 'Prentice's Song' (written in the 1720s) and further delighted when the Installing Master, Dr Timothy Ross Lloyd Myatt (St Anne's and Wolfson; Apollo, 2008), welcomed and conversed with his successor, Paul Gerstmayr (Balliol and St John's; Apollo, 2011), in Tibetan.

CONCLUSION

IN RECENT DECADES THE nature of the lodge's recruits has changed. There are fewer gilded youths now, fewer sportsmen and fewer soldiers. There are also fewer potential clergy. Still some recent Apollonians, by reason of their Masonic standing, have become public figures.

Two in particular lived public lives within the hierarchy of Freemasonry. First, Sir Philip Colville Smith (St John's; Apollo, 1886), Master of Apollo five times over, in 1891, 1893, 1896, 1919 and 1935–36;[242] and second, Sir James Stubbs (Brasenose; Apollo, 1930), grandson of Oxford's greatest historian: it fell to him in 1964 to initiate the debate which culminated in 1986 in the removal of the fearsome 'penalties' traditionally attached to Masonic 'obligations'.[243] Both these men served as Grand Secretaries to the United Grand Lodge of England. And both revelled in the administration of the English 'Craft' and in the minutiae of traditional Masonic ceremony. Colville Smith – 'the greatest of Secretaries Freemasonry has known' – was rumoured to have attended a stupefying 1,000 lodge meetings; and Stubbs, 'the Black Prince of Freemasonry' – very much in his grandfather's shadow – could even be said to have had Oxford's 'history in his genes'. In recent years, the Grand Mastership itself was held by no less a figure than the 11th Earl of Scarbrough (Magdalen; Apollo, 1920, Grand Master 1951–67). Scarbrough has his own niche in history: he was the last Lord Chamberlain to exercise the power of theatrical censorship.[244]

Much has changed in British society and Freemasonry since their time, but the University lodge can still boast among the UGLE's senior active officers the Deputy Grand Master (Jonathan Spence), the Provincial Grand Master of Oxfordshire (James Hilditch), the President of the Masonic Charitable Foundation (His Honour Richard Hone, QC), the Deputy President of the Board of General Purposes (James Long, TD), another member of the BGP as President of the Committee of General Purposes of the Royal Arch (Dr Malcolm Aish) and the Grand Secretary (Dr David Staples).

Finally, in matters of philanthropy and good fellowship, two names should certainly be recorded here. Tony Marchington (Brasenose and St Edmund Hall; Apollo, 1992) – saviour of the Flying Scotsman (see above) and of much else besides – lived out his years according to the best conventions of Apollo bonhomie.[245] And the 8th Earl Cadogan (Magdalen; a Past Deputy Grand Master, who joined Apollo in 2004), one of Britain's great philanthropists, has also practised in Apollo the charitable work for which he was knighted in 2012.

Charity remains fundamental to Masonic life. Each year the current membership gives away substantial sums in bursaries and subsidies, on grounds of need alone, without partiality. Just one example will do to illustrate the point. In the six years to 2015, the central Masonic charities distributed over £100 million to Freemasons and their families and to non-Masonic charities, including disaster relief.[246] In this respect Apollo fully shares the communal spirit of the 7,500 or so lodges gathered still under the direction of the United Grand Lodge of England. So the customs of Apollo live on. Since 1818 the spirit of Apollo has emphasized not just good fellowship – plenty of cakes and ale – but good citizenship too. Principle and enjoyment are by no means incompatible. It is, on balance, a record of which Oxford and Freemasonry can be proud.

NOTES

1 The 'secrets' are those traditional forms of recognition which are used by Freemasons essentially to prove their identity and qualifications when entering a Masonic meeting.

2 T.H. Aston (ed.), *History of the University of Oxford*, 8 vols (Oxford, 1984–94).

3 The idea of Freemasonry as a 'cultural agency' was first adumbrated in J. Roberts, 'Freemasonry: Possibilities of a Neglected Topic', *EHR*, vol. 84, no. 331 (1969), pp. 323–55. The application of Gramsci's concept of hegemony to Masonic lodges as instruments of social control has been sketched out in P.J. Rich, *Elixir of Empire* (London, 1989), and much expanded in J.L. Harland-Jacobs, *Builders of Empire: Freemasons and British Imperialism, 1717–1927* (Chapel Hill NC, 2007).

4 Roberts, 'Freemasonry: Possibilities of a Neglected Topic', p. 335.

5 The United Grand Lodge of England, *Masonic Year Book*; *Masonic Year Book, Historical Supplement*, 2nd edn, 1969, published by the UGLE and printed by Oxford University Press.

6 D. Knoop and G.P. Jones, *A Short History of Freemasonry to 1730* (Manchester, 1940), pp. 9, 127, 322. For general discussions, see also A.E. Waite, *Emblematic Freemasonry* (London, 1925) and J.S.M. Ward, *Freemasonry: Its Aims and Ideals* (London, 1923).

7 [James Anderson], *The Constitutions of the Free-Masons Containing the History, Charges, Regulations etc. of that most Antient and Right Worshipful Fraternity* (1723); ed. L. Vibert (1923).

8 What Anderson called 'The old Gothic Constitutions', e.g. BL Royal MS. 17 A. I [*c.*1390], ed. J. Halliwell-Phillipps (1840; 1844). Also BL Add MS. 23198 [*c.*1410], ed. M. Cooke (1861). For details, see W.J. Hughan, *The Old Charges of the British Freemasons* (1872; 1895; suppl. 1906); also L. Vibert, 'Anderson's Constitutions of 1723', *AQC* 36 (1923), pp. 36–85.

9 The Prince of Wales had been initiated at Kew Palace in 1737.

10 Facsimile of 1738 edn, ed. G.W. Speth, in *AQC* 3 (1890), pp. 143–4.

11 1738 facsimile, p. 147; D. Knoop and G.P. Jones, *The Genesis of Freemasonry* (Manchester, 1947), p. 179.

12 Knoop and Jones, *The Genesis of Freemasonry*, p. 179.

13 Quoted in ibid., pp. 179–80.

14 R.H.S. Rottenbury, 'The Pre-Eminence of the Great Architect in Freemasonry', *AQC* 97 (1984), pp. 192–9.

15 Quoted by W.J. Williams in *AQC* 56 (1943), p. 53.

16 T. Sprat, *History of the Royal Society* (1667), quoted in *AQC* 78 (1965), p. 68. There are echoes here of Thomas Hobbes.

17 D. Knoop and G.P. Jones, 'Freemasonry and the Idea of Natural Religion', *AQC* 56 (1943), p. 47.

18 For a clear explanation of this development, see Knoop and Jones, *The Genesis of Freemasonry*, chs 12–13.

19 J. Hamill, 'The Earl of Moira, acting Grand Master 1790–1813', *AQC* 93 (1980), pp. 31–48.

20 D. Knoop, 'University Masonic Lodges', *AQC* 59 (1946), p. 4 *et seq.*

21 W.N. Hargreaves-Mawdsley (ed.), *Woodforde at Oxford, 1759–76* (Oxford Historical Society N.S. 21; Oxford, 1969), pp. 217–18, 222, 237, 257, 280, 291, 323: 1774–76; J. Mordaunt Crook, *Brasenose: The Biography of an Oxford College* (Oxford, 2008; 2010), pp. 150–51.

22 Between 1769 and 1790 there were at least fifteen members from Brasenose, plus five from All Souls: Lord Edward Conway, son of the 1st Marquess of Hertford; Edward Isham, warden of All Souls and vice chancellor of Oxford; Robert Price, chaplain to George III; James Strode; and John Kynaston (E.L. Hawkins, 'Two Old Oxford Lodges', *AQC* 22 (1909), pp. 166–77).

23 Crook, *Brasenose*, pp. 151–2; R.L. Poole, *Catalogue of Oxford Portraits*, vol. 2 (Oxford, 1911–24), p. 243; J.P. Jenkins, 'Jacobites and Freemasons in Eighteenth-century Wales', *Welsh Historical Review* 9 (1979), pp. 391–406.

24 J. Melton, *The Rise of the Public in Enlightenment Europe* (Cambridge, 2001), p. 70; K. Whelan, *The Tree of Liberty: Radicalism, Catholicism and the Construction of Irish Identity, 1760–1830* (South Bend IN, 2000), p. 120; Harland-Jacobs, *Builders of Empire*, pp. 131, 140.

25 Lodges were numbered by date of formation. When lodges ceased to exist, the numbers of those remaining were sometimes adjusted downwards but that practice was later stopped.

26 J. Lemprière's *Classical Dictionary* (1804), which the founders of Apollo Lodge must have known well, tells us that 'Apollo was the

god of all the fine arts, of medicine, music, poetry and eloquence … He had … the power of knowing futurity … In every part of the world he received homage as the president of the Muses … and the patron of the liberal arts and sciences.'

27 His relation, Sir John St Aubyn, was the Provincial Grand Master for Cornwall 1785–1839.

28 The attack was combined with a shameless appeal to the electors of Glasgow University's Chair of Greek. This time he was successful (*Edinburgh Review* 35 (1821), pp. 308–11). See also *Letter to P. Elmsley in answer to the appeal made to Prof. Sandford as umpire between the University of Oxford and the Edinburgh Review* by D.K. Sandford et al. (1822); *The Pamphleteer* 21 (1822) [BL PP. 3557 w]; *A Letter to D.K. Sandford … in answer to the strictures of the Edinburgh Review on the open Colleges of Oxford* (1822) [BL T711 (10)]; Correspondence with Peel, BL Add. MSS. 40404–40423.

29 E.g. '£10 to the distressed Irish and Scotch' and 1 guinea each to the Masonic Girls' and Boys' Schools, and the Masonic Asylum (Apollo University Lodge, Register and Minute Book: 10 March 1847); 3 gns to 'Radcliff's Infirmary', 2 gns for the Dispensary, 1 gn each for Anti-Mendicity, Boys' School, Girls' School, Aged Masons Asylum and Blue Coat School (ibid.: 19 February 1851). In 1834, 10 guineas went to the church 'at the back of the Clarendon Press'; in 1835, £10 went to the building of St Clement's; in 1836, £10 went towards 'the remodelling of the interior of St Peter in the East' (ibid.: 3 June 1836).

30 Ibid.: 22 February 1849. The housekeeper was Martha Cox. Premises were shared with the City Book Club Library (*Oxford Directory*).

31 [Cuthbert Bede, pseud.], *Adventures of Mr. Verdant Green*, pt III, ch. X (1853). See *Oxford Dictionary of National Biography* (A. Sanders).

32 Apollo minutes: 4 May 1819.

33 Apollo *Centenary Meeting* (1919). BNC, M.P.P. 80 F1.

34 E. Hodder, *Life and Work of the Seventh Earl of Shaftesbury*, 3 vols (London, 1887); G.B.A.M. Finlayson, *The Seventh Earl of Shaftesbury, 1801–1885* (London, 1981); G. Battiscombe, *Shaftesbury: A Biography of the Seventh Earl, 1801–1885* (London, 1974).

35 *Complete Peerage*, quoting E. Yates, *Recollections and Experiences* (1874).

36 Crook, *Brasenose*, p. 204; Whitfield MSS, Diary of Caroline Clive: 10 January 1848 (*ex inf.* Edward Clive).

37 *Complete Baronetage.*

38 Leader inherited a fortune in 1828; went down without a degree after a few 'idle and spendthrift' terms at Oxford; pursued a prominent political career among the Philosophical Radicals until 1844; then retired to a life of connoisseurship on the Continent, where he restored notable properties in Cannes, Florence and Maiano (*Oxford Dictionary of National Biography*: S. Lee; H.C.G. Matthew).

39 Lists compiled from Apollo minutes.

40 K. Feiling, *In Christ Church Hall* (London, 1960), p. 188.

41 *Complete Peerage*; M. Maclagan, *Clemency Canning* (London, 1962).

42 See [C. Chauncy Burr], *Autobiography and Lectures of Lola Montez* (London, 1858); H. Wyndham, *The Magnificent Montez* (London, 1935); H. Célarié, *La Vie vagabonde et tumultueuse de Lola Montès* (1950). She died in New York in 1861.

43 *Oxford Dictionary of National Biography* (J. Parry).

44 *Complete Peerage*. His father, the 10th Duke, considered himself the rightful King of Scotland and was buried in a colossal mausoleum at Hamilton Palace (F. Boase,

Modern English Biography, vol. 1, col. 1296 (London, 1892)).

45 Portrait, R.F. Gould, *History of Freemasonry*, vol. 1 (New York, 1884), p. 200. Another Erskine, the 4th Earl of Rosslyn, was twice Grand Master of Grand Lodge, Scotland. For earlier phases, see D. Stevenson, *The First Freemasons: Scotland's Early Lodges and Their Members* (Aberdeen, 1989).

46 J. Kelly and M. Powell (eds), *Clubs and Societies in Eighteenth-Century Ireland* (Dublin, 2010), pp. 327, 329. See also P. Mirala, *Freemasonry in Ulster, 1733–1813* (Dublin, 2007), and A. Blackstock, *Loyalism in Ireland, 1789–1829* (Woodbridge, 2007).

47 Harland-Jacobs, *Builders of Empire*, pp. 150–56, 283.

48 For a photograph of the 1st Duke, see *Men of Mark*, vol. 1 (London, 1876). The 2nd Duke owned 76,500 acres in Ireland. His death in 1913 was preceded by Wyndham's Act (1903), which facilitated the sale of many Irish estates; it was soon followed by the cataclysm of civil war and partition.

49 J.W. Sleigh Godding, *A History of the Westminster and Keystone Lodge* (Plymouth, 1907), pp. 150–52.

50 *The Times*, 29 March 1884.

51 His brother C.L. Arkwright was also Apollo (1865).

52 Secretary 1877–87. See C. Petrie, *The Carlton Club* (London, 1955; ed. A. Cooke, 2007), p. 251.

53 Godding, *A History of the Westminster and Keystone Lodge*, pp. 169–70, 172.

54 Ibid., Register, pp. 184–93.

55 For an obituary, see *Masonic Journal*, December 1898.

56 J.W. Daniel, 'Pure and Accepted Masonry, 1843–1901', *AQC* 106 (1993), pp. 79–80. For the careers of Lathom and Limerick, see

Boase, *Modern English Biography*, vol. 6, cols 11 and 55.

57 G. Hamilton, *Parliamentary Reminiscences and Reflections, 1886–1906* (London, 1922), p. 10.

58 Daniel, 'Pure and Accepted Masonry, 1843–1901', p. 79; A. Hardinge, *The Life of Henry Herbert, Fourth Earl of Carnarvon, 1831–1890*, vol. 1 (Oxford, 1925), pp. 224–9: 30 March 1859. His private secretary in 1876–78 was John (Hely-Hutchinson), 5th Earl of Donoughmore (Apollo, 1867). His greatest ally was the Revd Canon George Portal (Apollo, 1848).

59 Quoted in Harland-Jacobs, *Builders of Empire*, p. 270: 1887–8.

60 Hardinge, *The Life of Henry Herbert*, vol. 1, p. 225: 8 January 1857; BL Add. MS 60945, fols. 109–10 (*ex inf.* Dr J.W. Daniel). Kipling's poem 'The Mother-Lodge' (1895) recalls the camaraderie of regimental lodges in provincial India (*Poems of Ruyard Kipling*, ed. T. Pinney, vol. 1 (Cambridge, 2013), pp. 443–5). Quotation from Harland-Jacobs, *Builders of Empire*, p. 258.

61 Harland-Jacobs, *Builders of Empire*, p. 3.

62 He had been a lecturer in Cape Colony 1876–84, before retreating to a parish in Somerset.

63 For Rhodes's 'Confession', see R.I. Rotberg and M.F. Shore, *The Founder: Cecil Rhodes and the Pursuit of Power* (Oxford, 1988), p. 90, and J. Flint, *Cecil Rhodes* (London, 1976), Appendix, pp. 248–52. Winwood Reade's *The Martyrdom of Man* was published in 1872. See *Oxford Dictionary of National Biography* (F. Driver), and W.S. Smith, *The London Heretics, 1870–1914* (London, 1967). Ruskin's Slade Lectures on Art were delivered early in 1870, and published later that year.

64 P. Magnus, *King Edward the Seventh* (London, 1964): 25 December 1868.

65 Apollo minutes, 2 March 1863.

66 Apollo minutes, 14 March 1860; 9 May 1860.

67 Report, Apollo minutes, 6 November 1863, 28 November 1863; *Illustrated London News* 1863. The Corn Exchange, designed by S.L. Seckham, did 'not appear to excite much admiration' (*British Almanack and Companion* 1864, p. 162).

68 Apollo minutes, 11 May 1866.

69 Ibid.

70 John Ruskin, *Works*, ed. E.T. Cook and A. Wedderburn, vol. 33 (London, 1908), pp. 363, 476 (Slade Lectures, 1883).

71 Apollo minutes, 18 June 1884. For garden party programmes (1857–1901), see Bodl. G.A.Oxon. 8vo 1120.

72 On 23 November 2013 a Grand Charity University Lodges' Ball was held in London to commemorate Apollo's royal ball of 150 years previously. Some 1,000 people attended (*ex inf.* G. Bourne-Taylor).

73 Apollo minutes, 7 June 1864; 9 and 13 February 1865; 12 February 1866. Bruton's practice in the Oxford area was considerable (e.g. 62 Banbury Rd, 1864–5; the apse of St Paul's, Walton St 1853; Banbury Town Hall, 1854). He was also surveyor to Christ Church and All Souls. His office was at 28 St John Street (*Oxford Directory*).

74 Apollo minutes, 26 November 1862.

75 Apollo minutes, 29 February 1872; 19 April 1872.

76 Daniel, 'Pure and Accepted Masonry, 1843–1901', p. 85.

77 C. Holland (ed.), *The Notebooks of a Spinster Lady, 1878–1903* (London, 1919): *ex inf.* Dr James Yorke.

78 *Oxford Dictionary of National Biography* (M. Pugh).

79 Bruce Robinson, citing 'Masonic membership records on ancestry.co.uk', in *Daily Telegraph*, 23 November 2015, p. 3.

80 Akers-Douglas – Lord Balcarres called him 'a most skilful wirepuller' – was 'a perfect foil to Balfour, playing tortoise to Balfour's hare' (Jane Ridley in *Oxford Dictionary of National Biography*). Later 1st Viscount Chilston. See E.A. Akers-Douglas, *Chief Whip: The Political Life and Times of Aretas Akers-Douglas, 1st Viscount Chilston* (London, 1961).

81 W.H. Long, *Memories* (London, 1923); *Oxford Dictionary of National Biography* (A. Jackson).

82 For the Burdett-Coutts family, see *Oxford Dictionary of National Biography* (E. Healey). She rests in Westminster Abbey; he at Frant, Sussex. He also founded Westminster Lodge.

83 V. Hicks Beach, *Sir Michael Hicks Beach*, vol. 2 (London, 1932), p. 280.

84 'Nestor' [Sir D.O. Hunter Blair] in the *Catholic Times*, 9 March 1928; reprinted in *Memories and Musings* (New York, 1929), p. 115.

85 Oscar Wilde, *The Complete Letters of Oscar Wilde*, ed. M. Holland and R. Hart-Davis (London, 2000), pp. 47, 60–62n.

86 Hunter Blair, 'Oscar Wilde as I Knew Him', *Dublin Review*, July 1938. See also *The Tablet* 174 (1939), p. 319, and *The Times*, 13 September 1939, p. 8. Hunter Blair became a privy chamberlain to Pope Pius IX.

87 For Wilde's Masonic career, see Y. Beresiner, 'The Wilde Oxford Mason', *Masonic Quarterly,* 4 January 2003, pp. 6–8.

88 Hunter Blair, *Memories and Musings*, pp. 110–17, 261.

89 Ibid.; Sir D.O. Hunter Blair, *A Last Medley of Memories* (London, 1936), p. 196.

90 For a contemporary critique of Leo XIII, see *London Quarterly Review* 69 (1887), pp. 144–55.

91 W. Read, 'The Church of Rome and Freemasonry, 1738–1983', *AQC* 104 (1992), pp. 51–94, and particularly J.A. Ferrer-Benimeli SJ, 'The Catholic Church and Freemasonry', *AQC* 119 (2006), pp. 234–55.

92 Williams to R.A.H. Morrow (Grand Secretary, United Lodge), 23 January 2003. See also N.B. Cryer, 'Freemasonry and the Church of England', in *Freemasonry and Religion* (London, 1985), and [R. Runcie], *Freemasonry and Christianity: Are They Compatible?* (London, 1987). For a critique of Masonic ritual, see W. Hannah, *Darkness Visible* (London, 1952).

93 *The Times*, 5 September 1874, p. 9. Ripon had to admit to Cardinal Manning that during his time as a Freemason he 'never heard a single word uttered against Altar or State' (*AQC* 69, pp. 324–5; *AQC* 98, pp. 76–80).

94 R.J. Galloway, *A Passionate Humility: Frederick Oakeley and the Oxford Movement* (Leominster, 1999), p. 36.

95 F.M. Turner, *John Henry Newman: The Challenge to Evangelical Religion* (New Haven CT, 2002), pp. 536–8; Galloway, *A Passionate Humility*, pp. 158–60, 174, 181, 188, 190–91, 194–200.

96 T. Mozley, *Reminiscences, Chiefly of Oriel College and the Oxford Movement*, vol. 2 (London, 1882), p. 5.

97 Apollo minutes, 11 June 1828. Oakeley's autobiographical MS makes no mention of Apollo (Balliol MSS 408–10). He remembered services at Christ Church Cathedral in the 1820s as dismal; those at Oriel as only a little better (F. Oakeley, in *Reminiscences of Oxford*, ed. L.M. Quiller Couch, *Oxford Historical Society* 22 (1892), pp. 329–30).

98 Compiled from *Crockford's* and Apollo minutes.

99 Other appointments at this time included: Jesus College, in 1839, appointing one of its graduates, Henry Watling (Apollo, 1823), to the Rectory at Tredington, Worcestershire (£558 p.a., plus house); University College in 1835 appointing one of its fellows, Peter Hansell (Apollo, 1826), as rector of Kingsdon, Somerset (£435 p.a., plus house); Exeter College in 1830 appointing one of its graduates, James Clutterbuck (Apollo, 1826), as vicar of Long Wittenham, Berkshire (£200 p.a., plus house); Merton College graduate William Chetwynd-Stapylton (Apollo, 1845) moved swiftly into a College living at Malden, Surrey (£447 p.a., plus house).

100 *Oxford Dictionary of National Biography* (H.E.C. Stapleton); H. Stapleton, *The Model Working Parson* (1976). His many writings include *Popery a Novelty* (1851), *Protestantism* (1852) and *A Simple Catechism for Protestant Children* (1877). See also C. Bullock, *W. Weldon Champneys, the Earnest Worker* (*The Crown of the World*, 1884, pp. 225-42). BL 4907 bbb5.

101 *Oxford Dictionary of National Biography* (G. Le G. Norgate; rev. C. Brown); T.E. Yates, *Venn and Victorian Bishops Abroad: The Missionary Policies of Henry Venn and Their Repercussions upon the Anglican Episcopate of the Colonial Period 1841–1872* (London, 1978); H. Cnattingius, *Bishops and Societies: A Study of Anglican Colonial and Missionary Expansion, 1698–1850* (London, 1952).

102 G.W. Cox, *Life of J.W. Colenso D.D. Bishop of Natal*, 2 vols (London, 1888); A.O.J. Cockshut, *Anglican Attitudes* (London, 1959); O. Chadwick, *The Victorian Church*, vol. 1 (London, 1960); P. Hinchliff, *J.W. Colenso: Bishop of Natal* (London, 1964); J. Guy, *The Heretic: A Study of the Life of John William Colenso, 1814–1883* (Pietermaritzburg, 1983).

103 *Oxford Dictionary of National Biography* (T. Seccombe; rev. M.C. Curthoys); Boase, *Modern English Biography*, vol. 3, cols 264–5. Rogers's *Reminiscences*,

ed. R.H. Hadden (London, 1888), make no mention of Apollo.

104 S.R. Hole, *The Memories of Dean Hole* (London, 1892), p. 348.

105 Crook, *Brasenose*, pp. 218–22.

106 A.P. Purey-Cust, 'Four Corner Stones of Freemasonry' (at Holy Trinity Church, Hull; 5 October 1881); 'The Aim and Spirit of Freemasonry' (at York Minster; 28 August 1884); 'Jubilee Sermon' (at Lincoln Cathedral; 2 June 1887); Jubilee Sermon (at York Minster; 14 July 1887). Library, Freemasons' Hall.

107 W.B. Woodgate, *A Modern Layman's Faith (*Nova Religio Laici*) Concerning the Creed and Breed of the 'Thoroughbred Man'* (London, 1893). See also *Oxford Dictionary of National Biography* (H.C. Wace; rev. E. Halladay).

108 F. Weatherly, *Piano and Gown: Recollections* (London, 1926), pp. 66, 69. See also *Oxford Dictionary of National Biography* (J.D. Pickles).

109 W.B. Woodgate, *Reminiscences of An Old Sportsman* (London, 1909), p. 444. For obituaries ('Sportsman and Bohemian'), see *The Times*, 2 November 1920, p. 15, and *The Field*, 6 and 13 November 1920. His pseudonym was 'Wat Bradwood'.

110 Crook, *Brasenose*, ch. 5 *passim*.

111 *Saturday Review*, 26 April 1873, p. 563.

112 *Edinburgh Review* 240 (1924), p. 330; portrait, *Graphic* 13 (1876), pp. 563–4; *Times Literary Supplement*, 2 January 1930, pp. 1–2. See also *Oxford Dictionary of National Biography* (W.H. Scheuerle).

113 J. Foster, *Alumni Oxonienses: The Members of the University of Oxford, 1715–1886* (Oxford, 1888), introduction.

114 V.H.H. Green, *Religion at Oxford and Cambridge* (London, 1964), p. 365.

115 Crook, *Brasenose*, p. 305.

116 J. Foster, *Men at the Bar* (London, 1885).

117 Boase, *Modern English Biography*, vol. 3, col. 851.

118 Briefly an Anglican curate; he switched to law after conversion to Catholicism in 1857 (Boase, *Modern English Biography*, vol. 2, cols 757–8).

119 Foster, *Men at the Bar*.

120 Boase, vol. 4, cols 620–21. Photograph in *Men of Mark*, vol. 7 (London, 1883); caricature in *Vanity Fair* 7 December 1893.

121 C. Cibber, quoted in H.B. Wheatley and P. Cunningham, *London Past and Present*, vol. 2 (London, 1891), p. 343.

122 G. Williams, *Death of a Circuit: Being Some Account of the Oxford Circuit and How It Was Abolished* (London, 2006).

123 Haig was initiated in Elgin's Lodge at Levens in 1881, but did not become a Master Mason until 1924.

124 This section on Apollo casualties in World War I is based on lists prepared by Colin Perrin (Perrin typescript, Apollo Archives). All quotations in this section are taken from Perrin's typescript. Apollo is most grateful to Mr Perrin for his researches.

125 *Oxford Dictionary of National Biography* (E. Rutherford; J.L. Heilbron); J.L. Heilbron, *H.G.J. Moseley: The Life and Letters of an English Physicist, 1887–1915* (1974); T. Downing, *Secret Warriors: Key Scientists, Code Breakers and Propagandists of the Great War* (London, 2014); *The Times*, 27 February 2016, pp. 19, 24.

126 Many a Whitehall office still bears the stamp of Sir Schomberg McDonnell.

127 *Oxford Dictionary of National Biography*.

128 B. Cherry and N. Pevsner, *London 4: North* (London, 1998), p. 267.

129 Ampthill's death in 1935, a day before his former rowing partner at Henley, prompted this epigram, published anonymously in *The Times*:

Oarsmen they lived, and silver goblets mark
The well-timed prowess of their trusty blades:
In death their rhythm kept, they now embark
To row their long last course among the Shades.

Lord Ampthill was also one of the founders of the National Party in 1917, a splinter group of right-wing Tories, which he revived in 1929 (after its demise in 1921) as the National Constitutional Association. See Tony Kushner and Kenneth Lunn, *Traditions of Intolerance: Historical Perspectives on Fascism and Race Discourse in Britain* (Manchester, 1989), p. 159.

130 Their first meetings were free; thereafter the charge was 2 guineas per meeting. By February 1917 the charge had already added £60 to Apollo's bank account (minutes, 27 October 1914 and 10 February 1917). The city lodges' thanks to Apollo were later recorded in the minutes for 1 May 1920.

131 Minutes, 27 October and 27 November 1914.

132 Minutes, 27 October 1914.

133 Sir James Stubbs, *Freemasonry in My Life* (London, 1985), p. 26.

134 When Baynes died the Provincial Grand Master ordered 'masonic mourning' (i.e. black rosettes on regalia) to be worn at the next lodge meeting, the last occasion on which this Victorian custom seems to have been observed.

135 Minutes, 5 March 1919.

136 At that time Grand Lodge knew of only 59, but recent research has discovered many others.

137 Halsey's father had been the Master of Apollo in 1835, and two of Halsey's sons succeeded him as Provincial Grand Master for Hertfordshire: the one who did not go to Oxford, Admiral Sir Lionel Halsey, GCMG, GCVO, KCIE, CB, from 1930 to 1949, and the Revd Canon Frederick Halsey from 1949 to 1952. In his eulogy (minutes, 5 March 1927) Colville Smith claimed that Halsey had also attended the lodge on his sixtieth anniversary as a member and had then been presented with a silver cup, but no contemporary mention of this was made in the minutes.

138 He also oversaw the granting of independence to a number of colonies as a minister in the Commonwealth Relations Office.

139 Several reasons for the general expansion have been advanced, the more persuasive of which seem to connect it with the continuing high social status of the English Craft and the need for the war's survivors to find or renew male friendships and a hobby that provided a peaceful occasional sanctuary, removed from the demands of everyday life.

140 See also p. 28.

141 *Independent*, 4 May 2005; www.independent.co.uk/news/obituaries/ johnnie-stewart-236547.html.

142 Minutes, 30 January 1926.

143 Minutes, 20 February 1926.

144 Obituary, *The Times*, 30 June 1969, p. 10.

145 Elected to Parliament (1910–28), he had been made Baron Bledisloe for his service as a junior minister in the Ministries of Food and then Agriculture and Fisheries.

146 The 6th Earl, who died in 1948, had been the Deputy Speaker in the House of Lords and had been elected the Grand Master of the Grand Lodge of Ireland in 1913.

147 Porritt appears in the film as 'Tom Watson'.

148 Hewetson was a fast bowler and a triple Blue, who became a schoolmaster at St Edward's School, Oxford. Stubbs, *Freemasonry in My Life*, p. 25.

149 The Prince of Wales (Prov. GM for Surrey, later King Edward VIII), the Duke of York (Prov. GM for Middlesex, later King George VI and a Past Grand Master) and the Duke of Kent (Prov. GM for Wiltshire and Grand Master). Porritt went on to become Serjeant Surgeon to the Queen from 1952 until 1967.

150 Porritt served as a surgeon with the 21st Army in North Africa and Europe, taking part in the D-Day landings in Normandy. He was awarded a CBE and a war-substantive rank of lieutenant-colonel.

151 Porritt to Griffith as Secretary of Apollo, 24 October 1982, appended to the minutes of 23 October 1982. Much of the above information can be found in the obituary in the *Independent* of 4 January 1994 and in J.W. Daniel's *History of Royal Alpha Lodge* (Rochester, 2006).

152 Obituary, *Independent*, 8 December 1992.

153 Obituary, *Daily Telegraph*, 27 October 2001.

154 Minutes, 4 February 1928.

155 See p. 127.

156 Obituary (by Warren Hoge), *New York Times*, 6 August 2001.

157 John Frederick Wolfenden joined Apollo from Churchill Lodge while he was a don at Magdalen. Minutes, 28 February 1931.

158 He succeeded to the earldom on the death of his father in 1940, his elder brother becoming the 14th Duke of Hamilton.

159 Elected as a Scottish representative peer from 1945 until 1963, Selkirk was the Conservative Paymaster-General 1953–55, Chancellor of the Duchy of Lancaster 1955–57 and First Lord of the Admiralty 1957–59.

160 Minutes, 3 February 1923.

161 The Master of Apollo (G. Bourne-Taylor) attended that meeting and presented Skipwith with facsimiles of the pages from the Minutes Book recording his Initation,

Passing and Raising. The Master commented that the year 1926 had begun with Baird's demonstration of the transmission of moving pictures by wireless and ended with the release of *The Jazz Singer*, starring Al Jonson and heralding 'talking pictures'. Minutes, 24 February 1996.

162 See letter inserted in place of the minutes for 23 October 1937 from the Provincial Grand Secretary of Suffolk.

163 See above, pp. 119-20.

164 'Luckhurst, Tim: War Correspondents', in *1914–1918-Online. International Encyclopedia of the First World War* (Freie Universität Berlin, 8 October 2014); https://encyclopedia.1914-1918-online.net/article/war_correspondents.

165 'In the 1920s he became a noted player of cricket, tennis and hockey, participating in international competitions, and in 1931 he toured Canada with the Marylebone Cricket Club; he was acknowledged as a master gamesman in Stephen Potter's book *Gamesmanship*' (Wikipedia).

166 By Chenevix-Trench: see Mark Peel, *The Land of Lost Content: The Biography of Anthony Chenevix-Trench* (Edinburgh, 1996), pp. 35-42. His brother, Frederick Temple KC (All Souls), took silk in 1915, married the master of Balliol's daughter and died as London's Metropolitan Magistrate in 1938, aged 57.

167 Obituary (by Peter Fullerton), *Independent*, 9 November 1996.

168 The Prestonian Lecture is the only official lecture of the UGLE. The lecturer is selected annually.

169 Minutes, 3 June 1972.

170 For further details of his legal career, see the sympatico website. www3.sympatico.ca/wfmcgee/Brett/Historical/Robert_Henry_Brett.html

171 When the war started, Grand Lodge

initially suspended the activitiy of all its lodges, but the order had been withdrawn by the time Grand Lodge met later in the same month (September 1939).

172 Unfortunately, the lodge records and an Internet search provide little information about Saxton himself beyond the facts that his book, *The Economics of Price Determination*, was published by Oxford University Press in 1942, and that he is shown as a D.Phil. in the minutes in 1945. Saxton's minutes are somewhat fuller than his predecessor's, though still too formal to attract a historian's interest very often – except for some written between June 1953 and May 1954, containing the longest record of discussions within the lodge since 1914. The matter discussed was the proposal to transfer the lodge's own 'Building Fund' to the Provincial Grand Lodge for its proposed new Provincial Masonic Hall.

173 Minutes, 22 November 1958.

174 Horlock's visits became less frequent in the 1960s and he died in 2009. His obituary was published in *The Times* on 27 August.

175 Minutes, 8 November 1941.

176 The John Griffith Memorial Fund was set up in 1993 by members of Jesus College in memory of John Griffith and may be applied to the support of a John Griffith Memorial Scholarship, normally awarded to a graduate/undergraduate of a university in Eastern Europe engaged in advanced study or research in Classics.

177 A.T.M. Myres was proposed for initiation by the Revd Miles Weight Myres DD, the UGLE's Grand Chaplain in 1931; his seconder was Professor John Linton Myres, who was the Master of Apollo in 1898.

178 Quoted by Sir James Stubbs in his eulogy, recorded in the minutes of 2 June 1990.

179 *The Times*, 3 September 2012. Mandleberg's major Masonic work was his

Ancient and Accepted (London, 1995).

180 White had succeeded P. Colville Smith as Grand Secretary in 1937.

181 *The Times*, 25 February 2000.

182 Chamberlain's death is recorded in the minutes of the meeting held in Magdalen in November 1944.

183 From Quicke's obituary in the *Daily Telegraph*, 4 January 2010.

184 Harewood had recently succeeded Prince George, Duke of Kent, KG, as Grand Master after the Duke's death on active service.

185 'The Airmen's Stories – S/Ldr. A P Hope', www.bbm.org.uk/airmen/HopeAP.htm.

186 Sir Julian Paget (ed.), *Second to None: The Coldstream Guards, 1650–2000* (Barnsley, 2000) ch. 7, n. 25.

187 Obituary, *Daily Telegraph*, 30 April 2008.

188 He later became the Conservative MP for Stroud (1955–87) and a junior minister; he was knighted in 1981.

189 Maurice Wiles, 'Lampe, Geoffrey William Hugo (1912–1980)', *Oxford Dictionary of National Biography* (2004), ch. 7.1.

190 Farley Mowat, *And No Birds Sang* (Toronto, 1979), p. 173.

191 For an account of his exploits in the SOE see his *Setting Europe Ablaze* (Surrey, 1983).

192 He left the European Parliament in 1975.

193 *Sydney Morning Herald*, 7 December 2005.

194 Obituary of Robert (Fleetwood) Hesketh, *Daily Telegraph*, 27 December 2004.

195 Reported in the obituary of his son, Robert (Fleetwood) Hesketh, published in the *Daily Telegraph* on 27 December 2004.

196 See also Daniel Byrne-Rothwell, *The Byrnes and the O'Byrnes*, vol. 2 (Colonsay, 2010), 366–7. Leicester-Warren eventually inherited Tabley House in Knutsford. He left it to the nation on his death.

197 Sir Ernest Cooper, born in Canada in 1877, had been the managing director of Gillette Industries Ltd and was inaccurately described by his obituarist in *The Times* of 8 February 1962 as 'the Chief Executive Officer of English Freemasonry'. (The President of the BGP is the equivalent of the chairman of a company's board of directors, while its employee, the Grand Secretary, is the chief executive officer.)

198 www.apollo357.com/index.php/history/1914-1969, 15 August 2015.

199 In October 1963 (when 'Bro Daniel … delivered a most interesting and informative talk on his experience of attending Masonic Lodges in Germany during the past academic year'), June 1964 (when 'the Ancient Charges were read in full'), October 1964 and June 1965.

200 *Virgin Islands News Online*, 7 May 2014, 'Hon. Ralph T. O'Neal OBE will not seek reelection!'

201 Minutes, 8 May 2010. The original article appeared in *AQC* 112 (1999).

202 Minutes, 11 June 2011.

203 Obituary, *Telegraph*, 11 April 2008.

204 These were mounted in a presentation box with a suitable inscription and deposited with the Provincial (Masonic) Museum. It is probable that Dr Spalding bought them from the lodge when they were sold off in 1973 to keep running costs down.

205 *The Times*, 2 March 2011, 'Register', p. 48.

206 See the minutes for February and October 1961 and Cartwright's entry in Frederick Smyth's *A Reference Book For Freemasons* (London, 1998).

207 'Lodged' there presumably by J.G. Griffith, the treasurer and a fellow of the College.

208 This little ritual is first recorded in the minutes of February 1961.

209 *The Times*, 13 June 1967.

210 *The Times*, 3 June 1948.

211 'The King as a Freemason', *The Times*, 13 February 1952, p. 6.

212 *The Times*, 'Services Notices' 21 March 1951, and 'News in Brief' 20 June 1951.

213 *The Times*, 9 May 1957, and 'Freemasonry: Scots Church Remains Uncommitted', 27 May 1965.

214 The committee consisted of Francis Leo Clark (the Master, from St Peter's, born in 1920 and later a judge), the Revd B. Williams (Senior Warden), Griffith (Treasurer), Saxton, Costin and Giles H. Rooke (born in 1930 and later His Hon. Judge Giles Rooke, PJGD).

215 Minutes: November 1942, April 1951, October 1953, January to 29 May 1954, October 1958, May and June 1960, March 1963 and February 1964.

216 Costin died in office a few months later and his successor, John Kiteley, had to be installed by a Past Master of the lodge, Paul Atyeo.

217 Minutes, 8 May 1970.

218 Minutes, October 1974.

219 Minutes, November 1976, November 1977. He had agreed to continue as Apollo's representative on the OMHC board after the building's purchase, commenting that 'this small duty … required but little attention' (minutes, February 1964).

220 Griffith included in the figure of £22 the costs of registering the new member with Grand Lodge, the Grand Lodge and Provincial Grand Lodge dues, and a copy of the *Book of Constitutions*.

221 Minutes, October 1982, February 1983, April 1984, June 1988, May 1989, January and

February 1991, May and October 1992, and February 1994.

222 Minutes, November 1975, March 1980, May 1989. The total raised by the Province as a whole for that appeal reached £1.1 million.

223 Minutes, February 1994.

224 At the time of writing (December 2016), Englefield is the senior member of the Supreme Council of the Ancient and Accepted Rite (see also fn 230).

225 Morrow was the fourth Apollonian to hold the office since 1900, the others being Sir Philip Colville Smith, Sir James Stubbs and J. W. Daniel.

226 Unusually, Cockin's eulogy in the Minute Book (May 1999) records his leading position in another masonic body, the Trinitarian Christian 'Ancient and Accepted Rite'; he became a member of its nine-man ruling body, the Supreme Council, joining two other Apollonians, Sir James Stubbs and J.W. Daniel.

227 Minutes, October 2001.

228 Bourne-Taylor's early minutes follow and then develop the lighter style adopted by Griffith and Cockin, but once he started to add 'glosses' they revert to the minimalist style of Colville Smith a century earlier. Unlike his minutes, however, these glosses will not be opened to public scrutiny until 50 years have elapsed since their deposit in the Bodleian Library.

229 While Geoffrey Bourne-Taylor was Secretary of the lodge one of his sons, Robin (see below, Chapter XII), was initiated in it and another, William, received his Second Degree there after his initiation in Westminster and Keystone Lodge in London.

230 Shilson joined the 'Masonic civil service' in 2015 when he was appointed as the Grand Secretary General of the Supreme Council of the Ancient and Accepted Rite, a post previously held by two other Apollonians, J.W. Daniel and A.E. Englefield. In 2018 Dr Staples was appointed as Grand Secretary and is thus the fifth Apollonian to hold that office.

231 Hillier B.A. Wise (see above) had been similarly honoured by the Grand Master in 1997.

232 Boys-Stones recently joined two other Apollonians on the Committee of General Purposes of Supreme Grand Chapter of Royal Arch Masons – Dr Malcolm Aish (President) and Professor Stephen Tucker.

233 See the Minutes of the meeting held in October 2005 when the Lodge considered 'the following emendations to the preamble to the By Laws [sic]: (i) By ancient tradition, membership of the lodge is normally restricted to matriculated members of Oxford University and to members of Congregation. (ii) By ancient tradition, the WM of the lodge is chosen from those brethren who are in residence. However, from time to time, this may not prove to be either possible, or in the best interests of the Lodge. Under such circumstances the Lodge Committee may recommend a worthy brother, appropriately qualified as a past Warden, who is able to demonstrate a clear commitment to the especial duties of this office.'

234 Obituary (by Geoffrey Bourne-Taylor), The Times, 29 October 2011.

235 Minutes, November 1999.

236 Minutes, for example: January 1976, March 1977, May 1981, February 1992, January 1995, May 1996 and June 1999.

237 On one such occasion, on 25 November 1995, when a party of French Masons from the Elias Ashmole Lodge in Paris attended, the Secretary read the minutes of the previous meeting in both French and English. There were also regular visits to and from Westminster and Keystone Lodge and

the Oxford and Cambridge University Lodge in London, and the Isaac Newton University Lodge in Cambridge (of which its Master is 'an honoured guest' at Apollo during his Mastership).

238 Minutes, November 2000.

239 www.universitiesscheme.com

240 See Stubbs, Freemasonry in My Life, p. 29: 'even though there may be some justification for describing the Apollo as a "sausage machine" one can adapt Sir Winston Churchill's remark and proudly say "Some machine, some sausages!"'

241 In June 2015 the ballroom could not be made available, and Apollo met in the debating chamber of the Oxford Union Society. Meetings are usually held in the Randolph's ballroom, a room large enough for the already laid dining tables to be clustered at one end during the ceremonies. Once the lodge is closed the brethren retire to the adjacent (private) bar, the tables are restored to their normal places and the hotel staff serve a three-course dinner, with wine, to rarely fewer than sixty and often more than a hundred members and visitors. The dining charge at the time of writing is about £38.

242 Obituary, The Freemason, 13 November 1937, pp. 338–9. See also The Freemason, 9 September 1917, p. 118.

243 Stubbs, Freemasonry in My Life. See also Masonic Records, August 1967; The Times, 4 April 2000.

244 Obituaries, Masonic Record, August and December 1969; AQC 81 (1968), pp. 254–5 (J.W. Stubbs). See also Sunday Times, 10 May 1953.

245 Obituary (by Geoffrey Bourne-Taylor), The Times, 29 October 2011.

246 United Grand Lodge of England, Freemasonry: An Approach to Life (London, 1989 and later), p. 11.

GLOSSARY OF MASONIC TERMS

(For a fuller glossary see Frederick Smyth, *A Reference Book for Freemasons* [1998].)

Board of General Purposes
The executive committee of the United Grand Lodge of England (see below).

Craft
'The Craft' is a synonym for the three fundamental degrees of Freemasonry ('Entered Apprentice', 'Fellow Craft' and 'Master Mason') which are 'worked' in lodges of Freemasons. A 'Craft' lodge owes ultimate allegiance to and receives its authority to work these degrees from a 'Grand Lodge', which may delegate some of its powers to a Metropolitan, Provincial or, overseas, a District Grand Lodge (see below).

Degrees
See 'Craft' above. There are also degrees beyond the Craft, organized under autonomous or 'sovereign' bodies. The closest to the Craft is the Royal Arch (see below), which, like the others, requires that an applicant is at least a Master Mason in the Craft. Other Masonic degrees, orders and rites mentioned in this history are 'the Rose Croix' (the 18th degree of the Ancient and Accepted Rite, supervised by the Supreme Council of the 33rd Degree) and the degree of Mark Master Mason under the Grand Lodge of Mark Master Masons (see below).

Director of Ceremonies
The officer within a lodge responsible for its ceremonial work.

District
Lodges in a territory overseas organized under a District Grand Lodge, itself subject to the Grand Lodge.

'English' Freemasonry
Freemasonry practised under the authority of the United Grand Lodge of England (UGLE).

Founding Master
The first Master of a lodge.

Grand
A prefix used to distinguish ranks and administrative bodies above those of a 'private' lodge. Officers in a Metropolitan, Provincial or District 'Grand' Lodge are styled 'Provincial/ District Grand' officers. A 'Grand Officer' is an officer of the Grand Lodge itself, 'Senior Grand Deacon' for example.

Grand Charity
One of the Grand Lodge's major charities.

Grand Lodge
The Masonic body that has the ultimate masonic authority over a group of lodges. The first Grand Lodge, the Grand Lodge of England, was formed in 1717 by four London lodges. Since its amalgamation

with its rival Grand Lodge in England in 1813 it has been known as the United Grand Lodge of England (UGLE). Today it has about 7,400 lodges within its jurisdiction and a membership of about 205,000.

Initiation

The ceremony at which a candidate is admitted into Freemasonry – as an 'Entered Apprentice Freemason'.

Installation

The annual meeting of a lodge at which its elected Master is installed in the Master's chair.

Join

A Freemason is initiated (see above) in his 'Mother' lodge but can then, if elected, join another lodge or lodges.

Lodge

A lodge (or 'Private Lodge' as it is termed in the UGLE's *Book of Constitutions*) is the smallest yet most important unit or group of Freemasons in the Craft, authorized to meet as such and to work the three degrees of Craft Freemasonry by the Grand Master of the Grand Lodge.

Mark Master Masons (Grand)

A major and independent offshoot of the 'Craft' (see above).

Master

One who presides over a lodge. He has to be a Master Mason (see below) and to have served as a Warden in a lodge for at least one year.

Master Mason

A Freemason who has taken the third of the three degrees of Craft Freemasonry, the preceding two being those of 'Entered Apprentice' and 'Fellow Craft'.

Metropolitan Grand Lodge

The umbrella organization for the 1,300 or so lodges in London. These have recently been organized under a Metropolitan (rather than a 'Provincial') Grand Lodge, headed by a Metropolitan Grand Master.

MW (Most Worshipful)

The prefix applied to the Grand Master and his Pro Grand Master.

Officers and Offices

The officers and offices of lodges (Grand, Metropolitan, Provincial, District and Private) mentioned in the text are shown in the table on page 201.

OSM

The Grand Master's Order of Service to Masonry, a rare distinction awarded for special service to the Craft.

Past

A prefix normally applied to a former holder of an active office, a Past Master of a lodge for example. However, the Grand Master and his Metropolitan/Provincial/District Grand Masters may honour members by appointing them directly to 'Past' rank even if they have not held active office, to 'Past Assistant Grand Director of Ceremonies' or 'PSGW' (Past Senior Grand Warden), for example.

Prestonian Lecturer

The Prestonian Lecturer is appointed annually on the nomination of the Board of General Purposes by the Trustees of the Prestonian Fund. His lecture is the only one given with the authority of the Grand Lodge.

Pro Grand Master

In the UGLE the office of Pro Grand Master can be filled only when the Grand Master is a prince of the blood royal. Until 1976 its holder had to be a peer of the realm. The office is second only to the Grand Master's, and its occupant is the royal Grand Master's right-hand man, a Masonic elder statesman to whom he can leave the oversight of the Craft's internal and external affairs, and who represents him when he is unable to preside over meetings of the Grand Lodge or to participate in public ceremonies.

Province/Provincial Grand Lodge

An administrative organization of lodges within the 'home' jurisdiction of the Grand Lodge, similar to a District Grand Lodge overseas.

Rose Croix

The Christian 'Rose Croix' degree, which had been worked in England since the 1770s, was incorporated into the 'Ancient and Accepted Rite of Freemasonry' as the eighteenth of its thirty-three degrees in 1845 when a Supreme Council of the rite for England and Wales was established. The rite, often referred to as 'the Rose Croix', is an autonomous organization with no formal relationship with the United Grand Lodge of England, though it requires that applicants for membership of the rite are Master Masons (see above) and profess the Trinitarian Christian faith.

Royal Arch

A supplementary Order of Freemasonry so closely related to 'the Craft' that the Grand Master and Pro Grand Master of the UGLE occupy *ex officio* its comparable offices ('First Grand Principal', 'Pro First Grand Principal'). It is administered from the offices of the Grand Lodge.

RW (Right Worshipful)

The prefix accorded to those immediately below the rank of Grand or Pro Grand Master, namely Deputy and Assistant Grand Masters, Metropolitan/Provincial/District Grand Masters and Grand Wardens.

Tyler

The Tyler of a lodge guards the entrance to its meetings so that none but Freemasons or candidates for admission as Freemasons can enter.

United Grand Lodge of England

See above.

Visitor

A member of another lodge attending a lodge's meeting.

VW (Very Worshipful)

The prefix applied to a few senior offices immediately below that of Grand Warden.

Worshipful

The prefix applied to the Master of a lodge and to those senior to him by virtue of their Metropolitan/Provincial/District or Grand rank.

THE STRUCTURAL ORGANIZATION OF THE UNITED GRAND LODGE OF ENGLAND

GRAND LODGE	METROPOLITAN, PROVINCIAL AND DISTRICT GRAND LODGES	A 'PRIVATE' LODGE
Grand Master	Metropolitan/Provincial/District Grand Master	Master
(Pro Grand Master)		Senior Warden
Deputy Grand Master	Metropolitan/Provincial/District Deputy Grand Master	Junior Warden
Metropolitan, Provincial and District Grand Masters		Chaplain
Senior Grand Warden	Metropolitan/Provincial/District Grand Wardens	Treasurer
Junior Grand Warden		Secretary
Grand Chaplain	Metropolitan/Provincial/District Grand Secretary	Director of Ceremonies
President, Board of General Purposes	etc.	Almoner
Grand Registrar		Charity Steward
Grand Secretary		Senior Deacon
Presidents of Masonic Charities		Junior Deacon
Grand Director of Ceremonies		Organist
Grand Sword Bearer		

(Private Lodges are the basic unit of the organization. They come within the immediate jurisdiction of a Metropolitan, Provincial or, overseas, a District Grand Lodge, which in turn reports to the Grand Lodge.)

APPENDIX 1: MASTERS OF
APOLLO UNIVERSITY LODGE

1819–21	Ireland, John
1822–23	Ogle, James Adey, Trinity College
1824	Ridley, Revd Charles John, University College
1825	Watling, Revd Charles Henry, Jesus College
1826–27	Harington, Richard, Brasenose College
1828–29	Ridley, Revd Charles John, University College
1830–31	Hansell, Revd Peter, University College
1832	Harington, Revd Richard, Brasenose College
1833–34	Ridley, Revd Charles John, University College
1835	Alston, Rowland Gardiner, Christ Church
1836	Sewell, Revd James Edwards, New College
1837	Bingham, Revd Charles William, New College
1838	Cox, Revd William Hayward, St Mary Hall
1839–40	Williams, Revd Henry Blackstone, New College
1841	Fox, William Edward Lane, Balliol College
1842–43	Thomas, Revd George Fuller, Worcester College
1844	Boyd, Frederick, University College
1845–46	Meredith, Revd Charles John, Lincoln College
1847–49	Burstall, Stephen, University College
1850	Portal, George Raymond, Christ Church
1851	Tyrwhitt, Richard St John, Christ Church
1852	Beach, William Wither Bramston, Christ Church
1853	Best, Thomas, Magdalen College
1854	Beach, William Wither Bramston, Christ Church
1855	Malcolm, John Wingfield, Christ Church
1856–57	Pickard, Revd Henry Adair, Christ Church
1858	Codrington, John Edward, Brasenose College
1859–60	Faber, Revd Arthur Henry, New College
1861–62	Norman, Revd Richard Whitmore, Exeter College
1863	Bedford, Revd William Kirkpatrick Riland, Brasenose College
1864–65	Cave-Browne-Cave, Fitzherbert Astley, Brasenose College
1866–67	Short, Revd Walter Francis, New College
1868	Dallin, Thomas Francis, The Queen's College
1869	Lamert, Capt. George Fead, Worcester College
1870	Wyndham, Thomas Heathcote Gerald, Merton College
1871	Jermyn, Revd Edmund, Christ Church
1872	Bird, Reginald, Magdalen College
1873	HRH the Prince of Wales, D.C.L., Christ Church (Bird, Reginald, Magdalen College, W. Deputy M.)
1874	Morrell, Frederick Parker, St John's College
1875	Pickard, Revd Henry Adair, Christ Church
1876	HRH Prince Leopold, D.C.L., Christ Church (Pope, Revd Richard William Massey, B.D., Worcester College, W. Deputy M.)
1877	Sackville-West, Lt-Col. the Hon. William Edward, Christ Church
1878	Hilton, Revd Louis Kercheval, Christ Church
1879	Deane, Revd Henry, St John's College
1880–81	Parratt, Walter, Magdalen College
1882	Hawkins, Edward Lovell, Merton College
1883	Penny, Revd Fraser Hislop, St John's College
1884	Angel-Smith, Revd Stuart Cecil Frank, Christ Church

1885	Morgan, William Lewis, Exeter College	1914	Cowley, Arthur Ernest, Magdalen College
1886	Baynes, Robert Edward, Christ Church	1915–16	Gamlen, John Charles Blagdon, Balliol College
1887	Pope, Revd Richard William Massey, Worcester College	1917	Mackworth, Arthur Christopher Paul, Magdalen College
1888	Wakeman, Henry Offley, All Souls College	1918	Proudfoot, Frank Grégoire, Major, The Queen's College
1889	Sayers, Revd Henry, Christ Church	1919	Smith, Philip Colville, G. Sec., St John's College
1890	Clark, Albert Curtis, The Queen's College	1920	Blockley, Revd Thomas Trotter, Magdalen College
1891	Smith, Philip Colville, St John's College	1921–22	Tawney, John Archer, Brasenose College
1892	Greenwood, Thomas, Exeter College	1923	Whitelocke, Hugh Anthony Bulstrode, Christ Church
1893	Smith, Philip Colville, St John's College	1924	Poole, Edgar Gerard Croker, Trinity College
1894	Wilson, George John, Christ Church	1925	Stewart, Haldane Campbell, Magdalen College
1895	Underhill, George Ernest, Magdalen College	1926	Wrong, Edward Murray, Magdalen College
1896	Smith, Philip Colville, St John's College	1927	Blagden, John Basil, Brasenose College
1897	Stride, William John Francis Keatley, Exeter College	1928	Costin, W.C., St John's College
1898	Myres, John Linton, New College	1929–30	Hewetson, Edward Pearson, Pembroke College
1899	Theodosius, Alfred Fletcher, University College	1931	Bathurst, Hon. William Ralph Seymour, Trinity College
1900	Bussell, Revd Frederick William, Brasenose College	1932	Johnson, Patrick, Magdalen College
1901	Brownrigg, Charles Edward, Magdalen College	1933	Amery, George Douglas, Brasenose College
1902	Davis, Revd Thomas Harold, University College	1934	Weldon, Thomas Dewar, Magdalen College
1903	Thompson, Charles Henry, The Queen's College	1935	Smith, Philip Colville, St John's College
1904	Carter, Albert Thomas, Christ Church	1936	Johnson, Patrick, Magdalen College
1905	Cowley, Arthur Ernest, Magdalen College	1937	Costin, W.C., St John's College
1906	Blockley, Revd Thomas Trotter, Magdalen College	1938–40	Griffith, John Godfrey, New College
1907	Biggs, Revd Charles Richard Davey, St John's College	1941–42	Saxton, Clifford Clive, Magdalen College
1908	Hall, Frederick William, St John's College	1943	Horlock, Henry Wimburn Webb Sudell, Pembroke College
1909	Hartley, Harold Brewer, Balliol College	1944	Gauntlett, John Mildred Deane, New College
1910	Cronshaw, Revd George Bernard, The Queen's College	1945	Horlock, H.W.W.S., Pembroke College
1911	Cowley, Arthur Ernest, Magdalen College	1946	Costin, W.C., St John's College
1912	Cronshaw, Revd George Bernard, The Queen's College	1947–48	Milburn, Robert Leslie Pollington, Worcester College
1913	Douglas, Claude Gordon, St John's College	1949	Gamlen, John Charles Blagdon, Balliol College

1950	Dashwood, John Rawdon, St John's College
1951–52	Lampe, Geoffrey William Hugo, St John's College
1953	Clark, Francis Leo, St Peter's Hall
1954–55	Williams, Thomas Brian, St John's College
1956	Spalding, John Michael Kenneth, New College
1957–58	Bownas, Geoffrey, The Queen's College
1959	Costin, W.C., St John's College
1960	Kiteley, John Frederick, Hertford College
1961–62	Gauntlett, John Mildred Deane, New College
1963	Pierce, Thomas Bryan, St Peter's College
1964–65	Ormerod, Alexander Edward, St Catherine's College
1966	Horn, Charles Bennett, St John's College
1967	Cochrane, John Atholl, St Edmund Hall
1968	Atyeo, Henry Paul Bingham, Exeter College
1969	Costin, W.C., St John's College
1970	Kiteley, John Frederick, Hertford College
1971	Merry, Denis Harry, St Catherine's College
1972	Hollinrake, Roger Barker, Merton College
1973	Webster, David, St John's College
1974	Mitchell, Peter John, St Edmund Hall
1975	Hobby, Roger Maurice, St John's College
1976–77	Griffiths, Robert Amos, University College
1978–79	Saunders, William Bransby Rees, Jesus College
1980	Good, Robert William, Mansfield College
1981	Englefield, Alan John, Worcester College
1984	Cockin, John, Hertford College
1985	Long, James Martin, Christ Church
1986	Parshall, Charles Ward, Trinity College
1987	Hilditch, James Robert Guy, St John's College
1988	Brown, Nigel Kenneth, Hertford College

1989	Baker, Jonathan Mark Richard, St John's College
1990	Tucker, Stephen John, Trinity College
1991	Sanders, James William Ashton, Exeter College
1992	Butler, Peter, MP, St Edmund Hall
1993	Sweeney, Robert Maxwell, Christ Church
1994	Burwood-Taylor, Basil Henry, OBE, St John's College
1995	Bourne-Taylor, Geoffrey Dennis, St Edmund Hall
1996	Marchington, Anthony Frank, Brasenose College
1997	Boys-Stones, George Robin, St John's College
1998	Shields, Derek, Trinity College
1999	Madden, Sebastian Charles Edward Amadeus, Keble College
2000	Lepper, Charles Francis, Lincoln College
2001	Smith, Philip Michael Russon, Lincoln College
2002	Borwick, Simon John, Brasenose College
2003–04	Brett, Justin Edward, Exeter College
2005	Forster, Richard, Trinity College
2006	Johnson, Daniel Miles, Corpus Christi College
2007	Deutschenbauer, Steffen, St Edmund Hall
2008	Noon, Christopher Philip, Christ Church
2009	Fellerman Robin Max, St Edmund Hall
2010	Wain, Alexis William, Keble College
2011	Robbins, Timothy David, Brasenose College
2012	Smithdale, James David Arthur, Christ Church
2013	Petzolt, Sebastian, St Hilda's College
2014	Worth, Jeremy Julian, Keble College
2015	Myatt, Timothy Lloyd, St Anne's College/ Wolfson College
2016	Gerstmayr, Paul Jinpa Gyatso, Balliol College/ St John's College

APPENDIX 2: SECRETARIES OF APOLLO UNIVERSITY LODGE

1818	Wyatt, Thomas, Exeter College; St Aubyn, William, Christ Church
1819	Waller, William, Brasenose College
1820–21	Ogle, James, Trinity College
1822–23	Floyn, Charles, Trinity College
1824	Proctor, Revd N., Jesus College
1825	Holden, C., Trinity College
1826	Paul, Robert, Exeter College
1827	Reid, D., University College
1828–30	Atkinson, William, University College
1831	Jeffreys, Henry, Christ Church
1832	Sutherland, A.J., Christ Church
1833	Williams, Robert, Oriel College
1834	Colbourne, N.W. Ridley, Christ Church
1835	Halsey, Thomas, Christ Church
1836	Holbeck, Hugh W., Christ Church
1837	Wilson, John, Corpus Christi College
1838	Burnett, William, New College
1839	Gee, Richard, Wadham College
1840	Mant, Frederick, New College
1841–42	Lempriere, Charles, St John's College
1843	Vernon, E.H., University; Landen, J.J.B., Worcester College
1844–45	Thompson, William, The Queen's College
1846–47	Williams, Philip, New College
1848	Tristram, Thomas, Lincoln College; Best, Thomas, Magdalen College
1849–50	Lechmere, E.W., Christ Church
1851	Walsh, Digby, Balliol College
1852	Ogle, Octavius, Wadham College
1853	Harrison, W.W., Brasenose College
1854	Fairborough, J.C., Magdalen College
1855	Orton, Hon. L.G., Magdalen College
1856	Wakeman, O.F., Christ Church
1857	Martyn, Charles, Balliol College
1858	Harrison, W.W., Brasenose College; Mitford, Algernon, Christ Church
1859–61	Williamson, Victor, Christ Church
1862	Cave-Brown-Cave, Fitzherbert, Brasenose College
1863–64	Latham, P.A., Brasenose College
1865	Galland, Basil, Lincoln College
1866	Robbins, Leopold, Trinity College; Thompson, William, The Queen's College (resigned)
1867–68	Stephenson, Henry Stillington, The Queen's College
1869	Borlase, William, Trinity College
1870–72	Churchill, Cameron, Worcester College; Conway, Sir John, Bt, Christ Church
1873	Riach, Hugh, Magdalen College
1874	Fletcher, W.R.B., Christ Church
1875	Sackville-West, Lt-Col. Hon. William, Christ Church and Keble College; Bodley, J.E. Courteney, Balliol College
1876–78	Bodley, J.E. Courteney, Balliol College; Paget, Cecil George, Christ Church
1879	Yule, C.J F., Magdalen College
1880–81	Hawkins, E.L., Magdalen College; Maguire, J.R., All Souls College

1882	Morgan, W.L., Christ Church
1883	Baynes, R.E., Merton College
1884	Darbyshire, Dr S.D., Balliol College
1885	Wakeman, H.O., All Souls College and Keble College; Bulley, F.P., Magdalen College
1886	Onions, J.H., Christ Church
1887	Clark, A.C., Queens' College, Cambridge
1888	Sayers, Revd H., Magdalen College and Christ Church
1889–92	Pope, Revd R.W.M., Worcester College
1893	Asst. Thompson, W.J., Exeter College
1894	Asst. Croxall, E.R.T., Hertford College
1895	Smith, P. Colville, St John's College; Asst. Collison, Harry, Merton College
1896	Wilson, G.J., Christ Church
1897	Asst. Leete, H.B., Worcester College
1898	Smith, P. Colville, St John's College; Asst. Brownrigg, C.E., Magdalen College
1899–1900	Asst. Thompson, C.H., The Queen's College
1901	Asst. Carter, A.T., Christ Church
1902	Asst. Cowley, A.E., Wadham College
1903	Asst. Mayer, F.H., Christ Church
1904	Asst. Frank, P.E., Magdalen College
1905	Asst. Hall, F.W., St John's College
1906	Asst. Hartley, H.B., Balliol College
1907	Asst. Lloyd, Revd R.H., Trinity College
1921–27	Smith, P. Colville, St John's College
1929–34	Smith, P. Colville, St John's College
1935	Corbin, P.G., Balliol College
1936	Smith, P. Colville, St John's College
1937–44	Johnson, P.
1945–57	Saxton, C.C., Magdalen College
1958–69	Griffith, J.G., Jesus College
1971–83	Griffith, J.G., Jesus College
1987–97	Cockin, J., Hertford College
1998–2011	Bourne-Taylor, G.D., St Edmund Hall
2012–present	Noon, C.P., Christ Church

APPENDIX 3: MEMBERS OF APOLLO UNIVERSITY LODGE KILLED IN THE FIRST WORLD WAR

List compiled by Geoffrey Bourne-Taylor with acknowledgement to Colin Perrin (from WW1 Remembered: Memories of and by Club Members, Oxford and Cambridge Club, *2015, pp. 35–9).*

2/Lt Horace Aubrey Back, age 35. Gloucestershire Regt; Brasenose College

Capt. Richard Vincent Barker, age 34. Royal Welsh Fusiliers; New College

Major Lord (Henry Gorell Barnes) Gorell, DSO, age 35. Royal Field Artillery; Trinity College

Lt Col. Percy William Beresford, DSO, age 42. Royal Fusiliers; Magdalen College

Lt Aubrey Francis Blackwell MC, age 27. Royal Field Artillery; Oriel College

Rev. Philip John Thomas Blakeway TD, age 50. City of London Yeomanry; Magdalen College

Lt Rowland George Reece Bowen, age 22. Royal Fusiliers; Exeter College

Lt Edward Fenwick Boyd, age 24. Northumberland Fusiliers; University College

Lt Michael Lloyd Braithwaite, age 34. Royal Flying Corps; New College

2/Lt Peter Handcock Broughton-Adderley, MC, age 27. Scots Guards; Exeter College

2/Lt William Jacob Bryan, age 27. Royal Fusiliers; Christ Church

2/Lt John Stamp Garthorne Burrell, age 31. Cheshire Regiment; Exeter College

Lt Col. Richard Chester Chester-Master, DSO & bar, age 47. Kings Royal Rifle Corps; Christ Church

Lt Esmé Fairfax Chinnery, age 28. Coldstream Guards/RFC; Brasenose College

Major Henry Francis Clifford, age 45. Gloucester Yeomanry; Christ Church

Capt. John Stanhope Collings-Wells VC, DSO, age 38. Bedfordshire Regt; Christ Church

Capt. William John Hutton Curwen, age 32. Royal Fusiliers; Magdalen College

Capt. George Arthur Murray Docker, age 37. Royal Fusiliers; Oriel College

2/Lt Alan James Ingram Donald, age 21. Manchester Regt; New College

Lt Henry Gamul Farmer, age 28. Seaforth Highlanders; New College

Lt Col. Earl of Feversham, age 37. Kings Royal Rifle Corps; Christ Church

2/Lt Reginald William Fletcher, age 22. Royal Field Artillery; Balliol College

2/Lt Charles Jefford Fowler, age 28. Royal Fusiliers; Trinity College

Major Philip Kirkland Glazebrook DSO, age 37. Cheshire Yeomanry; New College

Capt. Roby Myddleton Gotch, age 26. Sherwood Foresters; New College

Lt Reginald Cumberland Green, age 31. Bedfordshire Regt; Exeter College

Capt. Francis William Lindley Gull, age 28. Rifle Brigade; Christ Church

Lt Cyril Gwyer, age 32. Grenadier Guards; Christ Church

Lt Kenneth Rees Habershon, age 26. Rifle Brigade; New College

Capt. Archibald Robert Hadden, age 28. London Regt; Christ Church

Capt. Edward Hain, age 28. Devon Yeomanry; New College

Major Evan Robert Hanbury, age 30. Leicester Yeomanry; New College

Sapper William Hanna, age 25. Royal Engineer; The Queen's College

Lt George Edgcombe Hellyer, age 23. Hampshire Regt; Christ Church

Revd Oswald Addenbrooke Holden, age 43. Chaplain, Exeter College

2/Lt Lyulph Walter Mowbray Howard, age 29. The Queen's (Royal West Surrey Regt); New College

Capt. John Leslie Johnston, age 30. Ox and Bucks L.I.; Magdalen College

Lt The Hon. Edward James Kay-Shuttleworth, age 27. Rifle Brigade; Balliol College

Capt. Archibald Edward Kennedy, age 35. Arg. and Suth. Highlanders; Oriel College

Lt Henry Cyril Dixon Kimber, age 22. Royal Field Artillery; University College

Capt. William Gabriel King-Price, age 39. Manchester Regt; Merton College

Lt Andrew Brooks Knowles, age 31. 17th Indian Cavalry; Lincoln College

Capt. Ronald Owen Lagden, age 26. Kings Royal Rifle Corps; Oriel College

Lt Guy Francis Lawrence, age 25. Grenadier Guards; Trinity College

Capt. John Francis Leather, age 24. Royal Army Service Corps; Balliol College

Major Richard Percy Lewis, age 41. Devonshire Regiment; University College

Maj. The Hon. Charles Henry Lyell, age 43. Royal Garrison Artillery; New College

2/Lt Kenneth Fitzpatrick Mackenzie, age 24. Queen's Own Cameron Hrs; Trinity College

Lt Norman Lindsay Mackie, age 24. Machine Gun Corps; Hertford College

Lt Duncan Mackinnon, age 30. Scots Guards; Magdalen College

2/Lt Arthur Christopher Paul Mackworth, age 31. Rifle Brigade; Magdalen College

2/Lt Charles Robert Crighton Maltby, age 26. Rifle Brigade; Worcester College

2/Lt Ferdinand Marsham-Townshend, age 35. Scots Guards; Christ Church

2/Lt Myles Lewis Wigan Matthews, age 23. Royal W. Kent Regiment; University College

Maj. The Hon. Sir Schomberg Kerr McDonnell, GCVO, KCB, age 57. Queen's Own Cam Highldrs; University College

Lt Eric Archibald McNair, VC, age 24. Royal Sussex Regiment; Magdalen College

2/Lt Edward Guy Melland, age 26. Cheshire Regiment; New College

2/Lt The Hon. Charles Thomas Mills MP, age 28. Scots Guards; Magdalen College

2/Lt Henry Gwyn Jeffreys Moseley, age 27. Royal Engineers; Trinity College

Capt. John Norwood VC, age 38. Westminster Dragoons; Exeter College

Lt Rt Hon. Lord Henry Bligh Fortesque Parnell (5th Baron Congleton), age 24. Grenadier Guards; New College

Lt John Nicol Fergusson Pixley, age 29. Grenadier Guards; Merton College

Lt George Henry Fosbroke Power, age 21. Middlesex Regiment; New College

Lt Harold Leslie Rayner, age 26. Devonshire Regiment; Corpus Christi College

Lt Col Lord Ridley DL, age 41. Northumberland Yeom.; Balliol College

Lt Joel Harrison Seaverns, age 22. Royal Fusiliers; Christ Church

Capt. Herbert Shepherd Shepherd-Cross, age 39. Machine Gun Corps; University College

Lt Henry Langton Skrine, age 34. Somerset Light Infantry; Balliol College

Lt Lothrop Lewis de Berniere Smith, age 23. Rifle Brigade; Magdalen College

Lt Harold Rolleston Stables, age 28. Royal Fusiliers; New College

2/Lt Cyril Edward Seymour Stephenson, age 37. Queen's Royal Lancers; Magdalen College

2/Lt Daniel Pike Stephenson, age 25. N. Staffs Regiment; Lincoln College

2/Lt Arthur Amyot Steward, age 35. Royal Flying Corps; Magdalen College

2/Lt Kenneth Douglas Thomson, age 29. Argyll &Suth Highlanders; University College

Lt Col Lord Alexander Thynne DSO, age 45. Wiltshire Regiment; Balliol College

2/Lt Bruno Wolfgang Wahl, age 36. Indian Army; Balliol College

2/Lt Gordon Stafford Woodhouse, age 26. Royal Field Artillery; Lincoln College

Lt William Reginald Fitzthomas Wyley, age 24. Royal Field Artillery; Balliol College

Lt Edward John Henry Wynne, age 22. Grenadier Guards; Christ Church

Lt Raymond Gilbert Hooker Yeatherd, age 25. Queen's Bays; Christ Church

Capt James Hamilton Langdon Yorke MC, age 33. The Welch Regiment; Oriel College

APPENDIX 4:
APOLLO'S OLYMPIANS

WILLIAM HENRY GRENFELL, 1ST Baron Desborough (Balliol), Fencing (Epée team) silver medallist in 1906, and first ever flag bearer for Great Britain in the Parade of Nations, had been initiated in Apollo University Lodge on 23 February 1875. He was a Member of Parliament, had rowed twice for Oxford in the Boat Race (1877 – the only dead heat; 1878 – Oxford victory) and was president of the London Olympic Games in 1908.[†]

Guy Nickalls (Magdalen), Rowing (Eight) gold medallist in 1908, had been initiated in Apollo University Lodge on 24 February 1891.

Wilfrid Alexander Johnson (Trinity), Lacrosse silver medallist in 1908, had been initiated in Apollo University Lodge on 30 May 1899.

Duncan Mackinnon (Magdalen), Rowing (Coxless Four) gold medallist in 1908, was subsequently initiated in Apollo University Lodge on 9 February 1909. As a lieutenant in the Scots Guards he was killed in action at Ypres in the Battle of Passchendaele on 9 October 1917.

Harold Evelyn Holding (Oriel), Athletics (800 metres) competitor in 1908, had been initiated in Apollo University Lodge on 25 February 1902.

John Charles Field-Richards (Keble), Motor Boating (Mixed B Class and Mixed C Class) double gold medallist in 1908, had been initiated in Apollo University Lodge on 24 June 1897.

Sir William Lorenzo Parker, 3rd Baronet (New College), Rowing (Eight) silver medallist in 1912, had been initiated in Apollo University Lodge on 27 April 1909.

Arthur Frederick Reginald Wiggins (New College), Rowing (Eight) silver medallist in 1912, had been initiated in Apollo University Lodge on 4 June 1912, forty-five days before winning his silver medal on 19 July 1912.

Edgar Richard Burgess (Magdalen), Rowing (Eight) gold medallist in 1912, was subsequently initiated in Apollo University Lodge on 28 October 1912.

Colonel Arthur Espie Porritt, Baron Porritt (Magdalen), Athletics (100 metres) bronze medallist (for New Zealand) in 1924, was subsequently initiated in Apollo University Lodge on 13 June 1925. The 100 metres race in which he won bronze was the famous *Chariots of Fire* race, but his name was changed in the film to Tom Watson (apparently because of Porritt's modesty about this achievement). He was later Serjeant Surgeon to the Queen, president of the BMA, RCS and RCM, Governor General of New Zealand, Grand Master of the Grand Lodge of New Zealand, and received many honours (GCMG, GCVO, CBE).

John Edward (Jack) Lovelock (Exeter), Athletics (1500 metres) gold medallist (for New Zealand) in 1936, had been initiated in Apollo University Lodge on 18 November 1933. He set the world record in the 1500 metres final.

Derek James Neville Johnson (Lincoln), Athletics (800 metres and 4 x 400 metres relay) silver and bronze medallist in 1956, had been initiated in Apollo University Lodge on 30 April 1955.

Robin Edwin Bourne-Taylor (Christ Church), Rowing (Eight) competitor (9th place) in 2004 and Rowing (Pair) competitor (13th place) in 2008, had been initiated in Apollo University Lodge on 24 November 2001.

† The 1906 Games were known as 'Intercalated Games'. They were at the time considered to be Olympic Games and were referred to as the 'Second International Olympic Games in Athens' by the International Olympic Committee. Whilst medals were distributed to the participants during these games, the medals are not officially recognized by the IOC today.

BIBLIOGRAPHY

Akers-Douglas, E.A., *Chief Whip: The Politial Life and Times of Aretas Akers-Douglas, 1st Viscount Chilston*, London, 1961.

[Anderson, J.], *The Constitutions of the Free-Masons Containing the History, Charges, Regulations etc. of that most Antient and Right Worshipful Fraternity*, 1723; cd. L. Vibert, 1923.

Apollo University Lodge, 1818–2005, Oxford, Bodleian Library, MS. Eng. c. 7363-78, d. 3732-7, MS. Digital 7-22.

[Bede, Cuthbert, pseud.], *Adventures of Mr. Verdant Green*, 1853.

Beresiner, Y., 'The Wilde Oxford Mason', *Masonic Quarterly*, 4 January 2003.

Blackstock, A, *Loyalism in Ireland, 1789–1829*, Woodbridge, 2007.

Boase, F., *Modern English Biography*, 6 vols, London, 1892–1921; repr. 1965.

Bourne-Taylor, G.D., 'Members of the Apollo University Lodge killed in the First World War', *WW1 Remembered: Memories of and by Club Members*, Oxford and Cambridge Club, London, 2015.

[Burr, C.], *Autobiography and Lectures of Lola Montez*, London, 1858.

Byrne-Rothwell, D., *The Byrnes and the O'Byrnes*, House of Lochar, Scottish Booksellers & Publishers, Isle of Colonsay, Argyll, 4 vols., 2010-15.

Cartwright, E.H., *The English Ritual of Craft Masonry*, Penrose, 1936.

Cartwright, E.H., *Masonic Ritual: A Commentary on the Freemasonic Ritual*, 3rd edn, London, 1985.

Cnattingius, H., *Bishops and Societies: A Study of Anglican Colonial and Missionary Expansion, 1698–1850*, London, 1952.

Complete Baronetage.

Complete Peerage.

Cox, G.W., *Life of J.W. Colenso*, 2 vols, London, 1888.

Crockford's Clerical Directory.

Crook, J. Mordaunt, *Brasenose: The Biography of an Oxford College*, Oxford, 2008; 2010.

Cryer, N.B., 'Freemasonry and the Church of England', in *Freemasonry and Religion*, United Grand Lodge of England, London, 1985.

Daniel, J.W., 'Pure – and Accepted – Masonry: The Craft and the Extra-Craft Degrees, 1843–1901', *Ars Quatuor Coronatorum* 106, 1993, pp. 68-102.

Daniel, J.W., *History of Royal Alpha Lodge*, Rochester, 2006.

Daniel, J.W., *Masonic Networks and Connections*, London, 2007, ch. 3 'Canon Portal', pp. 68–100.

Daniel, J.W., 'The 4th Earl of Carnarvon (1831–1890) and Freemasonry in the British Empire', doctoral thesis, University of Sheffield, 2010.

Dodds-Parker, A.D., *Setting Europe Ablaze*, Ascot, 1984.

Ferrer-Benimeli, J.A., 'The Catholic Church and Freemasonry', *Ars Quatuor Coronatorum* 119, 2006, pp. 234–55.

Foster, J., *Alumni Oxonienses: The Members of the University of Oxford, 1715–1886*, 8 vols, Oxford, 1888.

Galloway, R.J., *A Passionate Humility: Frederick Oakeley and the Oxford Movement*, Leominster, 1999.

Godding, J.W. Sleigh, *A History of the Westminster and Keystone Lodge*, Plymouth, 1907.

Gould, R.F., *History of Freemasonry*, 2 vols, New York, 1884.

Hamill, J., 'The Earl of Moira, Acting Grand Master, 1790–1813', *Ars Quatuor Coronatorum* 93, 1980, pp. 31–48.

Hamilton, G., *Parliamentary Reminiscences and Reflections, 1886–1906*, London, 1922.

Hannah, W., *Darkness Visible*, London, 1952.

Hardinge, A., *The Life of Henry Howard Molyneux Herbert, fourth Earl of Carnarvon, 1831-1890*, 2 vols, Oxford, 1925.

Hargreaves-Mawdsley, W.N. (ed.), *Woodforde at Oxford, 1759–76*, Oxford Historical Society N.S. 21, 1969.

Harland-Jacobs, J.L., *Builders of Empire: Freemasons and British Imperialism, 1717–1927*, Chapel Hill NC, 2007.

Hawkins, E.L., 'Two Old Oxford Lodges', *Ars Quatuor Coronatorum* 22, 1909, pp. 166–77.

Heilbron, J.L., *H.G.J. Moseley: The Life and Letters of an English Physicist, 1887–1915*, Berkeley CA, 1974.

Hicks Beach, V., *Sir Michael Hicks Beach*, 2 vols, London, 1932.

Hinchliff, P., *J.W. Colenso*, London, 1964.

Hodder, E., *Life and Work of the Seventh Earl of Shaftesbury*, 3 vols, London, 1887.

Hole, S.R., *The Memories of Dean Hole*, London, 1892.

Holland, C. (ed.), *The Notebooks of a Spinster Lady, 1878–1903*, London, 1919.

Hollinrake, R., 'The Masonic Life and Times of W. Bro. Sir Walter Parratt, K.C.V.O., Master of the Music, Grand Organist', *Ars Quatuor Coronatorum* 112, 1999, pp. 182-221.

Hughan, W.J., *The Old Charges of the British Freemasons*, London, 1872; 1895; supp. 1906.

Hunter Blair, Rev. Sir D.O., *Memories and Musings*, New York, 1929.

Hunter Blair, Rev. Sir D.O., *A Last Medley of Memories*, London, 1936.

Hunter Blair, Rev. Sir D.O., 'Oscar Wilde as I knew Him', *Dublin Review*, July 1938, pp. 90-105.

Jenkins, J.P., 'Jacobites and Freemasons in Eighteenth-century Wales', *Welsh History Review* 9, 1979, pp. 391–406.

Kelly, J., and M. Powell (eds), *Clubs and Societies in Eighteenth-Century Ireland*, Dublin, 2010.

Knoop, D., 'University Masonic Lodges', *Ars Quatuor Coronatorum* 59, 1946, p. 4.

Knoop, D., and G.P. Jones, *A Short History of Freemasonry to 1730*, 1940.

Knoop, D., and G.P. Jones, 'Freemasonry and the Idea of Natural Religion', *Ars Quatuor Coronatorum* 56, 1943, p. 47.

Lemprière, J., *Classical Dictionary*, London, 1804.

Long, W., *Memories*, London, 1923.

Lunn, K., and T. Kushner (eds), *Traditions of Intolerance*, Manchester, 1989.

Mackworth, A.C.P., *Varsity Vices*, Oxford, 1908.

Magnus, Sir P., *King Edward the Seventh*, London, 1964.

Mandleberg, C.J., *Ancient and Accepted*, Q.C. Correspondence Circle, 60 Great Queen Street, London, 1995.

Melton, J., *The Rise of the Public in Enlightenment Europe*, Cambridge, 2001.

Mirala, P., *Freemasonry in Ulster, 1733–1813*, Dublin, 2007.

Mowat, F., *And No Birds Sang*, Toronto, 1979.

Mozley, T., *Reminiscences, Chiefly of Oriel College and the Oxford Movement*, 2 vols, London, 1882.

Oxford Dictionary of National Biography, 60 vols, Oxford, 2004.

Peel, M., *The Land of Lost Content: The Biography of Anthony Chenevix-Trench*, Edinburgh, 1996.

Petrie, C., *The Carlton Club*, London, 1955; ed. A. Cooke, 2007.

Poole, Mrs R.L., *Catalogue of Oxford Portraits*, 3 vols, Oxford, 1911–24.

Potter, S., *The Theory and Practice of Gamesmanship: Or the Art of Winning Games without Actually Cheating*, London, 1947.

Purey-Cust, A.P., 'Four Corner Stones of Freemasonry', 1881.

Purey-Cust, A.P., 'The Aim and Spirit of Freemasonry', 1884.

Read, W., 'The Church of Rome and Freemasonry, 1738–1983', *Ars Quatuor Coronatorum* 104, 1992, pp. 51–94.

Rich, P.J., *Elixir of Empire*, London, 1989.

Roberts, J.M., 'Freemasonry: Possibilities of a Neglected Topic', *English Historical Review*, vol. 84, no. 331, 1969, pp. 323-55.

Rotberg, R.I., and M.F. Shore, *The Founder: Cecil Rhodes and the Pursuit of Power*, Oxford, 1988.

Rottenbury, R.H.S., 'The Pre-Eminence of the Great Architect in Freemasonry', *Ars Quatuor Coronatorum* 97, 1984, pp. 192–9.

[Runcie, R.], *Freemasonry and Christianity*, London, 1987.

Sandford, D.K., *A Letter to Peter Elmsley*, Oxford, 1822.

Saxton, C.C., *The Economics of Price Determination*, Oxford, 1942.

Smith, W.S., *The London Heretics, 1870–1914*, London, 1967.

Smyth, Frederick, *A Reference Book For Freemasons*, Q.C. Correspondence Circle, London, 1998.

Srinivasan, K., *The Rise, Decline and Future of the British Commonwealth*, Basingstoke, 2005.

Stubbs, J.W., *Freemasonry in My Life*, Shepperton, 1985.

Trevor-Roper, H., *The Wartime Journals*, ed. R. Davenport-Hines, London, 2012.

United Grand Lodge of England, *Book of Constitutions* (occasional publication), 60 Great Queen Street, London.

United Grand Lodge of England, *Masonic Year Book*, 60 Great Queen Street.

United Grand Lodge of England, *Masonic Year Book, Historical Supplement*, 2nd edn, Oxford, 1969.

Vibert, L., 'Anderson's Constitutions of 1723', *Ars Quatuor Coronatorum* 36, 1923, pp. 36–85.

Waite, A.E., *Emblematic Freemasonry*, London, 1925.

Ward, J.S.M., *Freemasonry: Its Aims and Ideals*, London, 1923.

Weatherly, F., *Piano and Gown: Recollections*, London, 1926.

Whelan, K., *The Tree of Liberty: Radicalism, Catholicism and the Construction of Irish Identity, 1760–1830*, South Bend IN, 2000.

Woodgate, W.B., *Reminiscences of an Old Sportsman*, London, 1909.

Yates, T.E., *Venn and Victorian Bishops Abroad: The Missionary Policies of Henry Venn and Their Repercussions upon the Anglican Episcopate of the Colonial Period, 1841–72*, London, 1978.

Newspapers

Daily Telegraph, 27 October 2001, 27 December 2004, 11 April 2008, 30 April 2008, 4 January 2010, 23 November 2015.

Independent, 8 December 1992, 4 January 1994, 9 November 1996, 4 May 2005.

New York Times, 6 August 2001.

Oxford Chronicle, 14 November 1919.

Sunday Times, 10 May 1953.

Sydney Morning Herald, 7 December 2005.

The Times, 5 September 1874, 29 March 1884, 2 November 1920, 8 and 17 July 1935, 13 September 1939, 3 June 1948, 21 March and 20 June 1951, 13 February 1952, 5 September 1955, 9 May 1957, 8 February 1962, 27 May and 30 June 1965, 13 June 1967, 30 June 1969, 25 February and 4 April 2000, 27 August 2009, 2 March and 29 October 2011, 3 September 2012, 27 February 2016.

Virgin Islands News on Line, 7 May 2014.

Websites

www.apollo357.com/index.php/history/1914-1969, 15 August 2015

http://bbm.org.uk/the-airmen-stories

www.universitiesscheme.com/web/about

PICTURE CREDITS

INDEX OF NAMES

Williams, Robert, of Plas Gwyn 102
Williams, Abp Rowan 77
Williams, Revd Thomas Brian 159, 196
    n214, 204
Williamson, David 183
Williamson, Robert Isherwood 72
Williamson, Victor Alexander 41, 205
Willis, John 25
Wilmot, Anthony 39

Wise, Hillier B.A. 163, 197 n231
Wolfenden, John Frederick (Wolfenden),
    Baron 137, 146, 195 n157
Wolseley, Garnet (Wolseley), 1st Viscount 57
Wolverton, George (Glynn), 2nd Baron 40
Wood, Revd James 25–6
Woodforde, Revd James 25–6
Woodgate, Walter Bradford 91–2, *91*, 97
Woodhouse, Samuel 42

Wrigley, John 42
Wyatt, Matthew Digby 53
Wyfold, Sir Robert (Hermon-Hodge), 1st
    Baron 102

Yorke, Hon. Alexander Grantham 66

Zetland, Thomas (Dundas), 2nd Earl of 77
Zouche, Robert (Curzon), 14th Baron 40

INDEX OF SUBJECTS